# THE COMPLETE CRITICAL GUIDE TO
# SAMUEL BECKETT 822/B

Why did *Waiting for Godot* have such a radical impact on contemporary drama?

Was Beckett the last of the modernists, or was he the first post-modernist?

So many questions surround the key figures in the English literary canon, but most books focus on one aspect of an author's life or work, or limit themselves to a single critical approach. *The Complete Critical Guide to Samuel Beckett* is part of a unique series of comprehensive, user-friendly introductions which:

- offer basic information on an author's life, contexts and works
- outline the major critical issues surrounding the author's works, from the time they were written to the present
- leave judgements up to you, by explaining the full range of often very different critical views and interpretations
- offer guides to further reading in each area discussed.

This series has a broad focus but one very clear aim: to equip you with *all* the knowledge you need to make your own new readings of crucial literary texts.

'An extremely intelligent and very readable overview of Beckett's life, work and critical reception! … An excellent introduction to Beckett and worthwhile reading for those already familiar with him.'
Lois Oppenheim, *President, The Samuel Beckett Society*

**David Pattie** lectures in English and Drama at the University of Greenwich, UK.

THE COMPLETE CRITICAL GUIDE TO
# ENGLISH LITERATURE
Series Editors
RICHARD BRADFORD AND JAN JEDRZEJEWSKI

Also available in this series:

*The Complete Critical Guide to Geoffrey Chaucer*
Gillian Rudd
*The Complete Critical Guide to John Milton*
Richard Bradford
*The Complete Critical Guide to Alexander Pope*
Paul Baines

Forthcoming:

*The Complete Critical Guide to Robert Browning*
*The Complete Critical Guide to Charles Dickens*
*The Complete Critical Guide to Ben Jonson*
*The Complete Critical Guide to D. H. Lawrence*
*The Complete Critical Guide to William Wordsworth*

Visit the website of *The Complete Critical Guide to English Literature*
for further information and an updated list of titles
*www.literature.routledge.com/criticalguides*

# THE COMPLETE CRITICAL GUIDE TO
# SAMUEL BECKETT

*David Pattie*

London and New York

First published 2000
by Routledge
11 New Fetter Lane, London EC4P 4EE

Simultaneously published in the USA and Canada
by Routledge
29 West 35th Street, New York, NY 10001

*Routledge is an imprint of the Taylor & Francis Group*

Typeset in Schneidler by
HWA Text and Data Management, Tunbridge Wells
Printed and bound in Great Britain by
Biddles Ltd, Guildford and King's Lynn

*British Library Cataloguing in Publication Data*
A catalogue record for this book is available from the British Library

*Library of Congress Cataloging in Publication Data*
Pattie, David, 1963–
The complete critical guide to Samuel Beckett / David Pattie.
p. cm.
Includes bibliographical references and index.
1. Beckett, Samuel, 1906– 2. Authors, Irish–20th century–
Biography. 3. Authors, French–20th century–Biography. 4. Beckett,
Samuel, 1906—Outlines, syllabi, etc. I. Title.
PR6003.E282 Z7858 2001
848'.91409–dc21                                     00–055819

ISBN 0–415–20253–1 (hbk)
ISBN 0–415–20254–X (pbk)

# CONTENTS

# SERIES EDITORS' PREFACE

*The Complete Critical Guide to English Literature* is a ground-breaking collection of one-volume introductions to the work of the major writers in the English literary canon. Each volume in the series offers the reader a comprehensive account of the featured author's life, of his or her writing and of the ways in which his or her works have been interpreted by literary critics. The series is both explanatory and stimulating; it reflects the achievements of state-of-the-art literary-historical research and yet manages to be intellectually accessible for the reader who may be encountering a canonical author's work for the first time. It will be useful for students and teachers of literature at all levels, as well as for the general reader; each book can be read through, or consulted in a companion-style fashion.

The aim of *The Complete Critical Guide to English Literature* is to adopt an approach that is as factual, objective and non-partisan as possible, in order to provide the 'full picture' for readers and allow them to form their own judgements. At the same time, however, the books engage the reader in a discussion of the most demanding questions involved in each author's life and work. Did Pope's physical condition affect his treatment of matters of gender and sexuality? Does a feminist reading of *Middlemarch* enlighten us regarding the book's presentation of nineteenth-century British society? Do we deconstruct Beckett's work, or does he do so himself? Contributors to this series address such crucial questions, offer potential solutions and recommend further reading for independent study. In doing so, they equip the reader for an informed and confident examination of the life and work of key canonical figures and of the critical controversies surrounding them.

The aims of the series are reflected in the structure of the books. Part I, 'Life and Contexts', offers a compact biography of the featured author against the background of his or her epoch. In Part II, 'Work', the focus is on the author's most important works, discussed from a non-partisan, literary-historical perspective; the section provides an account of the works, reflecting a consensus of critical opinion on them, and indicating, where appropriate, areas of controversy. These and other issues are taken up again in Part III, 'Criticism', which offers an account of the critical responses generated by the author's work. Contemporaneous reviews and debates are considered, along with opinions inspired by more recent theoretical approaches, such as New Criticism,

# SERIES EDITORS' PREFACE

*The Complete Critical Guide to English Literature* is a ground-breaking collection of one-volume introductions to the work of the major writers in the English literary canon. Each volume in the series offers the reader a comprehensive account of the featured author's life, of his or her writing and of the ways in which his or her works have been interpreted by literary critics. The series is both explanatory and stimulating; it reflects the achievements of state-of-the-art literary-historical research and yet manages to be intellectually accessible for the reader who may be encountering a canonical author's work for the first time. It will be useful for students and teachers of literature at all levels, as well as for the general reader; each book can be read through, or consulted in a companion-style fashion.

The aim of *The Complete Critical Guide to English Literature* is to adopt an approach that is as factual, objective and non-partisan as possible, in order to provide the 'full picture' for readers and allow them to form their own judgements. At the same time, however, the books engage the reader in a discussion of the most demanding questions involved in each author's life and work. Did Pope's physical condition affect his treatment of matters of gender and sexuality? Does a feminist reading of *Middlemarch* enlighten us regarding the book's presentation of nineteenth-century British society? Do we deconstruct Beckett's work, or does he do so himself? Contributors to this series address such crucial questions, offer potential solutions and recommend further reading for independent study. In doing so, they equip the reader for an informed and confident examination of the life and work of key canonical figures and of the critical controversies surrounding them.

The aims of the series are reflected in the structure of the books. Part I, 'Life and Contexts', offers a compact biography of the featured author against the background of his or her epoch. In Part II, 'Work', the focus is on the author's most important works, discussed from a non-partisan, literary-historical perspective; the section provides an account of the works, reflecting a consensus of critical opinion on them, and indicating, where appropriate, areas of controversy. These and other issues are taken up again in Part III, 'Criticism', which offers an account of the critical responses generated by the author's work. Contemporaneous reviews and debates are considered, along with opinions inspired by more recent theoretical approaches, such as New Criticism, feminism, Marxism, psychoanalytic criticism, deconstruction and New Historicism.

The volumes in this series will together constitute a comprehensive reference work offering an up-to-date, user-friendly and reliable account of the heritage of English literature from the Middle Ages to the twentieth century. We hope that *The Complete Critical Guide to English Literature* will become for its readers, academic and non-academic alike, an indispensable source of information and inspiration.

RICHARD BRADFORD

JAN JEDRZEJEWSKI

# ACKNOWLEDGEMENTS

The author and publishers thank the Samuel Beckett Estate, The Calder Educational Trust and Grove/Atlantic, Inc. for permission to quote from the following copyright works by Samuel Beckett: *Dream of Fair to Middling Women, More Pricks than Kicks, Murphy, Watt, Mercier and Camier, The Trilogy, How It Is, Company, Worstward Ho, Collected Poems in English and in French, Disjecta, Proust* and *Three Dialogues with Georges Duthuit*. They would also like to thank Faber & Faber for quotes from *The Complete Dramatic Works*.

# ABBREVIATIONS AND REFERENCING

Throughout the text, references to Beckett's works are abbreviated as follows:

*CSD*   *Complete Shorter Prose 1929–1986* (ed S.E. Gontarski) New York: Grove Press

*DFMW*  *Dream of Fair to Middling Women* Dublin: Black Cat Press (1992)

*MPTK*  *More Pricks Than Kicks* London: John Calder (1970)

*M*     *Murphy* London: John Calder (1993)

*W*     *Watt* London: John Clader (1964)

*M&C*   *Mercier and Camier* London: John Calder (1974)

*T*     *The Trilogy (Molloy, Malone Dies, The Unnamable)* London: John Clader (1959)

*E*     *Eleutheria* (trans. Barbara Wright) London: Faber and Faber (1990)

*CDW*   *Complete Dramatic Works* London: Faber and Faber (1990)

*PTD*   *Proust* and *Three Dialogues with Georges Duthuit* London: John Calder (1965)

*D*     *Disjecta* (ed. Ruby Cohn) London: John Clader (1983)

*HII*   *How It Is* London: John Calder (1964)

*C*     *Company* London: John Calder (1980)

*ISIS*  *Ill Seen Ill Said* London: John Calder (1982)

*WH*    *Worstward Ho* London: John Clader (1983)

All references are to page numbers.

For all other references, the Harward system is used; full details of items cited can be found in the bibliography.

Cross-referencing between sections is one of the features of this series. Cross-references to relevant page numbers appear in bold type and square brackets **[28]**.

# INTRODUCTION

Samuel Beckett is generally regarded as one of the finest artists of the twentieth century. His work revolutionised our understanding of the nature and potential of both literature and drama, and provided some of the most resonant images of human existence in a troubled and confused historical period. This book brings together for the first time accessible discussions of Beckett's life and times, his work and the critical literature that he has inspired.

The book covers Beckett's early life and work as a young man adrift between his original home in Ireland, London and Paris; the various influences, both literary and cultural, that shaped his writing; the importance of his war-time experiences; and the period (1946–1953) during which he wrote the works which made him famous. It also contains a comprehensive account of the critical debates that have surrounded Beckett's work: the influence of Cartesian and existential philosophy; the influence of theoretical discussions, such as deconstruction and psychoanalytic criticism, on the reception of his work.

*The Complete Critical Guide to Samuel Beckett* has been designed to offer readers an accessible, up-to-date and comprehensive introduction to this key figure in literary and dramatic history.

# PART I

# LIFE AND CONTEXTS

## (a) THE EARLY YEARS: 1906–1927

Samuel Barclay Beckett was born on Good Friday, April 13th, 1906, in Cooldrinagh, the Beckett family home in Foxrock, County Dublin. He was the youngest child: a brother, Frank, had been born almost four years earlier, on the 26th of July 1902. Beckett was born into a reasonably wealthy family. His father, William Beckett (more commonly known as Bill) worked as a quantity surveyor in Dublin; the business was successful enough for the Becketts to own a large property relatively near the city, and Foxrock was a popular place for a Dublin businessman to set up house. His mother, May, had been a nurse before her marriage; indeed, she first met Bill Beckett when he was a patient in the nursing home where she worked. On both sides, Beckett's immediate ancestors had been pillars of Dublin life. The Becketts were master builders, and the Roes (his mother's maiden name) had been involved in the grain trade. The family had initially prospered; however, changes in the world market for grain in the 1880s had left the Roes in some financial difficulty, and the younger members, including May, were forced to work for a living.

Generally the date of a writer's birth, particularly that of a modern writer, should be an uncontroversial matter. However, in Beckett's case, establishing a definite date has not proved so easy; the day Beckett always celebrated was not the one on his birth certificate (the 13th of May). The confusion was compounded by the fact that his birth was registered on the 14th of June; as it was traditional for the family to register the birth of a child a month after the event, it has been assumed that Beckett was actually born in May, and that the April date, falling as it does on a date of great potential significance, was a story propagated by Beckett himself. However, in his recent biography, James Knowlson has provided crucial evidence in favour of the earlier date; Beckett's birth was announced in the Irish Times on April 16th, and the date given on the birth certificate would seem simply to have been a mistake.

Beckett's early childhood was comfortable; in its essentials it was no different from the early life of any middle-class Dublin Protestant before and during the First World War. His father worked in the city, returning home in the evening; his mother ran the household and devoted herself to good works in the local community. Even the Easter uprising of 1916, and the years of political turmoil leading up to the declaration of the Irish Republic, do not seem to have affected the Becketts materially; despite some local fears that Protestants would suffer in a land whose main religion was Catholicism, life in respectable suburbs such as Foxrock remained much the same as it always had. However, this is not to say that the events passed the young Beckett by: his father took him to see, from a distance, the centre of Dublin in flames, and the sight made a lasting impression on him.

As he grew, Beckett gradually acquired the skills and habits common to a child of his age and class; he learned to swim, to play tennis, golf, chess and cricket, and to play the piano (the first indication of a life-long interest in music). Neither was his education unique: from the age of five to the age of nine he attended a small, local school run by two sisters, the Misses Elsner (whose name and whose pet – a dog called Zulu – are used in the novel *Molloy*). Beckett's parents then sent him to a preparatory school, Earlsfort House, in Dublin: after Earlsfort House, Beckett followed his older brother first of all to Portora Royal School in Enniskillen in 1920, and then to the more prestigious of Dublin's two universities, Trinity College, in 1923.

On the surface, then, Beckett's early life does not seem to provide the kind of raw material for the extreme, idiosyncratic writing with which his name is associated (an impression that Beckett himself was at least in part to maintain)

> You might say that I had a happy childhood... although I had little talent for happiness. My parents did everything that could make a child happy. But I was often lonely. We were brought up like Quakers. My father did not beat me, nor my mother run away from home.
>
> (Bair 1980: 22)

As Deirdre Bair notes, this statement does hint at a rather more troubled childhood than the bare facts might suggest. It is tempting to build a full case history from the details of Beckett's home life, and in particular to make much of the at times difficult relationship with his mother. However, whatever the truth of the matter, it seems undeniable that Beckett was a solitary, rather self-contained child, fond of reading, and with a talent for placing himself in potentially difficult, not to say dangerous, situations. It also seems undeniable that this brought him into conflict with May in more than one occasion. For example, one of Beckett's childhood games involved climbing to the top of a sixty-foot fir tree, and throwing himself off, relying on one of the thicker, lower branches to break his fall. On another occasion, the ten-year-old Beckett dropped a lighted match into a petrol can, peering over to see the effect that his act would have; not surprisingly, his face was burned and his eyebrows singed. These actions seem to indicate, even at an early age, elements of Beckett's character that were to resurface later; the recklessness would abate somewhat, but the extreme independence and the stoic reaction to danger would remain with Beckett for the rest of his life.

Beckett's relationship with his father was warm. Bill Beckett was an active, enthusiastic, companionable man, with no pretensions toward an understanding of literature or art. Beckett later in life fondly remembered his father avidly consuming cheap detective novels in the evenings after work, and then being unable to remember anything about them once he'd finished. From his father, Beckett inherited his athleticism and his love of walking, especially in the countryside surrounding Dublin. Bill would spend most Sundays walking in the Wicklow hills while May and the rest of the family were at church; as he grew older, Beckett began to accompany his father, and came to know the surrounding countryside intimately. In particular, the view from the Wicklow hills across the city of Dublin to Kingstown (later Dun Laoghaire) harbour recurs frequently in his mature writing (in the novels *Mercier and Camier* and *Molloy*, for example). In the late text *Worstward Ho*, Beckett movingly evokes the image of an old man and child walking hand in hand

> Where then but there see now another. Bit by bit an old man and child. In the dim void bit by bit an old man and child. Any other would do as ill.
> Hand in hand with equal plod they go. In the free hands- no. Free empty hands. Backs turned both bowed with equal plod they go. The child hand raised to reach the holding hand. Hold the old holding hand. Hold and be held. Plod on and never recede. Backs turned. Both bowed. Joined by held holding hands. Plod on as one. One shade. Another shade.
>
> (*WH* 12–13)

Beckett's relationship with his mother was not so simple. May Beckett seems to have been a rather forbidding woman, with a tendency toward depression. She was not unbendingly stern, and was remembered by some acquaintances as kind and friendly; however, she was capable of great variations in mood, and at home she could be strict, obsessively concerned with politeness and decorum, and occasionally prone to bouts of an almost melodramatic hysteria. Again, it would be easy to inflate May's rather uneven character into full-blown neurosis, and to use this as the explanation for Beckett's own troubled development as a man and as a writer; to do this, though, would be to ignore the strong mutual affection between mother and son. Rather, Beckett's conflicts with his mother had more to do with a streak of self-will and stubbornness shared by both. May was a dominant woman, and Beckett, for much of his early life, behaved in a way almost calculated to arouse his mother's anger and concern; but he persisted, because to stop would have been to submit. These conflicts became more acute as Beckett grew; they seem to have been a source of great anxiety for mother and son

> [May's] anxiety about Samuel stemmed from what he later described as her 'savage loving'. Equally, it was not that Beckett disliked his mother or did not care what she thought of him. Rather he loved her almost as strongly and cared for her too much. So conflicts of will became heart-rending struggles with the loving side of himself as well as with his mother, as he saw her determinedly and diametrically opposed to him in her judgements or her expectations. And to feel the weight of her moral condemnation and disappointment, as well as to be distanced from her affection, was an additional burden for him to bear. For they rarely saw eye to eye on anything concerning himself.
>
> (Knowlson 1996: 22)

Beckett's schooldays were at first academically unremarkable. He was, by all accounts, a rather withdrawn student, forming few strong friendships (although the friendships he did form were long lasting; Geoffrey Thompson, a fellow pupil at Portora, became a lifelong friend). Beckett was at first more a sportsman than a scholar; he boxed, ran, swam, and played cricket well enough to represent Trinity College in first class tours of England in 1926 and 1927.

It was not until he entered Trinity in 1923 that Beckett began to fulfil his academic potential; and it was at Trinity, also, that he first encountered work that was to prove a lasting influence on his own writing. As an undergraduate Beckett studied French, a language he had begun to learn at his first school; at that time, the University stipulated that a student must study two languages, and Beckett accordingly chose Italian. The Professor of Romance Languages in Trinity at this time was Thomas Rudmose-Brown, who was to prove an important figure in Beckett's development both at and immediately after his time at Trinity. Beckett seems to have been a favourite of Rudmose-Brown's, although Beckett's thinly-disguised portraits of his old professor in his early work (Rudmose-Brown appears as the Polar

Bear in both *Dream of Fair to Middling Women* and the story 'A Wet Night' in *More Pricks than Kicks*) demonstrate that he was not an uncritical admirer of his tutor.

Rudmose-Brown introduced Beckett to the plays of Racine, the poetry of Ronsard and Verlaine, and the work of more modern authors such as Marcel Proust and Andre Gide. In contrast to the rather shy Beckett, Rudmose-Brown was a forceful, idiosyncratic man, outspokenly anti-clerical and possessed of a biting, epigrammatic wit. He was a man of strongly held prejudices, many of which his young protégé came to share. Articles written by Beckett in the late 1920s and the early 1930s ('Che Sciagura', published in *T.C.D.: a College Miscellany* in 1929, and 'Censorship in the Saorstat', written in 1934) attacked the Catholic Church's increasing influence on Irish political life; in 1928, Rudmose-Brown, seeking to establish contacts for his protege in Paris, recommended Beckett to the poet Valery Larbaud as 'a great enemy of imperialism, patriotism and all the churches'. (Knowlson 1996: 51).

Arguably, the other major influence on Beckett's academic development while at Trinity was not a member of the university's staff, but the private tutor who instructed him in Italian, Madame Bianca Esposito. She too appears in Beckett's early work in a lightly fictionalised form (as Signorina Adriana Ottolenghi, in 'Dante and the Lobster', the initial story in the collection *More Pricks than Kicks*). Beckett later credited Madame Esposito as the tutor who helped to nurture his profound love of the Italian poet Dante; *The Divine Comedy* (an allegorical poem about the soul's salvation, in which Dante journeys through Hell and Purgatory to Heaven) exercised a profound influence on Beckett's writing, providing him with images that were recur in his fiction and drama until the end of his life **[109–11]**.

Beckett was an avid, scholarly student, and was, by the end of his third year, sufficiently advanced in his studies to have gained a Foundation scholarship, the most prestigious undergraduate award at Trinity. His academic flowering was probably due to a variety of factors; the freedom of university, after the ordered learning regime of school; the influence of Rudmose-Brown; the fact that he was encountering texts that undoubtedly stimulated him (as well as Dante, Beckett engaged in a serious study of Shakespeare and Milton; and he also encountered the work of more controversial modern poets such as Guillaume Apollinaire, who had coined the term Surrealism only a few years before). Beckett's intellectual growth was also fuelled by the cultural life he encountered in Dublin; he became a dedicated theatre-goer, attending the premiere of Sean O'Casey's *Juno and the Paycock* and *The Plough and the Stars*, and W.B Yeats' versions of Sophocles' *Oedipus the King* and *Oedipus at Colonus*, at Dublin's Abbey Theatre, as well as revivals of the work of John Millington Synge **[112]**. Beckett also frequented other types of theatre; he regularly went to see the revues and music-hall turns that performed in the Olympia, the Gaiety, and the Theatre Royal. He would also go regularly to the cinema, to see Buster Keaton and Charlie Chaplin's silent comedies; Keaton's blank-faced stoicism seems to have made a great impact on Beckett, who later suggested the comic as the protagonist in *Film*. In addition, he developed what was to be a long-standing love and appreciation of fine art; in particular, he valued seventeenth-century Dutch painting, and was able, years later, to remember the paintings he had encountered in great detail.

Two other aspects of Beckett's life in Trinity deserve mention. As an undergraduate, he met, and fell in love with, a student in the year above him. Ethna MacCarthy was, by the standards of the time, a liberated woman; she spoke her mind, she smoked, she drank, and she enjoyed the company of men; moreover, she was fiercely intelligent and articulate. Beckett was captivated by her; but there is no evidence that their relationship was ever more than one-sided. MacCarthy never regarded Beckett as anything more than a friend; their friendship lasted until her death in 1959. However, as with many of the acquaintances of these days, MacCarthy (renamed the Alba) finds her way into Beckett's early writing; Knowlson also suggests that MacCarthy was the model for the girl with 'eyes ... like crysolite' (*CDW* 220) in *Krapp's Last Tape*.

It was during his time at Trinity that Beckett first began to suffer from the symptoms that were to plague him for most of his early adult life. From 1926 onwards, he was increasingly prone to what seems to have been a condition that was, at base, neurotic. His heart would race, making sleep impossible; later, his pounding heart would be supplemented by sweating and an accelerating sense of panic. In the later 1920s and 30s, these panic attacks would grow so severe that Beckett had to seek medical help.

As he neared the end of his undergraduate career, Beckett was at least clear about the direction he did not want his life to take. He did not want to work in the family business; nor did he want to be a clerk or a schoolmaster, two other career paths that had been suggested to him by his family (Knowlson 1996: 69). The only option open to him was therefore to pursue the academic course that his success at Trinity had made possible. As a leading student in modern languages, Beckett was an obvious candidate for the year-long exchange programme that

Trinity had organised with the École Normale Supérieure in Paris; the successful candidate would spend a year as a tutor at the École. His professor was, unsurprisingly, in favour of Beckett's candidature; his protégé was an outstanding student, and would, under normal circumstances, have been a considerable asset to the École and, when he returned from his time in Paris, a useful addition to the academic staff at Trinity. The successful candidate would be expected to engage in research; Beckett decided to study the poetry of Louis Jouve and the Unanimist school (a poet and movement that he had encountered first in his final undergraduate year). However, for various reasons (mostly concerned with the life that Beckett was to lead in Paris over the next two years, and the effect that it was to have on his development as a writer and as a man), this research was never completed.

## (b) THE YOUNG WRITER: 1928–1939

In 1928, therefore, Beckett's future seemed to be falling into a standard pattern. His candidature for the École lectureship was eventually accepted, but only after a row over the status of another Trinity lecturer currently in Paris. To fill in time between graduating and taking up the appointment at the École, Beckett accepted a teaching post at Campbell College in Belfast, at that time the largest public school in Northern Ireland. He was not a success; teaching was not liable to prove easy for the shy, self-contained, rather aloof young man that Beckett was becoming. At one meeting, the headmaster was moved to remind him that he was teaching the cream of Ulster. 'Yes, I know', Beckett replied; 'rich and thick'.

The lecturer already in Paris, occupying (at least in Rudmose-Brown's eyes) the position that was rightfully Beckett's, was an older Irishman, Thomas MacGreevey. When Beckett eventually took up his position in Paris in 1928 McGreevey was still at the Ecole, and the two became friends. Thirteen years Beckett's senior, MacGreevey was an outgoing, convivial man; a poet as well as an academic, he had a wide interest in modern European art and literature, and also a pride in being Irish that the younger man found more difficult to accept (although both men disliked the increasingly restrictive atmosphere in the Irish Free State). MacGreevey can lay claim to being the most important contact that Beckett ever made. Not only did the young Beckett have regular friendly contact with someone who knew and could discuss literature and art, he also benefited from MacGreevey's knowledge of Parisian cultural life. MacGreevey's list of friends and contacts was profoundly impressive. He knew both W.B Yeats and Jack Yeats, George Russell (A.E.), T.S Eliot, James Stephens, and Richard Aldington; and, crucially, MacGreevey was part of the circle of friends, admirers and disciples that had gathered around the most feted and the most controversial Irish artistic exile, James Joyce.

Joyce's influence on Beckett is undoubtedly important, but it is in some respects hard to gauge. What seems undeniable is that Beckett came under Joyce's spell; he ran errands for the older writer, whose eyesight was failing, and, as with most of Joyce's acquaintances, he was drawn into the composition of Joyce's last major work, *Finnegans Wake* (at this time known as *Work in Progress*). Although Beckett's role in the composition of the *Wake* was never an official one, he was happy to act as an unpaid researcher, taking notes and writing reports on books that Joyce might put to use in his work. He also read to Joyce, and, on a few occasions, took dictation for him. Moreover, Joyce provided an example for the younger man; Joyce was intimidatingly erudite, with a profound love of language (he, like Beckett, had studied French and Italian at university); despite the various distractions and difficulties he encountered, he remained quietly dedicated to his work, refusing to let external circumstances distract him; and he responded to criticism with a self-contained silence. This could not but impress a young man who, as he later confessed, had come to think of himself as apart from and in some senses superior to those around him, and who had already developed silence as a defence against the outside world.

Beckett's decision to become a writer also seems to have been at least influenced by his friendship with Joyce

> When I first met Joyce, I didn't intend to be a writer. That only came later when I found out that I was no good at all at teaching. When I found I simply couldn't teach. But I do remember speaking about Joyce's heroic achievement. I had a great deal of admiration for him. That's what it was; epic, heroic, what he achieved. But I realised that I couldn't go down that road.
>
> (Knowlson 1996: 105)

Joyce's influence on Beckett's development as a writer has been a matter of debate from the first. Reviewers of *More Pricks than Kicks* and *Murphy* noted a strongly Joycean flavour in these early works; and it is undoubtedly true that something of Joyce's love for neologisms and arcane references had transferred itself to Beckett. It might also be said that there are similarities between the protagonists in Beckett's early fictions and Stephen Dedalus in Joyce's *A Portrait of the Artist as a*

*Young Man* and *Ulysses*; Beckett's early protagonists are, like Stephen, intelligent young men at odds with the world. However, there are marked differences between the two. Joyce presents Stephen's artistic development in a series of increasingly complex, self-aware internal monologues. Beckett also uses the monologue form, but as a way of distancing the reader from his protagonists; the doings of Belacqua Shuah and Murphy are described by an ironic, mocking and self aware author, who on occasion finds it necessary to address the reader directly. Even at this early stage, Beckett's fiction draws attention to itself as fiction; the process of writing is at least as important as the substance of the text. This is at odds with Joyce's famous dictum, expressed by Stephen in *A Portrait of the Artist*

> The artist, like the God of creation, remains within or behind or beyond or above his handiwork, invisible, refined out of existence, indifferent, paring his fingernails.
>
> *(Portrait of the Artist as a Young Man,* 226)

It seems as though Beckett, although profoundly affected by Joyce's attitude to writing, realised early on that he could not simply imitate Joyce's style; their concerns were simply too different. The road Joyce took brought the unique artistic sensibility of Stephen back into contact with a world full of individuals equally, if differently, unique. Beckett's protagonists, as his writing developed, moved further and further away from the physical world. By the time of the trilogy, the mocking authorial voice of the early work has become the grimly ironic yet stoically determined monologue that the central characters cannot help but create, moment to moment, in an ultimately doomed and yet compulsive effort to finally make sense of their experience of the world; to finally have said all that can be said, so that the effort of speaking can finally be abandoned.

Joyce's friendship was the undoubted prize of Beckett's time in Paris; but he was equally influenced by the thriving cultural life of the city itself. He had got into the habit of frequenting galleries and the theatre in Dublin; in Paris he continued to do so, aided by the income he received from teaching, and by the allowance sent regularly from home. He had the good fortune to live in Paris at a time when it could justifiably claim to be the most important cultural centre in Europe; as well as the presence of writers such as Joyce, Paris was also home to the Surrealist movement (led by Andre Breton), and played host to avant-garde work from the rest of the continent and from America. As well as sampling modern art, Beckett increased his knowledge and appreciation of Racinian drama and seventeenth-century Dutch painting; and he also took the opportunity to study the work of Descartes and Schopenhauer **[105–6; 108–9]**. It was also home to a bewildering number of small presses and literary journals; and Beckett, through his friendships with Joyce and with MacGreevey, came to know many of the publishers, editors and writers who created, staffed and worked for them. When Beckett himself first began to write, he did so in a literary environment that was at least receptive to experimentation.

As well as a cultural environment that Dublin could not match, Paris also gave Beckett a greater opportunity to indulge in an active social life. In MacGreevey's company, Beckett began to drink and to keep late hours, only returning to his room in the early morning after the doors had been locked. Unsurprisingly, this meant that he did not rise early; his student, Georges Pelorson, found that his new English lecturer could not keep to an agreed timetable

> The day after I settled in, I found a note in pencil in my mailbox. It said, 'I am your English lecturer and I think that we should meet, so could you come to my place tomorrow morning at 11 o'clock'. So this next day I came up the stairs, knocked on the door and there was no answer, so I knocked again and again- no answer. I tried the knob, it worked and the door opened slightly. I saw an open window with shutters half-closed, the sun was pouring through that and falling right on the bed. On that bed, half-naked, was stretched a tall young man, very fair, who seemed to be even fairer because of the sun falling on him as he slept. I was very impressed by this spectacle. I didn't want to wake him so I scribbled a note to say that I had come to see him but as he was asleep, I had returned to my studies.
>
> (Knowlson 1996: 95–6)

They scheduled all subsequent meetings for the afternoon.

Beckett had not yet given up all idea of an academic life. For a while in Paris he studied for the proposed essay on Louis Jouve; although the essay is now lost, Beckett seems to have completed it in 1928 (it was, however, never submitted). Gradually, though, he began to produce critical work on other subjects; and gradually, too, he began to write short stories and poetry. As one might expect, Joyce figured largely in the kind of work that the young Beckett found himself producing. His first commission, indeed, was for an essay on Joyce's *Work in Progress* (published as *Finnegans Wake*); the essay, 'Dante ... Bruno. Vico ... Joyce' was first published in 1929. At the same time, Beckett wrote his first short story, 'Assumption', and the poem that was to be his first independently published work, *Whoroscope*. In 1930, he received a further commission, for a monograph on Proust **[111–12, 146–7]**. This monograph was eventually published by Chatto and Windus, one of whose editors, Charles Prentice, supported Beckett through the 1930s.

It is tempting to mine Beckett's early writing for clues to the path that his art would take. Certainly, Beckett's concerns do remain remarkably consistent from the beginning of his writing life to its end; but the form and style through which those concerns were expressed were subject to change, making the idea that Beckett's path is entirely marked out in his early critical work difficult to sustain. Finally, it should be remembered that much of this early material was produced to order; Beckett was instructed by Joyce to read Vico in preparation for his essay, and the commission on Proust was taken on board to earn its young author some money. Even the poem *Whoroscope*, a meditation on time and on Cartesian philosophy **[98, 105–6, 147–8, 150–1]** was produced as a last minute entry for a poetry competition sponsored by Joyce's friend, the publisher Nancy Cunard; submitted on the competition's closing day, it won the £10 prize. It is possible, therefore, to see Beckett's later writing prefigured in these texts; but, at the same time, it must be remembered that they are first the works of a very young man, and that, second, they are not entirely a pure reflection of the state of Beckett's mind nor of his art. Perhaps their main importance to the young Beckett was that they represented his first attempt to find a form for his own particular artistic concerns; they are the first signs that Beckett was beginning to think of himself as at least a potential, if not an actual, writer.

Nevertheless, the earliest writings do contain clues not only to the young Beckett's ideas on art and writing, but to his future development as an author; statements such as 'here form is content, content form', (*D* 27), and the teasing and often quoted sentence from *Proust* ('Tragedy is the statement of an expiation... the expiation of original sin... the sin of having been born' (*PTD* 67)) do seem to lead the reader naturally into the world of the later work. The comments on Dante's *Purgatory* in the essay on Joyce provide an interesting gloss on the cyclical, unending torments endured by so many of the characters in the mature fiction and drama

> Hell is the static lifelessness of unrelieved viciousness. Paradise the static lifelessness of unrelieved immaculation. Purgatory a flood of movement and vitality released by the conjunction of these two

elements. There is a continual purgatorial process at work, in the sense that the vicious cycle of humanity is being achieved ....

(D 33)

The description of habit in *Proust* could, perhaps, be applied equally to the world of *Waiting for Godot*

The laws of memory are subject to the more general laws of habit. Habit is a compromise effected between the individual and his environment, or between the individual and his own organic eccentricities, the guarantee of a dull inviolability, the lightning-conductor of his existence. Habit is the ballast that chains the dog to his vomit. Breathing is habit. Life is habit. Or rather life is a succession of habits, since the individual is a succession of individuals; the world being a projection of the individual's consciousness (an objectivation of the individual's will, Schopenhauer would say), the pact must be continually renewed, the letter of safe conduct brought up to date. The creation of the world did not take place once and for all time, but takes place every day. Habit then is the generic term for the countless treaties concluded between the countless subjects that constitute the individual and their countless correlative objects. The periods of transition that separate consecutive adaptations ... represent the perilous zones in the life of the individual, dangerous, precarious, painful, mysterious and fertile, when for a moment the boredom of living is replaced by the suffering of being ...

(*PTD* 19)

These statements seem to be unambiguous statements of a developing artistic credo, in which the individual's life is a painful progress through an unending purgatory, deadened only by habit. However, the very certainty in Beckett's authorial voice in these early texts is itself an indication that they are products of a mind quite different from that of the mature writer. As we shall see, the older Beckett only began to produce the work that ensured his fame after he had come to accept uncertainty as a guiding principle. Joyce and Proust, in the early critical works, are artists who succeed in conveying the substance of a purgatorial universe; Beckett the mature artist would come to accept the idea that, as an artist, he could only fail.

By his early twenties, Beckett had grown into an attractive man; and, although his rather distant, reserved manner prevented him from forming easy relationships with women, he had, in the summer before he went to Paris, fallen in love with his cousin Peggy Sinclair. Peggy was the daughter of Beckett's maternal aunt Frances, also called Cissie, and his uncle William, who was known to his friends as Boss. The Sinclairs had left Dublin in the early twenties for Kassel in Germany, where Boss had hoped to establish himself as an art dealer. Peggy, seventeen in 1928, travelled with her younger sister Deidre back to Ireland to visit her relatives; when she and Beckett met, the attraction seems to have been instantaneous on both sides. For the next eighteen months, Beckett travelled regularly to Kassel to see his cousin, much to the chagrin of his parents, who expressed their extreme disapproval; nevertheless, Beckett was initially entranced by a young woman who was pretty, clever and direct, capable of flights of bizarre humour

> The Smeraldina [the name given to a character closely based on Peggy Sinclair in Beckett's early fiction] never looked like being able to play the piano, but she had a curious talent for improvisation, which came up in her conversation. When she was in form, launched, she could be extremely amusing, with a strange feverish eloquence, the words flooding and streaming out like a conjuror's coloured paper ...
>
> (*DFMW* 14)

However, by the winter of 1929, the love affair had waned. Peggy, it seems, was increasingly frustrated by Beckett's taciturn manner, and Beckett seems to have been uncomfortable both with Peggy's attitude to literature, and, if the largely autobiographical *Dream of Fair to Middling Women* is a truthful reflection of his state of mind, with Peggy's openly physical, sexual nature. Whatever the reason, by early 1930 the relationship had ended; it left its mark on his fiction, both in the lightly veiled character of the Smeraldina-Rima in his early work, and in references *in Krapp's Last Tape* to a girl in a green beret, whose memory Krapp invokes with a mingled melancholy and regret.

In Paris, Beckett had also drawn the attention of Joyce's daughter Lucia. Although Beckett admitted that he found Lucia attractive, her advances were unwelcome for a number of reasons; because of Peggy; because of Beckett's friendship with Joyce, which did not stretch to Joyce's family (with the exception of Joyce's son, Giorgio); and because of Lucia herself. By the late twenties, she was already displaying signs of the schizophrenia that would plague the rest of her life; her behaviour was, to say the least, variable, and she seemed unable to concentrate on any one task for very long.

Joyce, however, did not recognise his daughter's illness until her condition had deteriorated further; and when Beckett, in May 1930, finally told Lucia that he was not interested in her, Joyce and his wife took their daughter's side. The rift in Beckett's and Joyce's friendship was never absolute, but it did not truly heal until Joyce finally accepted the fact of his daughter's illness.

In September of that year, after delivering the manuscript of *Proust* to his publishers in London, Beckett returned to Dublin to take up a post in modern languages at Trinity. He had no choice (he was poor, and the post at Trinity was waiting for him), but he was not pleased at the prospect. Something of his mental state can be gauged from the psychosomatic illnesses that he developed immediately before his return home; he had contracted an embarrassing and painful rash that stretched disfiguringly across his face, and a large cyst had grown at the back of his neck, and would require painful lancing. His family, and especially his mother, welcomed him home (even though they were rather upset by his appearance), and for the first few weeks he accepted and enjoyed their attentions. After a while, though, he began to chafe; he had been altered by his experiences in Paris, and was not likely to settle back into the life that had been mapped out for him. The atmosphere at Cooldrinagh became, over the next year, increasingly fragile; in the summer of 1931 Beckett and his mother had a blazing argument, apparently about the obscenity of his writing (he was at that time working on stories that would eventually find their way into *Dream of Fair to Middling Women* and *More Pricks than Kicks*). Neither Beckett nor his mother were inclined to apologise to each other afterwards; and, after a visit to Germany later in the year, Beckett moved out of his family's home completely, taking up residence in Trinity College.

Although Anthony Cronin contends that initially students were rather impressed by this new, obviously profoundly intelligent lecturer, Beckett himself found, in the words of the quote given above, that he 'simply couldn't teach'. In a letter to Charles Prentice in 1930, he talked of 'the grotesque comedy of lecturing' (Knowlson 1996: 126); writing to MacGreevey, he confessed 'I don't get on well with my classes... and that flatters me and exasperates my pride ... How long it will drag on, Tom, I have no idea'(Knowlson 1996: 126). Partly, this was the natural response of an extremely shy and rather withdrawn young man to the innately public nature of teaching; partly, to, it reflected Beckett's growing realisation that academic life was not for him. He could not concentrate on research, because he was preoccupied with the kind of fiction and poetry that he had begun to produce in Paris. Between 1930 and 1933 he completed *Dream* and *More Pricks*; he wrote poetry, most of which was collected and published in 1935, as *Echo's Bones and Other Precipitates*; and he received regular commissions for translations of modern French. In other words, he continued to work in the same style and in the same forms that he had first explored in Paris; and, as he realised later, he had begun to think of himself as a writer first of all.

During his spell at Trinity, two incidents demonstrated something of Beckett's increasing impatience with academia. In November 1930 he delivered a mock lecture on a fictional modern French poet, Jean du Chas; the lecture, much enjoyed by the faculty to whom it was delivered, was an elaborate academic joke on modern poetry, and on the pedantic, overly rational academic study of literature in general. Beckett also agreed to take part in a version of Corneille's *The Cid*; *The Kid*, written largely by Pelorson. Beckett played the part of the Cid's father, Don Diegue. In a monologue that satirised the notion found in classical French drama that all theatre should conform to a strict schedule (the play should take place, as far as possible, in real time), his character was forced to speak faster and faster as Pelorson manipulated the hands of a giant clock at the rear of the stage. Parallels were later drawn between Beckett's delivery and Lucky's speech in *Waiting For Godot*; at the time, though, the joke was not appreciated. Rudmose-Brown in particular was scathing; after spending the following afternoon drinking, Beckett had to be dragged to the theatre for the second performance.

One of the few happy events of Beckett's time at Trinity was the friendship that he struck up with the painter and writer Jack B. Yeats, who was in his sixties by the time that he and Beckett met. Beckett and Yeats had a mutual acquaintance – the ubiquitous MacGreevey – and Beckett gained an invitation to attend one of Yeats' 'at homes' (the term given at the time to relatively informal social or artistic gatherings). Yeats and Beckett soon established a rapport; the younger man was impressed both by Yeats' rather diffident personality and by his art, although he seems to have had a rather idiosyncratic notion of it. For Beckett, Yeats' late paintings displayed the essential solitude of man in the face of an indifferent nature; he also approved of Yeats' fiction, couched as it was in monologue, and the older man's nearly eventless dramas, which Beckett also saw during his stay in Dublin. Over the next few years, whenever Beckett found himself in Ireland, Yeats' friendship was a continuing source of great comfort.

Given the events at home and his increasing dissatisfaction with Trinity, it is no wonder that Beckett began to withdraw more and more both from his family and from his work. He returned to Paris briefly in

1931, and effected a partial reconciliation with Joyce; although the relationship with Peggy was over, he continued to pay visits to her family in Kassel; and he took long, solitary walks in the mountains around Dublin, along the country roads that would figure so heavily in his mature writing. The illnesses that had first manifested themselves in his undergraduate days returned; he suffered from recurring cysts, was overly susceptible to colds (during 1931 he developed pleurisy) and he found himself once again prone to heart palpitations and night sweats. His life, for the moment, seemed to lack any direction; given this, his decision to resign from his lectureship at Trinity in 1932 was at least an attempt to deal with the growing crisis in his life, even though the decision, once taken, left him with a strong residue of guilt over the response of his parents and his old professor.

From 1932 to 1937, when he settled permanently in Paris, Beckett led a rather rootless life, marked at regular intervals by tragedy and instability. He emerged from this period in some ways a profoundly changed man; calmer, more stable, with much of the arrogance of his younger self erased. Resigning from Trinity was the first step; Beckett had taken an irrevocable decision that would unambiguously demonstrate that he did not intend to follow a conventional career. He would continue to feel guilt over his decision for the rest of his life; but at the time it was perhaps the only solution to the growing burden that academic life had become. However, he had to endure the censure of his parents and his own growing feelings of inadequacy and instability; if the resignation from Trinity had been Beckett's first response to a growing sense of personal crisis, it would take him some time to assert his new found independence and to overcome the sense that he was, in leaving Trinity against his parents' wishes, something of a failure.

After deciding to resign his position, he took refuge with the Sinclairs in Germany, before returning to Paris for a few months. There he met with the acquaintances that he had made in his previous visit; naturally, this included Joyce, who had come to accept the fact that Lucia was seriously ill. He and Beckett resumed their old friendship, taking long walks together along the banks of the Seine by the Isle of Swans. While in Paris, Beckett also had the opportunity to search for some remunerative translation work; for example, near the end of his stay in Paris he sold a translation of Rimbaud's *Le Bateau Ivre* to Edward Titus, the editor of the journal *This Quarter*. Translation, though, was not the only type of writing that Beckett did in Paris. He had begun to write his first extended work, *Dream of Fair to Middling Women*, a lightly veiled (and in places intimidatingly learned) autobiographical fiction. The novel was largely composed in Paris, from February to June 1932, using some of the material that he had written in Dublin the previous year; Beckett sent it to various publishers, but their response was largely negative. Later, Beckett was to claim that *Dream* was an immature work, and did not sanction its publication until a few years before his death (it finally appeared in 1992). Immature though it may be, *Dream* has provided Beckett's biographers with invaluable material about his early life; at the time, it served a more immediate purpose. It was, in itself, a substantial piece of writing; and it provided material for the collection *More Pricks Than Kicks*, published by Chatto and Windus in 1934. [51–7]

At the time, though, the progress of *Dream* from publishing house to publishing house served only to depress Beckett; he seemed unable to place any of the work that he was doing. Publications were few; and his status in Paris was itself under threat, as the French government took an increasingly hard line on immigrants. The money from his Rimbaud translation enabled him to spend a little time in London; but, eventually, he succumbed to the inevitable, and he 'crawled home ... with [his] tail between [his] legs' (Knowlson 1996: 163). The atmosphere at Cooldrinagh was, initially, not as strained as one might have expected; Beckett was given a warm welcome by his family, but he soon came to feel as though he was a burden on them, and his guilt over the resignation kept him from re-establishing a social life in Dublin. He stayed at home, feeling increasingly isolated, and worked on his writing, producing, in addition to translations commissioned by Nancy Cunard, many of the stories later collected in *More Pricks*. His health worsened; the cysts returned, making an operation imperative, and Beckett entered hospital in May 1933. The operation took place on the 3rd; on the same day, Peggy Sinclair died of tuberculosis in Germany. Her health had been failing for some time, but her death was still a considerable shock.

Worse was to come. Beckett, recuperating from the operation, found that his writing was drying up; depressed and frustrated, he began to drink heavily. Once, arriving home late, he smashed the plates in the kitchen after a quarrel with May. In the aftermath of this incident, Beckett began to consider once more the possibility of leaving Ireland; he thought of turning to his father for an allowance to enable him to live in either Spain or Germany. During this difficult period, Bill Beckett had been a great comfort to his son, who wrote to MacGreevy, saying 'I'll never have anyone like him' (Knowlson 1996: 170). In mid-June, Bill suffered a major heart-attack; his younger son helped to take care of him, washing and shaving his father. At first, Beckett's father seemed to rally, but he had another, fatal heart attack on 26 June. Beckett described his father's death in the moving short poem 'Die Taghte Es'; mourning the death, he told MacGreevey 'I can't write about him. I can only walk the fields and climb the ditches after him' (Knowlson 1996: 171).

The gloom of the year was lightened somewhat by the news that Chatto and Windus had accepted his stories for publication; but the strain that Beckett had endured could not be alleviated so easily. He came close to a complete breakdown; according to Bair, by the end of the year Beckett's night panics were so severe that he could only sleep if Frank shared his bed. The situation was clearly untenable; and Beckett sought a cure

> After my father's death I had trouble psychologically. The bad years were between when I had to crawl home in 1932 and after my father's death in 1933. I'll tell you how it was. I was walking down Dawson Street [in Dublin]. And I felt I couldn't go on. It was a strange experience I can't really describe. I found that I couldn't go on moving … and I felt I needed help. So I went to Geoffrey Thompson's surgery … When he got there … he gave me a look over and found nothing physically wrong. Then he recommended psychoanalysis for me. Psychoanalysis was not allowed in Dublin at that time. It was not legal. So, in order to have psychoanalysis, you had to come to London.
>
> (Knowlson 1996: 172–3)

After some rather tense negotiations with May about his finances, Beckett left for London shortly after Christmas 1933.

Beckett's psychoanalyst was a Dr Wilfred Ruprecht Bion, an ex-army officer whom Beckett found engaging, if rather intimidating. The therapy lasted until Christmas 1935; its value to Beckett seems to have been not so much that it held out the promise of a cure for his afflictions, but that it enabled him to reflect on his experiences up to this point. Those experiences, Beckett told Bion, started before birth; he could remember life in his mother's womb – a feeling of enclosure, entrapment, with little possibility of escape. More immediately, Beckett began to realise that his physical condition was indissoluably linked to his mental state

> For years I was unhappy, consciously and deliberately ever since I left school and went into T.C.D., so that I isolated myself more and more, undertook less and less and lent myself to a crescendo of disparagement of others and myself. But in all that there was

nothing that struck me as morbid. The misery and solitude and apathy and the sneers were an index of superiority and guaranteed the feeling of arrogant 'otherness', which seemed as right and natural and as little morbid as the ways in which it was not so much expressed as implied and reserved and kept available for a possible utterance in the future. It was not until that way of living, or rather negation of living, developed such terrifying physical symptoms that it could no longer be pursued, that I became aware of anything morbid in myself. In short, if the heart had not put the fear of death into me I would still be boozing and sneering and lounging around and feeling that I was too good for anything else.

(Knowlson 1996: 179–80)

In 1935, Bion took Beckett to hear the noted psychoanalyst C.G. Jung deliver that year's lecture at the Tavistock Clinic (the clinic that Beckett was attending). Jung told his audience of a case he had treated; a young girl, convinced that she was going to die, who in fact died soon after the treatment ended. According to Jung, she died because she had never properly been born. The story made a great impact on Beckett, who later used it in the post-war radio play *All That Fall*. In the same lecture, Jung showed a model of the mind as a series of concentric spheres, leading to a dark circle at the centre: Beckett adopted this model for the sixth section of *Murphy*, the novel he was shortly to begin writing.

1934 was marked by the publication of *More Pricks than Kicks*; but Beckett produced little that was new. The publication itself was not something that he regarded with absolute delight. The portraits of those he knew in Dublin were liable to cause offence; one of the stories ('The Smeraldina's Billet-Doux') was based on the kind of letter that Beckett used to receive from Peggy Sinclair, and the possible reaction of Peggy's parents was a source of some concern to him. As it turned out, the Sinclairs were initially upset, but soon forgave him (Beckett later told James Knowlson that he had regretted the decision to publish the story ever since). The book garnered some positive reviews, (although reviewers could not resist the conclusion that the book was heavily influenced by Joyce) but its sales were disappointing.

In 1935, Beckett began *Murphy* **[57–60; 137]**, the last of his novels to be set in a recognisable location (a minutely detailed London). To prepare for the novel, part of which was set in an asylum, Beckett accompanied his friend Geoffrey Thompson on his rounds at the Bethlem Royal Mental Hospital; other characters were formed in the same manner as those in *More Pricks*; in particular, the drunken bard

Austin Ticklepenny was a potentially libellous portrait of Austin Clarke, an Irish poet known to Beckett. Stylistically, *Murphy* was an advance on Beckett's previous writing; it was clearer, sparer, and the arcane references of the earlier fiction were balanced by Beckett's dry, cool wit.

*Murphy* was begun and substantially written in London in 1935, the year that a collection of his poetry (*Echo's Bones and other Precipitates* **[98]**) was published, again without much success; Beckett finished the novel in Ireland the next year. A short time after returning home he fell ill with a recurrence of the pleurisy that had plagued him at Trinity. After this illness abated, he began to suffer once more the attacks of extreme panic that had driven him to seek psychiatric help in the first place. He wrote to MacGreevey that he felt defeated by his return; according to James Knowlson, he also suspected that his mother was manipulating his finances in an attempt to keep him in Ireland. However, during this period he did not sink into gloomy isolation; he at least made the effort to participate in Dublin literary society, even though he remained rather ill at ease in company. As in previous years, however, he found that he simply could not stay in Ireland. He fell in love with a younger woman, Betty Stockton, who was visiting Ireland from Boston, and wrote the poem 'Cascando' for her; she, however, was not attracted to him. Feeling lonely, he began a short, intense affair with his married cousin, Mary Manning Howe; when their respective mothers found out, the affair was terminated, and Beckett left, with his mother's approval, on a tour of Germany that lasted from September 1936 to April 1937.

In Germany, Beckett spent most of his time looking at art. The Nazi government had begun its purge of decadent modern painting, and it was hard to find the work of contemporary German painters; he was, however, able to see some modern collections and to be impressed by the work of Otto Dix and Karl Ballmer. He was however, more deeply affected by two older paintings; Giorgione's self portrait, seen in Hanover, in which the artist's face is placed against a dark background (an image which calls to mind the intently listening faces in the later drama), and Caspar David Friedrich's *Two Men Looking at the Moon*, which probably gave him the central image for *Waiting for Godot*. Travelling in Germany at this time, Beckett could not help but be aware of the increasing persecution of the Jewish population. The persecution had affected his own family; the Sinclairs had been forced back to Ireland, partly because the increasingly ailing Boss could not make a profit from his business, but also because of the increasing anti-Semitism they encountered. His private journals reveal that he was profoundly angered by the Nazis; the groundwork for Beckett's later involvement in the French resistance was laid during his time in Hitler's Germany.

From Germany, ill once more, he returned to Ireland; but life with his mother was more unbearable than ever. Although he continued to socialise, and although he began to experiment with a new form, writing the dramatic fragment *Human Wishes* (an aborted project on Samuel Johnson), May and Beckett rowed frequently. The tension was not eased by other events; Boss Sinclair was terminally ill, and died on the 4th of May; *Murphy* was still without a publisher, and Beckett had nothing else to send off. In such an atmosphere, it is unsurprising that his symptoms recurred; he told MacGreevey that '[the] heart bursts about one night in the seven …'(Knowlson 1996: 265). He began to drink excessively once more (there was a particularly memorable occasion a few days before his brother's wedding, that left Beckett nursing a gash on his forehead). Finally, Beckett and May had a fight (the precise details of which are unknown) and he decided to leave Ireland for good. Beckett wrote of this confrontation

> I am what her savage loving has made me, and it is good that one of us should accept this finally. As it has been all this time, she wanting me to behave in a way agreeable to her …, or to her friends …, or to the business code of Father idealised and dehumanised – ('Whenever in doubt what [to] do, ask yourself what would darling Bill have done') – the grotesque can go no further…
>
> (Knowlson 1996: 273)

In the middle of October 1937, Beckett left for Paris; from then onwards, he regarded France as his permanent home.

However, his new life in Paris was interrupted almost immediately. Shortly before his death, Boss Sinclair had read a memoir by the Dublin wit Oliver St. John Gogarty (a former friend of Joyce's, who provided the model for the character of Buck Mulligan in *Ulysses*) that contained libellous references to the Sinclairs. Beckett, much to his mother's disapproval, was called upon as a witness by the Sinclair family; he had to return to Dublin in late November to testify at the trial. His treatment at the hands of Gogarty's lawyer, one J.M. Fitzgerald, was sufficiently damaging (and entertaining) to make the front pages of the Dublin press the following day. Fitzgerald, adopting a phrase from the opposing lawyer's deposition, called Beckett a 'bawd and blasphemer' from Paris; it is unlikely that this description, and the experience of the trial, served either to make Beckett reconsider his decision to leave Ireland, or to bring about a reconciliation between himself and May.

Returning to Paris, Beckett involved himself once more in the circle surrounding Joyce, whose *Work in Progress* was finally nearing completion. He searched once more for literary commissions; and, once more, he started to write – this time in French. He produced a series of short poems (given the collective title 'Petit Sot') that seem in retrospect nothing more than a first attempt to create literature in a different language. They were not published at the time, but at the end of 1937 Beckett learned that *Murphy* had finally finished its tour of publishers, and was to be brought out by Routledge (who had been shown the manuscript by Beckett's friend Jack Yeats).

Between the signing of the contract and the novel's publication, Beckett's life took an unexpected and rather alarming turn. Beckett and an English couple, the Duncans (friends from his first trip to Paris in the 1920s) had been returning from a restaurant late at night, when a pimp, ironically named Prudent, fell into step beside them asking for money. Beckett refused; Prudent stabbed him, narrowly missing both his heart and his lung. The Duncans managed to move him to their flat; from there, the unconscious Beckett was taken to the Hospital Broussais. His Parisian friends, led by Joyce, rallied around him, visiting regularly, and Beckett seems to have been overwhelmed by the amount of affection in which his friends held him. His mother also came to visit, and he later wrote 'I felt great gusts of affection and esteem and compassion for her when she was over …What a relationship!' (Knowlson 1996: 282). Prudent was soon arrested, and Beckett found himself sitting next to his assailant while they waited for the trial to begin. Beckett asked Prudent why he had stabbed him; Prudent replied 'I don't know why, sir, I'm sorry'. Beckett seems to have been greatly amused by the response; he later wrote of Prudent

> There is no more popular prisoner in the Sante (a prison in Paris). His mail is enormous. His poules (prostitutes) shower gifts on him. Next time he stabs someone they will promote him to the Legion of Honour. My presence in Paris has not been altogether fruitless.
> (Knowlson 1996: 284)

Beckett's visitors in hospital included a Frenchwoman, seven years his senior, named Suzanne Deschevaux-Dumesnil. The two had first met in the late 1920s, when Beckett was at the École; as Beckett recuperated, they spent an increasing amount of time together, and soon after he left hospital they had decided to live together. Suzanne was, by all accounts, something of a contradiction; strong and practical, but with a surprising belief in the unorthodox (she championed alternative medicine, for example), she was both generous to the underprivileged and sharply slighting of those she disliked. Her relationship with Beckett was not always an easy one; but she provided the stability that his life had lacked, and, crucially, she always believed in the value of his work. She was also a politically committed woman, with contacts in the French Communist Party; these contacts were to play a crucial role in Beckett's life in the first few years of the Second World War.

## (c) WAR AND *WATT*: 1939–1946

As war became inevitable, Beckett's dislike and distrust of the Nazis hardened; he had many Jewish friends who were directly threatened by a possible German invasion, and he soon realised that, in this case, 'you couldn't just stand by with your arms folded' (Knowlson 1996: 304). When the German army invaded France in May 1940 Beckett, who had already offered his services to the French authorities as an ambulance driver, initially decided to join the flood of people leaving Paris. He and Suzanne fled to Vichy, where Joyce and his family were now staying; this was to be Beckett's last meeting with the ailing Joyce, who died in January the following year. Joyce arranged a loan from his friend Valery Larbaud for the penniless couple; this helped to tide them over until Beckett's brother was able to arrange his allowance. They finally decided, however, to return to Paris; and once they arrived in the French capital, it was not long before they both became involved in the fledgling French Resistance.

The cell they joined was codenamed Gloria SMH; it had been set up to organise the escape of British airmen who had been shot down over Paris, but by the time that Beckett and Suzanne joined it had become an information network, providing evidence of German troop movements for Allied intelligence. Beckett's job was one to which he was uniquely suited; he received information, translated it into English, compiling and editing a concise document that could be placed on microfilm and smuggled out of the country. The work was very dangerous. Although the group soon learned to be as secretive as possible there were many close calls, and the cell members found that, in practice, they could not ensure that security was as tight as they would like it to be. Beckett, Suzanne and the other members of the cell worked steadily through 1941; their luck deserted them the following year, when the cell was betrayed by a French priest, Fr Abeche, who had been recruited by the Germans. Beckett and Suzanne narrowly escaped Paris, and after a perilous journey through occupied France, they eventually found a safe refuge in the village of Roussillon, in the Vaucluse region of Vichy (a part of France nominally unoccupied, but in reality ruled by a puppet government on the Germans' behalf). Other members of the cell were not so fortunate. Albert Peron, (a close friend of Beckett) was arrested and interned, dying soon after the concentration camp in which he was imprisoned was liberated in 1945. For his resistance work, Beckett was awarded the Croix de Guerre and the Medaille de la Reconaissance Française after the war.

Life in Roussillon was necessarily constrained; it was a small agricultural village, and as such was rarely visited by the German army, but people who sought refuge there were tied to it for the duration of the war. According to Bair, Beckett responded to his enforced imprisonment in the village by having a nervous breakdown; however, this has been contested by Knowlson, who could find no evidence for a decline in Beckett's mental health at this time. Whatever the truth of the matter, it does seem that Beckett and Suzanne found their enforced exile in Roussillon frustrating. There were others in the village with whom they could share their days; the painter Henri Hayden and his wife, and a Miss Beamish, whose background (as her name suggests) was Irish. Beckett grew to love Hayden's painting, and he took to drinking with Miss Beamish; they could be heard drunkenly singing Irish songs late at night. He could also occupy his time in more physical ways; he worked for a local farmer named Aude, who in return supplied the couple with fresh food. Later, as the allied forces came closer to the village, Beckett took part in resistance activities, harrying the retreating Germans, but he found that he had no stomach for this kind of war.

In Roussillon, Beckett substantially wrote his final novel in English. *Watt* was begun in Paris before Beckett and Suzanne fled; its composition was completed during their stay in Roussillon. *Watt* has been held (by Deidre Bair) to be prime evidence of the disintegration of Beckett's mind; and it does, on the surface at least, seem to be a uniquely fragmented text **[60–2; 116–17, 151]**. Knowlson, though, locates the development of the work in a series of arguments that Beckett had with another refugee in Roussillon, Marcel Lob. Lob was an arch-rationalist, believing in the human mind's ability ultimately to understand the world; Beckett, perhaps drawing on his immediate experience of the war, disagreed. Perhaps something of this found its way into the novel, whose central character, the eponymous Watt, compulsively tries (and fails) to arrive at a precise understanding of his time in Mr Knott's house.

Roussillon was liberated in 1945; Beckett's and Suzanne's first impulse was, understandably, to resume their lives in Paris. They quickly moved back to the apartment they had shared in the Rue des Favorites before the war, finding it miraculously untouched. Beckett's next priority was to re-establish contact with his family. Later in the year, he travelled to Ireland, finding that his brother was now a happily married businessman and growing closer to their father as he aged; that his mother was frail, and that she had moved from Cooldrinagh to a smaller house. His acquaintances in Ireland in turn noted that Beckett was emaciated, and that, for the first time, he would finish any meal that was placed in front of him.

It was while he was visiting his family in 1945 that Beckett had the insight that was to change his writing decisively. A version of the revelation is presented in *Krapp's Last Tape*

> Spiritually a year of profound gloom and indigence until that memorable night in March, at the end of the jetty, in the howling wind, never to be forgotten, when suddenly I saw the whole thing. The vision at last. This I fancy is what I have chiefly to record this evening ... What I suddenly saw then was this, that the belief I had been going on all my life, namely [Krapp switches off impatiently, winds tape forward, switches on again]– great granite rocks the foam flying up in the light of the lighthouse and the wind-gauge spinning like a propeller, clear to me that the dark I have always struggled to keep under is in reality my most [Krapp curses, switches off ...]
>
> (*CDW* 220)

So persuasive was this fictional description that Beckett's first biographer took it as the literal truth, and claimed that the location of the revelation was Dun Laoghaire harbour near Dublin. Anthony Cronin states that it took place not at Dun Laoghaire but at a smaller harbour near the city; Knowlson, with Beckett's own authority, sites it in Beckett's mother's room. Wherever it happened (and Knowlson's case is the most persuasive) the insight had two facets. First, Beckett decided that, rather a rational attempt to order the outside world, his fiction should deal with the 'darkness' of the inner self. Second, and following on from this, Beckett was at last able to place his writing against that of Joyce, and in doing so to mark out his own zone of artistic exploration. As he told Knowlson in 1989:

I realised that Joyce had gone as far as he could in the direction of knowing more, [being] in control of one's material. He was always adding to it; you only have to look at his proofs to see that. I realised that my own way was in impoverishment, in lack of knowledge and in taking away, in subtracting rather than adding.

(Knowlson 1996: 352)

Of course, this was not the once and for all transformation that it might at first appear. From the first, as noted above, Beckett's writing had taken a different path from Joyce's and the events of the 1930s and 1940s had forced him to reconsider both his own psyche and his view of the world. Analysis had revealed to him his own weakness and he had lived through a time when the entire world seemed to be collapsing, carrying him along with it.

He had changed from the polite but rather arrogant young man that had first encountered Paris in the 1920s. Those who met him at this time spoke of his shyness, but also of the courtesy and concern that marked his dealings with other people. After visiting his family, he worked for a time in Saint-Lo as part of a team from the Irish Red Cross, who were building a hospital; Beckett was the quartermaster, and impressed the rest of the team with his efficiency, his dedication, his quiet friendliness, and his stoic determination to get the job done.

## (d) BREAKTHROUGH: 1945–1953

After the hospital was built, Beckett returned to Paris, and embarked on the most intense period of creative work in his life. It lasted from 1946 to 1953, and during it he produced the works that were to establish him as an internationally famous writer. In a short, intense burst of writing he finished four lengthy short stories ('First Love', 'The Expelled', 'The Calmative' and 'The End' **[65–6]**), four novels (*Mercier and Camier,* **[64–5]** and the novels of the trilogy – *Molloy, Malone Dies,* and *The Unnamable* **[66–72, 137, 191]**), and two plays (*Eleutheria,* **[73–4]** and the play that more than any work has become identified with him, *Waiting for Godot* **[74–6, 117, 143–4]**). The period is the more remarkable, because at its beginning Beckett was further away from literary fame than he had ever been. *Murphy* sold badly, and was remaindered; a French translation was prepared, but Beckett had his usual difficulty in finding a publisher for the manuscript. When Pierre Bordas finally took it on in October 1946, its sales were as disappointing as the English version's had been. *Watt* was doing the rounds of publishing firms to general incomprehension, even if Beckett's skill as a writer was at least acknowledged; rejecting the book, Frederick Warburg wrote

> Puns would be too easy but the book itself is too difficult. It shows an immense mental vitality, an outrageous metaphysical skill, and a very fine talent for writing. It may be that in turning down this novel we are turning down a potential James Joyce. What is it that the Dublin air does to these writers?
>
> (Knowlson 1996: 343)

If Beckett was remembered at all, it was as a member of Joyce's old cabal in a pre-war Paris that could not be recreated. If anything, his position had worsened considerably; the value of the money that he received from home was shrinking, and both he and Suzanne had to work to support themselves – Suzanne by sewing and teaching piano, and Beckett by taking on as much translation work as he could find. He wrote with no definite hope of publication, far less of recognition and remuneration; rather, the work seemed to be forcing itself out of him. It seemed as though he had no real choice in the matter.

The type of writing he produced was markedly different to that of the pre-war work. In fiction, only the short novel *Mercier and Camier* was written in the third person; the short stories and the trilogy were written as monologues. This new style grew directly from Beckett's revelation of the previous year; later, he said that he was able to write 'Molloy and what followed on the day I became aware of my own stupidity. Then I began to write the things I feel' (Bair 1978: 312). In a famous, frequently quoted passage from 'Three Dialogues with Georges Duthuit' **[134]**, written at the same time as the trilogy, Beckett mapped out the territory that he was now intent on exploring. He noted that, previously, the problem for the artist had been one of expression; how does one arrive at an image of the world. He defined a new art, one that would be

> ... weary of pretending to be able, of being able, of doing a little better the same old thing, of going a little further along a dreary road.
>
> D: And preferring what?
>
> B: The expression that there is nothing to express, nothing with which to express, nothing from which to express, no power to express, no desire to express, together with the obligation to express.
>
> (*PTD* 103)

In other words, it was no longer possible to create a fictional equivalent of the world; all that the artist could do would be to come to terms with his or her own ultimate failure, and to create art out of that failure. Beckett knew that this was a radical step for the artist; speaking to Israel Shenker in the 1950s, he drew a familiar parallel

> The more Joyce knew the more he could. He's tending toward omniscience and omnipotence as an artist. I'm working with impotence, ignorance. There seems to be a kind of aesthetic axiom that expression is achievement- must be an achievement. My little exploration is that whole zone of being that has been set aside by artists as something unusable – as something by definition incompatible with art.
>
> (Feyderman and Graver 1979: 148)

The work of this period was remarkable for two reasons beyond the sheer dedication that Beckett brought to the creation of his texts. First, the narrative voice was radically different. For one thing, although these new works were definitely set in a version of Ireland, the thinly disguised portraits and settings of the early work had given way to a more impressionistic, dreamlike evocation of Beckett's memories of the country. For another, the intimidatingly erudite tone of the earliest fiction had been disappearing gradually from his writing; as the novels moved into the first person, Beckett evolved a deceptively simple prose style, that was flexible enough to move from passages of high comedy (for the *Trilogy* is, amongst other things, blackly funny), through dispassionate descriptions of cruelty to passages of lyrical beauty

> ... Yes, it is quite dark. I can see nothing. I can scarcely even see the window- pane, or the wall forming so sharp a contrast that it often looks like the edge of an abyss. I hear the noise of my little finger as it glides over the page and then that so different of the pencil following after. That is what surprises me and makes me say that something must have changed. Whence that child I might have been, why not? And I hear also, there we are at last, I hear a choir, far enough away from me not to hear it when it goes soft. It is a song I know I don't know how, and when it fades, and when it dies quite away, it goes on inside me, but too slow, or too fast, for when it comes on the air to me again it is not altogether mine, but behind, or ahead ...
>
> (*T* 208)

It is frequently said of Joyce that he was never more a poet than when he wrote prose; the same has also been said of Beckett, and with good reason.

Finally, the new work was in a new language **[132–3, 167–8]**. The switch from English to French was not a complete or absolute one; Beckett had composed in French before the war, returning to English for *Watt*, and he was to return to English sporadically for the rest of his writing life. The turn to a new language should not be understood as an effort to facilitate publication in his adopted country; Beckett was, after all, skilled in languages, and had been immersing himself in French as a literary language for most of his adult life. Furthermore, it was a choice partly dictated by the demands that his new subject matter made on him. He needed a language that was not burdened, as he felt, with the weight of associations and the tendency toward inflated rhetoric that he identified in English

> It was ... easier, Beckett maintained, to write in French 'without style'. He did not mean by this that his French had no style, but that, by adopting another language, he gained a greater simplicity and objectivity. French offered him the freedom to concentrate on a more direct expression of the search for 'being' and on an exploration of ignorance, impotence and indigence. Using French also enabled him to 'cut away the excess, to strip away the colour', and to concentrate more on the music of the language, its sounds and its rhythms.
>
> (Knowlson 1996: 357)

The work accumulated; but it was as yet unpublished, and Suzanne took it upon herself to tout the manuscripts around Paris. Beckett himself was persistently unwell; the couple were too poor to feed themselves properly, and the sheer effort of writing had an undeniable effect on him. He was not the only one in his family to be ill; his mother had been diagnosed as having Parkinson's disease, and each time he visited her, her deterioration was more marked and more painful. He wrote of her

> I gaze into the eyes of my mother, never so blue, so stupefied, so heart-rending – the eyes of an issueless childhood, that of old age ... These are the first eyes I think I truly see. I do not need to see others; there is enough here to make one love and weep.
>
> (Knowlson 1996: 367)

May died in 1950, on the 25th of August; Beckett was with her at the end.

Beckett's post-war fame was due mainly to the efforts of two younger Frenchmen, the publisher Jerome Lindon, and the actor and director Roger Blin. Lindon was the owner of a small Parisian press; he first read *Molloy* in manuscript, and was so impressed (and amused) that he agreed to publish both it and *Malone Dies*. Lindon and Beckett soon formed a close working relationship, and Lindon became Beckett's main publisher in France. Beckett later formed the same kind of close friendship with two other publishers who took a keenly proprietorial interest in his work: John Calder in Britain and Barney Rosset in America.

Roger Blin was a Parisian actor and director known for his association with the Surrealists, and in particular with the theatrical theorist Antonin Artaud. Beckett and Suzanne, looking for a potential director for both *Eleutheria* and *Godot*, first encountered Blin's work in 1949, when they saw a poorly attended production of Strindberg's difficult late play *Ghost Sonata* directed by Blin. Beckett, though initially not impressed by Blin as an actor or director, was taken by a man who possessed some artistic courage, and who was receptive to difficult or challenging texts. Suzanne showed Blin both *Eleutheria* and *Godot*; Blin decided on the second play, in part because it would be cheap to mount. *Eleutheria* had a cast of seventeen characters, and demanded a complex stage set; *Godot* could be produced using just five actors and a tree.

It took time for such a radical play to be produced. Blin committed himself to the project in 1950, but *Godot* was not staged until January 1953, at the Theatre de Babylone, a small, 250 seat Paris theatre; Lucien Raimbourg played Vladimir, Pierre Latour Estragon, Blin himself Pozzo, and, in a celebrated performance, Jean Martin played Lucky. Martin, who had come to the production at the last minute, decided after research that the symptoms that Lucky manifested during the play were those of Parkinson's disease – the illness that had claimed Beckett's mother soon after the writing of *Godot*. After an uncertain start, *Godot* became one of the most fashionable plays in Paris, even though, every night, a proportion of the audience left well before the end. This pattern was repeated on its first London production in 1955, and its first American production in 1956; with each restaging, the play seemed to provoke the same questions – chief amongst them the question of Godot's identity. Beckett generally refused to engage in such discussions, but his reluctance did not stem what was becoming, even at this early stage, a tide of critical speculation.

## (e) FAME: 1953–1969

After the scandal of *Godot's* first production, Beckett became a recognised part of the Parisian literary scene, and his life was more and more taken up with the social side of fame; the visits from old friends, the requests from editors, producers and academics for new material and comments on the material already published. In the early fifties, such intrusions were not as frequent as they later became, but they were already a strain on a man as private as Beckett. He needed to find a retreat where he could write; with the money left after his mother's death, he paid for a house to be built in Ussy-sur-Marne, some thirty miles from Paris. The house at Ussy provided Beckett with the seclusion he needed to work; most of the later texts were written there. Fame, however, did not simply alter the pattern of Beckett's writing life; it also altered his relationship with Suzanne. Suzanne was not comfortable company for his friends; they found her less sociable even than the notoriously shy Beckett. The couple also kept different hours. He had been nocturnal since his student days, preferring to sleep in the mornings and to socialise sometimes until the early morning; this, and the increasing attention that he received, ensured that they lived lives that eventually became at least partly separate.

With the completion of *The Unnamable* and the short sections of prose Beckett entitled *Texts for Nothing* **[80–1]** , the period of intense creativity came to an end. Beckett himself described the fragmentary *Texts for Nothing* as an attempt to break out of the impasse that he had reached in his previous work. He wrote to McGreevey

> I feel very tired and stupid, more and more so, in spite of my often resting in the country, and I feel more and more that I shall perhaps never be able to write anything else ... I can't go on and I can't go back ...
>
> (Bair 1978: 386)

Much though Beckett was aware that he had written himself into a corner at the end of *The Unnamable*, there were other contributing factors to his mood of depression in the middle fifties. First, there was the tiring schedule, initiated by *Godot's* success, in which he had immersed himself; he had begun to take a strong interest in the details of theatrical production, an interest which was to be reflected in the increasingly detailed technical notes in his theatre texts, and in the work that he was later to direct in the 1960s, 70s and 80s. Second, there was the increasingly onerous task of translating his own work (a task that, after a couple of unsatisfactory collaborations, he undertook on his own). But mainly, his depression may be attributed to the death of the last surviving member of his immediate family; his brother Frank, who died of lung cancer in September 1954. As with his father and his mother, Beckett helped to nurse Frank during the final stages of his illness. As Frank neared death, Beckett wrote to Pamela Mitchell that he would sometimes sit on his own after Frank had gone to sleep, 'drinking a last beer before going to bed ... and the sound of the sea on the shore, and [his] father's death and [his] mother's, and the going on after them'. (Knowlson 1996: 402) The sound of the sea running over the shore became a recurring motif in the radio play *Embers*, submitted to the BBC in 1959.

As was to happen more than once in the succeeding years, when Beckett found that he could not write fiction, he turned to the theatre. His next play, *Endgame*, **[76–8, 125, 164]** was begun in the aftermath of his brother's death in 1955; at first, Beckett conceived of it as a two act play, but as the text was revised he slimmed it down, before arriving at its final form (a long one-act play). *Endgame* remained one of Beckett's favourite dramas; it was the first play to show, in great detail, the kind of care and attention to detail that he was to bring to his subsequent dramatic writing. But also, and perhaps unsurprisingly given the events in Beckett's life, the play is haunted by the prospect of universal death; the world outside Hamm's refuge is 'corpsed', and those inside the refuge seem eager to attain the same state (Clov: 'When I fall, I'll weep for happiness' (*CDW* 132)). The same atmosphere hangs over another play, written at the same time; the radio script *All That Fall*, **[78–9, 151–2]** commissioned by the BBC, and delivered in September 1956. *All That Fall* is the most obviously autobiographical of Beckett's mature plays, at least in terms of its setting, which is, as Beckett himself noted, that of his childhood

> Have been asked to write a radio play for the [BBC] and am tempted, feet dragging, and breath short and imprecations from the Brighton Road and Foxrock station and back, insentient old mares in foal being welted by the cottagers and the Devil tottered in the ditch- boyhood memories.
>
> (Knowlson 1996: 428)

The landscape of *All That Fall* might have been a familiar one for Beckett but, arguably, his evocation of the rural Ireland of his youth is haunted by the deaths of his father, his brother and his mother; the play is structured around the idea of mortality, from the snatch of music heard at its opening (Schubert's song 'Death and the Maiden) to the final revelation that a child has been crushed beneath the wheels of a train.

However death-obsessed the material, Beckett's dramatic writing was developing rapidly; he was increasingly in command of his medium, creating work that showed an acute awareness of the requirements and opportunities of the stage. In addition to *Endgame* and *All That Fall*, Beckett wrote the mime *Act Without Words* (1956), *Krapp's Last Tape* (1958) **[79–80]** , and the radio play *Embers* (1959) **[80]**. Each work relies for its effect, not only on the predicament of the characters, but on the increasingly sure and precise way in which the predicament is dramatised. In *Krapp's Last Tape*, Beckett dramatised the confrontation between an old man and his past by exploiting the possibilities inherent in the tape recorder; in *Embers*, Henry's monologue and memories are played off against the naggingly persistent sound of the sea.

Drama as extreme as Beckett's was not likely to establish itself without some resistance; and the history of the early productions is to some extent a history of missed opportunities. Although written in French, *Endgame* could not find a home on the Parisian stage; Beckett and Blin (who directed the play) had to wait until 1957 before it could be staged in London, at the Royal Court Theatre. Ralph Richardson was mooted for the first production of *Godot*; however, he and Beckett could not agree on the correct way to interpret the character. Beckett's judgement of Richardson gives an acute summary of the constraints that the Beckett actor would encounter

> [Richardson] wanted the low-down on Pozzo, his home address and curriculum vitae, and seemed to make the forthcoming of this and similar information the condition of his condescending to illustrate the part of Vladimir. Too tired to give satisfaction I told him that all I knew about Pozzo was in the text, that if I'd known more I would have put it in the text, and that this was true also of other characters ... I also told Richardson that if by Godot I had meant God I would [have] said God, and not Godot. This seemed to disappoint him greatly.
>
> (Knowlson 1996: 412)

In other words, for Beckett the ideal actor was one who concerned him or herself with the text as written and did not look for meanings that could not be enacted. When he came to direct his own work, Beckett would insist on an almost musical rendition of the text, with most attention being paid to the rhythm and pacing of the lines; he did not look for an overly emotional or unnecessarily naturalistic acting style, and would find himself at odds with actors whose training led them to look for the kind of realistic information that Beckett found himself unable and unwilling to provide. He found that in working with an actor, he was more likely to respond to an actor's physical and vocal presence. The actors Jack MacGowran and Patrick Magee, both closely associated with Beckett's early drama, both possessed distinctive voices and faces; furthermore, they both approached Beckett's drama as a practical proposition, rather than as a fully fledged philosophical statement that had to be understood before it could be enacted.

The pair had been associated with early productions; MacGowran played Clov in the first English language production of *Endgame* at the Royal Court in 1958, Magee had played in the BBC's *All That Fall*. Beckett's appreciation of and fondness for the pair was demonstrated by the fact that he created work specifically with them in mind (*Krapp's Last Tape* for Magee, the unfinished *J.M. Mime* and the television play *Eh Joe* **[94, 152]** for MacGowran). The rapport that the three had was clearly apparent in 1964, when Beckett came to London to assist in a production of *Endgame*, nominally directed by Michael Blake, in which Magee played Hamm and MacGowran Clov

> Both Pat Magee and Jack MacGowran, though at first politely sceptical, had little time for Blake's 'ardent commentaries', with Magee in particular showing a measure of contempt for what he thought was the director's too intellectual approach. The young man would explain what he thought a particular line meant, at which point Magee would growl in his throaty, County Armagh accent, 'yes, that's fine, man- but how do you play it?
>
> (Knowlson 1996: 513)

Beckett's attitude to his own work was profoundly different, and this showed itself clearly in rehearsals; he instructed the actors not to look for symbols in the text, and told them that the information they needed was already in the play itself. His directorial instructions were concrete and simple, sometimes almost pedantically so

> 'Sam, how would I say to Hamm, "If I knew the combination of the safe, I'd kill you"? MacGowran asked.
> Beckett answered quietly, "Just think that if you knew the combination of the safe you would kill him."
> MacGowran paused, then spoke the line perfectly...
>
> (Bair 1978: 480)

When Beckett did not encounter this attitude in the actors with whom he worked, the rehearsal process could be fraught; but if the actors shared Beckett's concern with the detail of the text and the staging, the results could be memorable. MacGowran and Magee were the first actors with whom Beckett formed a close relationship; later, there were others – Billie Whitelaw, David Warrilow, Pierre Chabert, Nancy Illig. Joining them was the director Alan Schneider, who mounted the first American productions of most of Beckett's plays. He too had realised that metaphysics and staging were difficult to reconcile on stage, and that the director's role was to realise the text as exactly as possible (a response that endeared him to Beckett, who proved increasingly unable to accept stagings that deviated from the text he had created).

The impasse in Beckett's prose was finally breached in 1959, when he began a piece entitled 'Pim', the first version of what became *How It Is* **[81–2]**. This curious work, written in short blocks of unpunctuated prose broken only by the narrator's gasps for breath, proved to be one of the most difficult texts Beckett had created, and progress was slow. *How It Is* prefigures the short prose pieces of the 1960s ('All Strange Away', 'The Lost Ones', 'Imagination Dead Imagine', 'Ping' et al), in which enclosed figures are described in a language that veers between agonised objectivity and mathematical rigour. These prose fragments, which Beckett allowed to be published piecemeal during the next two decades, are never less than striking, and are frequently extremely beautiful; but Beckett did not see them as a logical development in his writing. Rather, to him they represented failure; the prose fragments that he eventually allowed to be published were what remained after a rigorous process of rewriting and compression **[85–8, 130, 137–8, 163–4]**. He would complain to friends about the brevity of the work that he was producing: of *Ping*, quoted above, he wrote

> I succeed in hanging on ... to try and squeeze a last wheeze from the old bag and pipes. Seem to have got something suitably brief and outrageous all whiteness and silence and finishedness. Hardly publishable which matters not at all... months of misguided work have boiled down to 1000 words .
>
> (Knowlson 1996: 542)

He would return, time and time again, to the idea that his work was now produced on the point of its own exhaustion; that the prose pieces that appeared were the last few drops of his art, and that the time when he would finally fall silent was not very far away. In 1969, he completed another compressed prose piece, *Lessness*; on its completion he wrote to his friend, the critic Lawrence Harvey, 'fear I've shot my bolt on me and the work both shadowier than ever'. (Knowlson 1996: 564)

Something of the same tendency toward compression was now becoming apparent in the drama that Beckett produced in the 1960s. He began his last full-length play *Happy Days* **[83–4, 143, 181–2, 183–4]** in 1960, taking meticulous care that the staging of the new work was as precise as he could make it; the text was substantially rewritten the following year, and was shown to an enthusiastic Alan Schneider, who offered to direct it in New York. As with *How It Is*, the play is something of a transitional work. *Happy Days*, like the plays that follow it, is built around a simple yet striking central image; it is also the first of Beckett's plays to be intricately patterned, with physical action balanced precisely against the spoken text. So closely did Beckett entwine the physical and verbal aspects of this and future texts, that any deviation from the text as printed would radically affect the production of the play. As productions of his texts proliferated, Beckett became notoriously exact about the director's fidelity to the text that he wrote. Partly, this could be put down to the innate protectiveness of any writer faced with at times a radical reworking of his or her text; but it is also true that Beckett's texts were far more of a unified whole than the work of other dramatists. He was not so much a playwright as a maker of theatrical events

> For me, the theatre is not a moral institution in Schiller's sense. I want neither to instruct nor to improve nor to keep people from getting bored. I want to bring poetry into drama, a poetry which has been through the void and makes a new start in a new room-space. I think in new dimensions and basically am not very worried about whether I can be followed. I couldn't give the answers that were hoped for. There are no easy solutions.
>
> (Knowlson 1996: 447)

*Happy Days* was followed by *Play* (1962) **[89]**, in which a man and two women, trapped up to their necks in urns, are forced to pick over the details of their triangular relationship by an inquisitorial light that flicks from face to face. His next stage play, *Come and Go* (written in 1965) **[88–9]** underwent the same process as the prose pieces of the same period; pages and pages of draft versions to arrive at a short, four minute performance script. At the decade's end, Beckett produced his shortest work, *Breath*, a wordless, characterless gloss on Pozzo's lines in *Godot* ('they give birth astride of a grave, the light gleams for an instant, then it's night once more'.(*CDW* 83)) for Kenneth Tynan's erotic revue *Oh Calcutta*. *Breath* has become somewhat notorious. It has been read as though it is the final despairing summary of Beckett's position on the human condition; but it is more likely that Beckett meant the short sketch ironically, as a reductive comment on the review that was to follow. However, Tynan's decision to add naked bodies to the miscellaneous rubbish indicated in the text aroused Beckett's fury, and after a protracted wrangle, the sketch was withdrawn from the London production. **[88–93, 170–1** for a discussion of Beckett's late theatrical works]

Beckett continued to experiment in other forms. At the beginning of the 60s, he wrote two plays for radio – *Words and Music* and *Cascando* (both 1961) – both of which used music as a character. In the middle of the decade, unhappy with the way in which *Godot* had been transferred to television (even though the director was Donald MacWhinnie, a personal friend) he wrote a television play for MacGowran, *Eh Joe* (1965). The decade also saw Beckett's first and only foray into film. *Film* (1964) was the result of a request from Barney Rosset, Beckett's American publisher, for experimental filmscripts from noted Grove Press authors. Beckett was the only one to complete a script, which was filmed in New York in 1964, with Buster Keaton in the central role.

Beckett travelled to America for the filming; he and Alan Schneider (who was to direct the film) met the ageing Keaton in his hotel suite

> When Sam and I arrived, Keaton was drinking a can of beer and watching a baseball game on TV; his wife was in the other room. The greetings were mild, slightly awkward somehow, without meaning to be. The two exchanged a few general words, most of them coming from Same, then proceeded to sit there in silence while Keaton kept watching the game. I don't think he offered us a beer. Not out of ill-will; he just didn't think of it. Or else maybe he thought that a man like Beckett didn't drink beer.
>
>   Now and then Sam – or I – would try to say something to show some interest in Keaton, or just to keep the non-existent conversation going. It was no use. Keaton would answer in monosyllables and get right back to the Yankees – or was it the Mets? ... it was harrowing. And hopeless. The silence became an interminable seventh innings stretch.
>
> (Quoted in Knowlson 1996: 552)

Schneider was a novice film director, and had trouble realising the complex demands of the shooting script (the first shots had to be jettisoned; some film stock had to be reshot because the camera movement had produced an unpleasant strobing effect; and the film itself had warped in the intense New York heat). The interior scenes passed off more rewardingly, however; and Beckett was fascinated by the editing process (a fascination that led to the technically detailed and exact shooting scripts he produced for the later TV plays). [**93–4** for a discussion of Beckett's later media plays]

During the 1960s Beckett's celebrity increased markedly. It had been difficult to find time to concentrate on work before; now it was sometimes impossible, as he was sought out not only by the professionally interested but also by potential acolytes and by the merely curious. It was not that the attention was entirely unwelcome; Beckett made friends relatively easily, and there was a part of him that enjoyed the convivial life that his fame had made possible. He socialised with old friends (Con Leventhal, an acquaintance from Dublin, who had married Ethna McCarthy, the artist and sculptor Giacometti, Henri Hayden) and newer ones (Harold Pinter, who would send Beckett each new play for comment and advice, the playwright Robert Pinget, and Roger Blin). His manner (for he was genuinely solicitous and generous to his friends) and his international fame ensured that he also had networks of friends in Ireland, in Britain, in America, and later in the decade in Germany. With increasing fame came financial and other rewards; and Beckett developed the habit of surreptitiously providing for those friends who were not as fortunate as he was. His own lifestyle was rather more comfortable (he and Suzanne could now holiday abroad), but was in most respects unchanged. Perhaps the most consistent source of anxiety, though, was the state of his health. He had an operation to his jaw; and, as the decade wore on, his sight began to fail him, as cataracts grew in each eye (the cataracts were a source of great anxiety to Beckett, who had seen the deterioration of Joyce's sight at first hand).

He married Suzanne in England in 1960. This seems to have largely been for legal reasons; as he became wealthier, he began to worry about Suzanne's position should anything happen to him. The service was conducted in absolute secrecy, and only a very few of their friends knew of it. The marriage, however, did not change their relationship to any great extent; Beckett's life and Suzanne's diverged in some respects quite markedly. He never lost his sense of loyalty to his wife; but he began to have affairs, the longest lasting of which was with Barbara Bray, whom he met in London in the late 1950s. Their relationship lasted until Beckett's death, but there were others; and at certain points in the 1960s Suzanne came close to leaving him, claiming that the situation had become untenable. She did not; despite difficulties, they managed to retain enough in common for the marriage to survive. In 1960 Beckett shared the Prix Formentor with the Argentinean author Jorge Louis Borges; and he began to be talked about as a potential candidate for the Nobel Prize. In 1969 came the news that he had won; he and Suzanne were holidaying in Tunisia when the news reached them, in the form of a telegram from Jerome Lindon

> Dear Sam and Suzanne. In spite of everything, they have given you the Nobel Prize – I advise you to go into hiding. With affection.
>
> (Knowlson 1996: 570)

Beckett did not collect the award himself (he sent Lindon to Stockholm) and he dispersed the prize money amongst his needier friends. The publicity associated with the Nobel seems to have been nothing more than an irritant to Beckett. His work had reached another impasse; and the added fame that the prize brought made even more demands on his time.

## (f) LAST YEARS: 1970–1989

As had happened before in his creative life, Beckett found that the theatre provided an escape route from the impasse that his writing had reached. His vision was restored when his cataracts were successfully removed in 1970; the following year, he and Suzanne took a holiday in Malta. It was there that he saw Caravaggio's *Decollation of St. John the Baptist*. He later said that the painting provided him with the central image for the short play *Not I*, one of the most striking of the later plays. A spotlit mouth eight feet above a darkened stage spills out a fractured monologue while a cowled figure listens, periodically lifting its arms 'in a gesture of helpless compassion' (*CDW* 375) when the mouth refuses to adopt the first person. **[90, 185]** The cowled figure was seen by Beckett in 1972 in Morocco; and the idea for the monologue came from his own past

> I knew that woman in Ireland, I knew who she was- not 'she' specifically, one single woman, but there were so many of these old crones, stumbling down the lanes, in the ditches, beside the hedgerows. Ireland is full of them. And I heard 'her' saying what I wrote in Not I. I actually heard it.
>
> (Knowlson 1996: 590)

The play was produced for the first time in America in 1972. It is one of the most powerful of Beckett's plays, capable of having an almost visceral impact on an audience. When Beckett himself directed Billie Whitelaw in the British premiere, he encouraged her to speak at great speed, too fast for the audience to understand the text; he seems to have been more concerned with the impact of the image and the rhythm of the delivery than the words themselves.

*Not I* was the first of a series of plays that took the experiments of the 1960s to their conclusion; the tendency in the earlier plays toward patterned speech and movement, and toward an evocative rather than a dramatic text reaches its apogee in *Not I*, *That Time* (written in 1974) **[90–1]**, *Footfalls* (begun in 1975) **[91]** and the plays that follow them. These texts are as brief as the rejected fragments of dramatic work that he produced in the 1960s (these are reprinted in the *Complete Dramatic Works* as *Rough for Theatre 1* and *2*), but they are as formally intricate and as austerely beautiful as anything that Beckett ever wrote.

Beckett's keen interest in the staging of his plays naturally led him towards direction. He began to stage his own texts in the 1960s, and the 1970s he was used to receiving requests from theatres to supervise premieres and revivals of his work. He agreed only to a few of these requests, generally from actors and theatres that he knew. In addition to *Not I*, Beckett directed Whitelaw in the British premiere of *Footfalls*, and later on a revival of *Happy Days*. She found Beckett a courteous but demanding director; he insisted on complete fidelity to the written word, and he was adamant that the actor should not impose him or herself on the text

> When we rehearsed eyeball to eyeball, he opened up in me whatever there was to open up ... I can still hear him saying 'Too much colour, Billie, too much colour'. That was his way of saying 'Don't act'. He wanted the essence of what was in you to come out.
>
> (Knowlson 1996: 624)

Whereas another director might concern himself mainly with the actor's interpretation of the character, Beckett's approach to direction was rather more akin to that of the conductor or the painter. Preparing May for the premiere of *Footfalls*, Whitelaw remarked that she felt

> ... like a moving, musical Edvard Munch painting – one felt like all three – and in fact when Beckett was directing *Footfalls*, he was

not only using me to play the notes, but I also felt that he did have the paintbrush out and was painting, and, of course, what he always has in the other pocket is the rubber, because as fast as he draws a line in, he gets out that enormous India-rubber and rubs it all out until it is only faintly there.

(Knowlson 1996: 624–5)

Such an intense and idiosyncratic way of working could (and did) cause problems between Beckett and some of his actors; but he brought to each production a clear, detailed and practical sense of the way in which each play worked. His preparations were meticulous (some of the preparatory notebooks have been published; they show in great detail how carefully Beckett planned each production), and he preferred to deal with the text as a blueprint for production rather than as a puzzle that had to be unravelled before the actors could begin work. Any discussion of the meaning of the play was severely curtailed; any wider explanations were designed to help the actors realise rather than simply understand the text. For example, when working with the actors of the Schiller Theatre in Berlin, with whom he staged a very successful production of *Waiting for Godot* in 1975, he dealt with a query about the staging of the second act by stressing the non-naturalistic nature of the production

It is a game, everything is a game. When all four of them are on the ground, that cannot be dealt with naturalistically. That has got to be done artificially, balletically. Otherwise everything becomes an imitation, an imitation of reality ... It should become clear and transparent, not dry. It is a game in order to survive.

(Knowlson 1996: 607)

To mark Beckett's seventieth birthday, the BBC decided to mount a series of dramatic productions; they asked him to consider the filming of some of his work. He allowed the production of *Not I*; the auditor was cut, and the camera focused tightly on Whitelaw's mouth. The other suggestions were not so acceptable; and so Beckett created two new television plays, *Ghost Trio* and *... but the clouds ...* to form a trio with *Not I*. The three plays, given the collective title *Shades*, were broadcast in 1977. In them, one can see Beckett's by-now detailed grasp of the medium; in *Ghost Trio* and *... but the clouds ...*, the camera moves are choreographed as tightly and as rhythmically as the actions of the characters. **[94]**

Producing a prose work of any length, however, was still proving an elusive goal; the texts that emerged in the 70s were as compressed and as short as those of the 1960s. His attitude to many of them is summed up in the title he gave to a collection, published in 1976 – *For to End Yet Again and Other Fizzles* (Bair quotes the OED definition of fizzle – '1. The action of breaking wind quietly … 2. A failure or fiasco'. (Bair 1978: 538)). It was, then, something of a surprise that, at the end of the 1970s, he produced the first of three substantial prose works, written in what was for Beckett quick succession. *Company* **[94–5]**, begun in English in 1977 but not published until 1980, begins from a situation similar to that found in *How It Is*; a man lies in the darkness, remembering fragments of his previous life. Some of the memories are clearly Beckett's own; for example, the description of the protagonist's birth is almost identical to that of his author's

> You first saw the light in the room you most likely were conceived in. The big bow window looked west to the mountains. Mainly west. For being bow it looked also a little south and a little north. Necessarily. A little south to more mountain and a little north to more foothill and plain. The mid-wife was none other than a Dr. Hadden or Haddon. Straggling grey moustache and hunted look. It being a public holiday your father left the house soon after his breakfast with a flask and a package of his favourite egg sandwiches for a tramp in the mountains … When he returned at nightfall he learned to his dismay from the maid at the back door that labour was still in swing. Despite its having begun when he left the house full ten hours earlier. He at once hastened to the coachhouse some twenty yards distant where he housed his DeDion Bouton. He shut the doors behind him and climbed into the driver's seat … Though footsore and weary he was on the point of setting out anew across the fields in the young moonlight when the maid came running to tell him it was over at least. Over!
>
> (*C* 15–18)

Quite what moved Beckett to produce this work is hard to ascertain. As contemporary letters to the critic Ruby Cohn confirm, he felt that he had to produce something more substantial than the fragments of the past two decades; but also, *Company* might have been a response to the knowledge that Deidre Bair was preparing his biography. Certainly, *Company* is the most autobiographical of Beckett's works, even though the autobiographical element is filtered through the prose style of his later writing. *Company* was followed by *Ill Seen Ill Said* (begun in French in 1979) **[95–6, 165]** and *Worstward Ho* (written in English in 1981) **[96–7]**; the three works were collected together in the volume *Nohow On*, published in 1989.

Beckett continued to produce work almost until his death; the plays *Ohio Impromptu, Rockaby, A Piece of Monologue, Catastrophe* (dedicated to Vaclav Havel, the Czech dissident playwright) and *What Where* **[92–3]**; the television plays *Quad* and *Nacht und Träume* **[94]**; and *Stirrings Still* **[97]**, his last prose work, finished in 1987. These late works are in the simple, spare style that he had developed for *Not I* and the late trilogy; they show no noticeable diminution of his skill as a writer. The only sign of his increasing frailty was the infrequency with which new work appeared; the end of the 1970s and the beginning of the 1980s appear in retrospect to have been a late recapitulation of the creative outburst of the post-war years. From then on, work became as difficult as it had ever been. Beckett was ageing; the effort of writing, and the strain of being involved in productions of his own work, was becoming too much for him. His mood was not lightened by the death of many of his close friends. In particular, the two directors most associated with him, Roger Blin and Alan Schneider, had both died within months of each other in 1984.

In 1986, he began to complain of difficulties in breathing; emphysema was diagnosed, and by the following year he could not travel any distance without using oxygen. In 1988, after a series of falls, he collapsed at home and was taken to hospital; although his condition was not definitely diagnosed, he seemed to be suffering from Parkinson's disease, the same illness that was responsible for his mother's death. His last work, the poem *what is the word*, was begun in hospital, and completed in the retirement home where he was to die the following year. The establishment was a plain one, to the surprise of his frequent visitors, who knew that he could afford somewhere more comfortable; but he seemed content to his visitors, feeding the pigeons that gathered regularly outside his door

> He kept biscottes in his dressing-gown pocket to give to the pigeons. What was noticeable was that he could easily have thrown the crumbs to them while standing up. But, unsteady on his feet as he was, he had to risk falling over by bending down to feed them almost out of his hand.
>
> (Knowlson 1996: 701)

Suzanne Beckett died on 17th of April 1989; although their marriage had not been a particularly easy one, Beckett grieved for her. He did not outlive her long. He collapsed once more on the 6th of November 1989; on the 8th he was admitted to a neurological unit, after the initial tests for a suspected heart-attack had proved negative. Over the next few weeks he gradually drifted further and further into a coma, dying at 1pm on the 22nd of December.

Shortly before his death, he was visited by the Irish poet John Montague

> Most of our conversation had been circumspect, cautious and courteous, but now, sensing an opening, I feel brave enough for a direct personal question, even without the ritual glass before me.
>
> 'And now it's nearly over, Sam, can I ask you, was there much of the journey that you found worthwhile?'
>
> The blue eyes briefly ignite.
>
> 'Precious little'. And in case I did not hear or comprehend, he repeats it again with redoubled force, 'Precious little', and adds, 'For bad measure, I watched both my parents die'.
>
> (Cronin 1996: 590)

Montague had asked Beckett to copy out a poem for inclusion in *The Great Book of Ireland*, an illustrated compendium of Irish poets. Beckett had agreed to write out the early poem 'Da Tagte Es', composed after his father's death. Copying the poem was a laborious exercise, but eventually it was finished; 'with a gesture of finality' (Cronin 1996: 590) Beckett swept the drafts, the inkpot and the pen into the waste-paper basket.

---

## Further Reading

There are now three biographies of Beckett generally available: Bair (1979), Cronin (1996) and Knowlson (1996), which is probably the most comprehensive of the three. In addition, there are two subsidiary studies: Brater (1987) and Gordon (1996). Interviews with Beckett can be found in Graver and Feyderman (1979), and the correspondence beween Beckett and Alan Schneider has been collected in Harmon (1998). **[199–202]**

# PART II

# WORK

# (a) THE EARLY PROSE: 1929–1945

## i: 'Assumption' to *More Pricks than Kicks*

In the first years of his fame, Beckett proved rather reluctant to revisit his earliest work, despite the pressure brought to bear on him by publishers and academics. For example, he resisted offers to publish his first collection of short stories, *More Pricks than Kicks*, until the late 1960s; the unfinished novel *Dream of Fair to Middling Women* did not appear until after his death; the early short stories 'Assumption', 'Sedendo et Quiescendo', 'Text' and 'A Case in a Thousand' remained uncollected until the publication of the collected shorter prose in 1995; another story ('Echoes Bones', a continuation of Belacqua Shuah's story after death and burial), is as yet unpublished. He resisted publication, not so much because he was afraid of the harm that the widespread availability of work he regarded as inferior might do to his reputation, but because he felt that his earlier work was simply not good enough. He didn't destroy old manuscripts, and he made the early unpublished work available to academics, but in general it took some time for Beckett to overcome his unwillingness to allow the earliest of his experiments in prose to stand alongside the mature work. **[14–22]**

Now that most of the texts are available, it is easy to see why. Even if one makes no judgement about the relative merit of the early writing, it is radically different in tone and approach than the work that Beckett produced in the aftermath of WW2. The author's own judgement, that the work was written by a young man 'with the itch to make and nothing to say' (Bair 1978: 84), might seem rather harsh, but it has been echoed in the analyses of such eminent Beckett scholars as John Pilling, who called the earliest of Beckett's writings

> ... a forced growth: extremely ambitious, courageously experi-
> mental, but a little too exotic ... to take root and be widely admired.
> (Pilling 1994: 18)

As mentioned in the first section, Beckett was indebted to Joyce as an artistic example and role model **[12–13]**, and even though the tone and underlying preoccupations in Beckett's work are radically different from those of the older writer, the young Beckett shared Joyce's love of arcane, obscure and highly allusive language. It is difficult, for the unwary reader, to make sense of passages such as this:

Up to a time then after this little railway-station rectification she advanced up the railway-platform like a Gozzi-Epstein, being careful not to lose the platform ticket that yet ten pfennings cost had, insisting on the Garden of Eden in Mammy's furcoat, scarcely suggesting within the mild aphrodisiac of cheap loose black leather Russian boots legs that flexed nervously in black stockings stretched to the absolute limit of intensity and viewed from a very special Blickpunkt against a very special quality of hard light during a period of oestruation were not alas reasonably exciting. The truly tremendous bowl of the hips (frequent and easy) breaking out and away from the waistroot (she won't need no Lupercus) like a burdocked bulb of Ruffino and the two great melons of the buttocks received an almost Rhineline from the dark peltsheath ...

(*CSP* 8–9)

This passage from the story 'Sedendo et Quiescendo' is by no means the most obscure in the early prose; but it is a fair example of the style that Beckett first adopted. It is inconsistent, to say the least; at this stage in his career, Beckett characteristically juxtaposed the most learned references with a prose that was, if anything, aggressively colloquial. This not only makes the sense of the passage difficult to discern; it also puts a great strain on the structure of the sentences themselves. In Joyce, references are incorporated into the prose; in early Beckett, one sometimes gets the sense that references (and the more obscure the reference the better) are nailed on to phrases and sentences that are already fully formed. Although this can, on occasion, give rise to passages of memorable comedy (as it does in the best stories in *More Pricks than Kicks*), it is undoubtedly true that his earliest works are frequently rather tiring on the casual reader.

However, beneath the rather overworked surface of the prose, one can already see the young author developing those concerns that will later on come to be thought of as typically Beckettian. In his first published short story, 'Assumption', published in 1929, a young artist who has the unusual ability to reduce those around him to silence is visited by a woman who provokes him into a 'storm of sound'; as the tide of sound overwhelms him, he passes through a mystically described process of self-abnegation before dying. Silence is peace, and expression is annihilation. The style of the story, though, is rather awkward (Pilling calls 'Assumption' Beckett's worst piece of writing) and the central confrontation between the young man and the woman is too self-consciously poetic for the story to be anything other than a piece of marginally interesting juvenilia. It is an indication of Beckett's striking development as a writer that, only a few years later, he was able to write stories and novels as controlled and effective as 'Dante and the Lobster', and *Murphy*.

The prose of 'Assumption' might be pretentious, but it is not overburdened with learning; later, Beckett was able to blend references drawn from the history of Western literature, philosophy and art seamlessly into his writing, but in the work that immediately followed (*Dream of Fair to middling Women* and *More Pricks than Kicks*) the references frequently threaten to swamp the narrative. **[20–1]** The problem is complicated further, at least in *Dream*, by Beckett's stated desire to avoid the constraints imposed by a normal narrative structure ('The only unity in this story is, please God, an involuntary unity' (DFMW 132) the narrator wryly notes). *Dream*, even in its unfinished state, does not have a particularly coherent plot; it follows a young Dublin intellectual, Belacqua Shuah, in his travels in Dublin and around Europe; the novel is loosely structured around his various encounters with a number of young women (the Smeraldina-Rima, the Frica, the Syra-Cusa, the Alba) who are modelled, as noted in the first section, on the women that Beckett knew at this time (Peggy Sinclair, Mary Manning Howe, Lucia Joyce, Ethna MacCarthy). **[10–21]** Belacqua takes his name and manner from the Belacqua of the *Purgatorio* **[109–11]**. He prefers solitude and disengagement: the women that surround him are, in various ways, a threat to his isolation. Belacqua's preferred life takes place, as does Murphy's, in the darkness of his mind; the threat the women pose is that they will drag him back from the internal, mental world to the external physical world.

Such a passive hero presents a problem to any author; how can a non-dramatic, inert central character be used to generate the events of the novel? In his early work, Beckett's solution to this apparently intractable problem is twofold. First, he surrounds the central character with a troupe of fundamentally comic grotesques; these characters are not only themselves a source of narrative energy, but also help to indicate the sheer uncontainable material chaos of the world that the Beckett protagonist wishes to escape. Second, the author himself becomes entangled in the workings of the prose. In *Dream*, Beckett's voice is at its most intrusive

> The fact of the matter is we do not quite know where we are in this story. It is possible that some of our creatures will do their dope all right and give no trouble. And it is certain that others will not. Let us suppose that Nemo [a character introduced by the narrator who has only the most marginal connection to the events in

*Dream*] John, most of the parents, the Smeraldina-Rima, the Syra-
Cusa, the Alba, the Mandarin, the Polar Bear, Lucien, Chas, are a
few of those that will, that stand, that is, for something or can be
made to stand for something. It is to be hoped that we can make
them stand for something. Whereas it is almost certain that Nemo
cannot be made, at least not by us, stand for something. *He is
simply not that kind of person.*

(DFMW 9)

*Dream* has proved a fascinating site for those engaged in Beckettian
archaeology; it does contain much in the way of relatively unvarnished
autobiography, and it does lay out the philosophical and artistic
concerns of the young Beckett as comprehensively as in *Proust* and the
other early critical works. **[15–16]** However, in terms of the overall
development of his art, it is perhaps most notable because it contains
elements of Beckett's writing that will remain constant (although the
use that he will make of them will change) until the end of his life.
The narrator, bound up in the problems of narrating: the hero, searching
for an escape from the physical world; and the desire on the part of
both to turn away from the everyday. These elements, although
present, are present in fragmented form; in *Murphy*, *Watt*, and finally
in the novels of the trilogy, Beckett moves toward a unification of
these diverse concerns, finally arriving at a formal solution that is both
simple and surprisingly elegant.

*Dream* was also an archaeological treasure-trove for Beckett himself.
Sections of the unpublished novel were cannibalised for some of the
stories in the collection *More Pricks than Kicks,* the short story 'Sedendo
et Quiescendo', and the prose poem 'Text'. The Belacqua of *More Pricks*
is, however, a slightly different man than his namesake in the earlier
novel. He is more a part of the world than any other Beckettian
protagonist: uniquely for Beckett's male characters, he marries not once
or twice but three times. He is also presented rather more ironically
than the earlier Belacqua; in the second story, 'Fingal', Belacqua and
his current 'girl', Winnie, contemplate the view from the Hill of Feltrim
near Dublin

'When it's a magic land' he sighed 'like Saone-et-Loire'.
'That means nothing to me' said Winnie.
'Oh yes he said, 'bons vins et Lamartine, a champaign land for
the sad and serious, not a bloody little toy Kindergarten like
Wicklow.'
You make great play of your short stay abroad, thought Winnie.

(MPTK 26)

54

If, however, he is a part of the everyday world, he is also at the mercy of it; and in *More Pricks* Beckett creates an external reality that is threatening, not only to the protagonist's peace of mind (as was the case in *Dream*) but also to his physical and mental well-being. The characters in the collection are constantly under threat from an uncaring, unfeeling, brutally yet comically dangerous world. Belacqua's wives die grotesque deaths (Lucy, his first wife, dies two years after a riding accident cripples her; his second wife, Thelma, dies of 'sunset and honeymoon' (*MPTK* 189)). Belacqua's own death is treated in the same abrupt manner; he dies by mistake, on the operating table, during what should be a simple procedure. In light of this, Belacqua's decision, described at the opening of 'Ding-Dong' (the third story in the collection), to '... [toe] the line and beg(i)n to relish the world' (*MPTK* 39) carries its own weight of black irony; the world, after all, treats its inhabitants with casual cruelty

> ... All day the roadway was a tumult of buses, red, blue and silver. By one of these a little girl was run down, just as Belacqua drew near to the railway viaduct. She had been to the Hibernian Dairies for milk and bread and then she had plunged out into the roadway, she was in such a childish fever to get back in record time with her treasure to the tenement in Mark Street where she lived. The good milk was all over the road and the loaf, which had sustained no injury, was sitting up against the kerb, for all the world like a pair of hands had taken it up and set it there. The queue standing at the Paris Cinema was torn between conflicting desires: to keep their places and to see the excitement. They craned their necks and called out to know the worst, but they stood firm. Only one girl, debauched in appearance and swathed in a black blanket, fell out near the sting of the queue and secured the loaf. With the loaf under her blanket she sidled unchallenged down Mark Street and turned into Mark Lane. When she got back to the queue her place had been taken of course. But her sally had not cost her more than a couple of yards.
>
> (*MPTK* 43)

In this passage, Beckett creates a fundamental confusion, not over the event itself, but over the relative importance of the elements within the event. The little girl's death is not given as prominent a place as the fate of the loaf; and the loaf itself is described in almost human terms (it is 'sitting up against the kerb', having 'sustained no injury'). The accident happens, moreover, in front of an uncaring audience; the

queue treat the death as though it were part of the afternoon's enter-
tainment, and their only concern is whether this occurrence is
important enough to lower their chances of entry to the cinema. The
external world, outside the confines of the protagonist's mind, is a
world in which there is no clear distinction between people and things,
and where suffering and death are reducible to the simplest, most
callous, and most brutal terms.

The comically reductive fate of all creatures in this uncaring world
is described most memorably in the collection's first story, 'Dante and
the Lobster'. The story begins appropriately: Belacqua, who as we learn
in a later story is, like his Florentine namesake, 'sinfully indolent'
(*MPTK* 39), is first described at a moment of stasis:

> It was morning, and Belacqua was stuck in the first of the canti of
> the moon.
>
> (*MPTK* 9)

The only thing that can rouse him from this intractable passage in
Dante is the thought of his lunch, which he prepares in a passage full
of the bizarre comedy that marks later works such as *Watt* and the
trilogy. Lunch over, he picks up a lobster for his aunt, with whom he is
to dine at the end of the day. After an Italian lesson with his professor,
Signorina Ottolenghi [9], he takes the lobster, which he has been
assured is 'lepping fresh' (*MPTK* 17) (although Belacqua does not fully
understand the meaning of the term) to his aunt's house, where, to his
horror, he realises that it will be boiled alive

> In the depths of the sea it had crept into the cruel pot. For hours,
> in the midst of its enemies, it had breathed secretly. It had survived
> the Frenchwoman's cat and his witless clutch. Now it was going
> alive into scalding water. It had to. Take into the air my quiet breath.
>
> Belacqua looked at the old parchment of her face, grey in the
> dim kitchen.
>
> 'You make a fuss' she said angrily, 'and upset me and then lash
> into it for your dinner'.
>
> She lifted the lobster clear of the table. It had about thirty
> seconds to live.
>
> Well, thought Belacqua, it's a quick death, God help us all.
>
> It is not.
>
> (*MPTK* 21)

Belacqua, unable at the story's beginning to comprehend the workings of Paradise, is at the story's end unable to reconcile himself to the workings of Hell. One would think that a student of Dante would understand the infinite nature of torment; but, when faced with a fate that might come from the pages of the *Inferno*, all that Belacqua can do is to take refuge in a conventional piety ('... it's a quick death'). The narrator's conclusion is both a simple declaration, and a richly allusive reference to the unending suffering that is the lot of living creatures, in Belacqua's Dublin as in Dante's Hell.

---

## ii: *Murphy*

---

'Dante and the Lobster' is perhaps the first of Beckett's writings to be wholly successful. The tone is well controlled throughout, moving from the (ironically handled) erudition of Belacqua's private meditations, to the unforced comedy of the dialogue, before the sudden, sombre shift into the stark prose of the last section. This increasing control over his chosen medium is also readily apparent – is, in fact, even more apparent – in *Murphy*, his first novel, begun in London in 1935. **[23–4, 137]** Before *Murphy*, Beckett wrote the short story 'A Case in a Thousand', which remained uncollected until the publication of the *Collected Shorter Prose* in 1995. It is a curious story, containing elements that would find more successful expression in later work: the figure of Mrs Bray, keeping vigil over her sick child from the banks of a canal near the hospital in which he is being treated, echoes Krapp's vigil over the house of his dying mother. The relationship between Mrs Bray and the story's central character, a young doctor named Nye, is perhaps an early draft for the bizarre couplings in the later work (Watt and Mrs Gorman, Molloy and Lousse, Macmann and Molly).

Beckett never disowned *Murphy*. It was the first work to be translated from English into French; and Murphy himself appears in the trilogy, as the first in the line of solitary outsiders that terminates in the Unnamable. Murphy is, however, still recognisably a 'citizen of the world'; he lives in West Brompton in London in the 1930s, and his travels, and those of the other characters, take him and them on a geographically accurate tour of the city streets. The various journeys around London described so minutely in the novel are only one of the potential routes open to its central character; and they are definitely not the ones he prefers. Murphy is the first of Beckett's protagonists actively to seek to escape from his world; when we first encounter him, he is naked and bound to a rocking chair

He sat this way because it gave him pleasure! First it gave his body pleasure, it appeased his body. Then it set him free in his mind. For it was not until his body was appeased that he could come alive in his mind ... And life in his mind gave him pleasure, such pleasure that pleasure was not the word.

(*M* 6)

Murphy seeks a particular kind of stasis; a state in which he will be able to abandon not simply the external world but also the self that is bound up in that world. Murphy's mind is in the novel pictured as a series of concentric circles, and Beckett devotes the sixth chapter of the novel to a description of their operation, beginning with the outside ring, and moving in to the formlessness contained within the central circle. This is, as one might guess, Murphy's preferred destination

The third [circle], the dark, was a flux of forms, a perpetual coming together and falling asunder of forms. The light contained the docile elements of a new manifold, the world of the body broken up into the pieces of a toy; the half light, states of peace. But the dark neither elements nor states, nothing but forms becoming and crumbling into the fragments of a new becoming, without love or hate or any intelligible principle of change. Here there was nothing but commotion and the pure forms of commotion. Here he was not free, but a mote in the dark of absolute freedom. He did not move, he was a point in the ceaseless unconditioned generation of and passing away of line.

(*M* 65–6)

Murphy, naturally, has an abiding interest in the life of the mind and the spirit; he is knowledgeable about psychiatry, and has an interest in spiritualism (neatly combining the two discourses, he follows the prompting of a horoscope and becomes a nurse in a mental hospital). His quest is to attain nothingness: to pursue the Cartesian split (see section 3) between the mind and the body to its logical conclusion, and to achieve a perfect isolation in the endlessly mutable chaos of his innermost thoughts. This is, of course, a paradoxical wish: he is determined, through an act of will, to achieve a state in which he can will nothing.

However, the nothingness to which Murphy aspires is not the only state of nothingness in the novel. His stint in the Magdalene Mental Mercy seat brings him into contact with a Mr Endon, described as 'the most biddable little gaga in the entire insitution'. (*M* 134) Mr Endon is, it seems, completely unreachable: he interacts with the external world without acknowledging it, behaving as though the activities of those around him do not make the slightest difference to his life. Murphy is understandably fascinated by this patient, who seems to have already achieved a state of absolute willessness; he makes an attempt to contact Mr Endon, engaging him in a game of chess. Beckett reproduces the moves in conventional notation in the text of the novel; by following the moves, one can seen that Murphy and Mr Endon are following two mutually incompatible strategies. Murphy throws pieces into Mr Endon's path, in an increasingly desperate attempt to provoke his opponent into a clear response; Mr Endon moves his pieces in a pre-set pattern, that does not require any engagement with Murphy's forces. Murphy himself comes to acknowledge this; at the point where an engagement might possibly take place, when the movement of Murphy's pieces threatens to disrupt the inscrutable pattern Mr Endon is following, Murphy resigns. No wonder, in an attached note, Beckett describes Murphy's first move as ' the primary cause of all [his] subsequent difficulties' (*M* 137); he is fundamentally mistaken in thinking that, through his actions, he can reach a state in which action is no longer necessary. Mr Endon has already reached that state: but Mr Endon is a closed system, and cannot be understood. After his failed attempt to contact the uncontactable, Murphy retreats to the solace of his chair, and while rocking comes as close as he ever can to the perfect isolation he seeks: but he is killed by a gas leak, and, in a bathetic postscript, his ashes are eventually scattered across the floor of a London public house.

The tone of *Murphy* is more restrained than in the earlier work, and the overarching tone of dry irony that Beckett adopts allows him to create memorable moments of absurd comedy; and, as he did in *More Pricks than Kicks*, Beckett surrounds his central character with a variety of grotesques (Murphy's spiritual guide Neary, the pot poet Austin Ticklepenny **[23–4]**, the head nurse of the asylum, Bim Clinch, whose first name will recur in the original version of *Godot*, and in *How It Is*). Some of the names pun on the hopelessness of Murphy's quest (the paradoxically named Mr End/on, for example, whose name also recalls the Greek word for 'within') while some pun on the interconnection, in the Beckettian universe, of birth and death (Miss Carridge).

Of a different order is the central female character of the novel, Celia, whose prostitution supports both Murphy and herself; she alone can find something of the same peace as he does in will-less meditation (she uses his chair to calm herself after he departs for the asylum), and she is the only character in the novel who is able to deal with Murphy on more or less equal terms. Beckett gives her the final chapter of the novel: after Murphy's death, she takes her grandfather, Mr Kelly, to Hyde Park to fly his kite. As the park rangers cry 'all out', the line slips from the old man's fingers, and he is not quick enough to recover it: his attempts to recapture the kite take him to the edge of the Round Pond

> Celia caught him on the margin of the pond. The end of the line skimmed the water, jerked upward in a wild whirl, vanished joyfully in the dusk. Mr Kelly went limp in her arms. Someone fetched the chair and helped to get him aboard. Celia toiled along the narrow path into the teeth of the wind, then faced north up the wide hill. There was no shorter way home. The yellow hair fell across her face. The yachting-cap clung like a clam to the skull. The levers were the tired heart. She closed her eyes.
> *All out.*
>
> (*M* 158)

---

### iii: *Watt*

---

It took some time for Beckett to return to full-scale composition: the unsettled nature of his life, the experiments in a new form (theatre, in the unfinished piece *Human Wishes*) and later in a new language (the 'petit sot' poems in French) are perhaps evidence of a dissatisfaction with his work up to this point, especially given the relative commercial failure of *Murphy*. It was not until he had fled to exile in Rousillon that he was able to concentrate on his next large work, the novel *Watt*. **[28, 116, 150–51]**

The difference between Beckett's second and third novels is, first, stylistic. The learned, ironic, detached tone of *Murphy* is gone: in its place is a narrative voice that is pedantically and comically caught up in the precise nuances of the everyday

> ... they then began to look at one another, and much time passed, before they succeeded in doing so. Not that they looked at one another long, no, they had more sense than that. But when five men look at one another, though in theory only twenty looks are necessary, every man looking four times, yet in practice this number is seldom sufficient, on account of the multitude of looks that go astray. For example, Mr Fitzwein is looking at Mr Magershon, on his right. But Mr Magershon is not looking at Mr Fitzwein, on his

left, but at Mr O'Meldon, on his right. But Mr O'Meldon is not looking at Mr Magershon, on his left, but, craning forward, looking at Mr MacStern on his right but three at the far end of the table. But Mr MacStern is not craning forward looking at Mr O'Meldon, on his right but three at the far end of the table, but is sitting bolt upright looking at Mr de Baker, on his right. But Mr de Baker is not looking at Mr Mac Stern, on his left, but at Mr Fitzwein, on his right ...

(W 173–4)

And so on, and so on. *Watt* is periodically punctuated by similar blocks of prose, in which all the possible permutations (or as many permutations as can be expressed before the writer's exhaustion catches up with him) have been explored. However, simply to explore all the permutations of the physical world is not even to begin to understand it: in fact, the opposite seems to be true – the closer one looks at the world, the less comprehensible it becomes. *Watt,* it could be said, is a philosophical farce on the theme of rationality; the world will not shake itself into sense for even the most determined mind.

*Watt*'s plot is simple. A man, Watt, takes up the post of servant at the house of a Mr Knott, first on the ground floor and then, after an abrupt promotion, on the top floor. After repeated attempts to understand, or failing that to codify his employer and his location, he leaves, later to appear in an asylum where he relates in garbled fashion his experiences to the novel's author, a fellow inmate called Sam. The novel can be thought of as an extended variation on the final encounter between Murphy and Mr Endon in Beckett's previous novel: in a last attempt to communicate with his patient, Murphy holds Mr Endon's face in his hands and gazes directly into his eyes, only to find that 'Murphy is a speck in Mr Endon's unseen' (*M* 140). Similarly, Watt never understands his employer: everything about Mr Knott, his size, his shape, his dress, his speech, changes not only from day to day, but from moment to moment. As Watt in the asylum tells Sam, his quest to the source 'of nought', is ultimately fruitless; untangling Watt's last recorded speech (which is spoken backwards), we find:

Sid by sid, two men. Al day, part of nit. Dum, num, blin. Knot look at Wat? No. Wat look at Knot? No. Wat talk to knot? No. Knot talk to Wat? No. Wat den did us do? Niks, niks, niks. Al day, part of nit. Sid by sid, two men.

(W 166)

The eternal question suggested by the name Watt is met by the eternal answer of Knott, a name that suggests not only negation but also inextricable entanglement (Knott = not = knot).

This incommunicability extends to the novel itself: *Watt* is punctuated by gaps in the text, as parts of the manuscript are supposedly unintelligible or have gone missing: Sam himself informs us that, due to Watt's garbled way of talking, much of the information about Mr Knott's house is lost. The novel has a list of addendae, not included in the main text because of the author's 'fatigue and disgust' (*W* 247). Characters are introduced only to be abandoned; Watt's predecessor, Arsene, appears only at the moment when he is about to leave the house; before doing so, though, he delivers a 'short statement' of some twenty-five pages. An entire family, the Lynches, spring into existence, it seems, as a by-product of Watt's determinedly rational attempt to understand what happens to the scraps from Mr Knott's table. The Galls, a piano-tuning father and son, appear and then disappear; Watt, meditating compulsively on their visit, finds that he cannot assign any meaning to it. Watt himself is a strangely contingent character: we accept him as the main questing intelligence in the novel, and yet he himself is one of a series of more or less identical servants who pass through Mr Knott's household, and as such is indistinguishable in kind from his fellows.

The process whereby the central character in a Beckett work removes himself from the external world, already begun in *Murphy*, is taken further in *Watt*. Although the novel begins in a world of comic grotesques that would not be out of place in the earlier novel, this world is abandoned as soon as Watt abruptly begins his journey to Mr Knott's house. Belacqua and Murphy are young men down on their luck, always at the mercy of the everyday world: Watt is perhaps the first of Beckett's unworldly protagonists, the long line of tramps and indigents whose aimless, dreamlike wanderings will preoccupy him from the composition of *Watt* to the end of his writing life.

---

## Further Reading

Beckett's early prose has rarely been treated as an object of study in itself: critics have tended to mine it for clues to the post-war work. Cohn's (1962), Kenner's (1961), and Fletcher's (1964) studies, although written at the beginning of critical interest in Beckett, still provide a good introduction to the author's world; Federman (1965) is the first to study the early fiction in its own right; Robinson (1970) gives the clearest description of the early fiction as the first stage in an existential quest; Kennedy (1971) discusses in depth the symbolic structure of *Murphy*; and DiPierro (1981) provides a close analysis of *Watt*. More recently, Acheson (1997) and Pilling (1998) provide good introductions to Beckett's work up to 1946.

## (b) BECKETT'S POST-WAR WORK: 1945–1960

### i: The turn to monologue

At the end of the Second World War Beckett took two decisions that proved crucial for the development of his art. He decided to create an art that dealt directly with failure: and he turned from English to French, because French as a language gave him the simplicity of expression that his writing required **[33]**. Working in a language that forced him toward simplicity would also enable Beckett to create work that resolved the problematic content of his early novels; the contrast between the demands of a prose narrative and the tendency of his central characters towards stasis and impotence. In *Murphy* and *Watt*, the central characters' lives had been described by a narrator who made no claim to omniscience; in the nouvelles and the Trilogy, Beckett simply united the narrator and the central character, making the narrator's inability to describe and account for himself the central dilemma that his writing explored

> ... I shall not answer any more questions. I shall even try not to ask myself any more. While waiting I shall tell myself stories, if I can. They will not be the same type of story as hitherto, that is all. They will be neither beautiful or ugly, they will be calm, there will be no ugliness or fever in them any more, they will be almost lifeless, like the teller. What was that I said? It does not matter. I look forward to them giving me great satisfaction, much satisfaction ...
>
> (*T* 180)

Thus Malone; and his situation – a man in a room telling himself stories about himself, or about another, to fill in time and to have done with speaking, is a paradigm of Beckett's work not only in fiction, but also in theatre, film, radio and television. The situation is not unvarying, but the central dilemma remains remarkably consistent. A story or a course of action is adopted because it promises to structure an otherwise chaotic life; but that structure itself either disintegrates, or is found to be too constricting, or simply, because of the narrator's own weakness, cannot be pursued to its end. Language, too, is itself a structure; and Beckett's characters find themselves increasingly unable to find a linguistic form that will even begin to describe their lives truthfully and clearly. For all his talk of telling himself stories, at the novel's end Malone has only managed to complete one, and that by default (he dies as his central character, Macmann, drifts out to sea). The turn to monologue, then, not only allows Beckett to speak more directly and more simply about his characters' struggles with the essentially cruel chaos of their worlds; it also introduces into his work a central tension between structure and content, a tension that Beckett will carry into his work in other media over the succeeding decades. Put simply, the content tends toward disintegration, toward shapelessness, whereas the structure that Beckett builds to house the content is increasingly tightly organised. This gives his work its characteristic atmosphere; of writing almost but not quite at the point of complete disintegration.

## ii: *Mercier and Camier* and the *Nouvelles*

However, the transformation in Beckett's writing was not as clear-cut as the above description might suggest. As noted in the first section, he had already composed work in French (the series of poems written in the late 1930s); the first draft of 'The Expelled', then known as 'Suite', was begun in English and then recreated in French. The first extended work in French, the novel *Mercier and Camier*, was a third person narrative, written in the style Beckett had created for the opening and closing sections of *Watt*. Both *Mercier and Camier* and the four nouvelles can be seen as dry runs for the trilogy and the works that followed it: *Mercier and Camier* introduces the Beckett protagonist as inconclusive wanderer, his quest always at the mercy of events; the *nouvelles* accustom us to that protagonist's habitual tone of voice. The works also prefigure Beckett's development in other ways; like Valdimir and Estragon, Mercier and Camier are bound together so closely that they seem frequently to be speaking with the same voice; like the protagonists of the trilogy, they are obsessively concerned with their possessions, which, nevertheless, they constantly lose or mislay. Their journey is inconclusive, yielding at its end only fragmentary memories:

> I miss my stick, said Camier, it was my father's.
> I never heard you speak of it, said Mercier.

Looking back on it, said Camier, we heard ourselves speak
everything but ourselves.
We didn't bring it off, said Mercier, I grant you that. He took
thought a moment, then uttered this fragment, Perhaps we might–
What a deathtrap, said Camier, wasn't it here we lost the sack?
Not far from here, said Mercier.

(*M&C* 199)

Beckett did not agree to the publication of *Mercier and Camier* until
1970; he placed more faith in the short series of stories he produced at
the same time. These stories – 'First Love', 'The Expelled', 'The Calmative', and 'The End' – trace the life of an unnamed indigent, a man in
flight, either voluntary or enforced. He escapes the woman who is giving
birth to a child that is possibly his; he is expelled from the house and
the hospital in which he has been sheltered, albeit momentarily; perhaps
approaching death, he envisions himself on a boat, slowly sinking, only
to find that, after death, he has to continue to tell himself stories to
escape the process of his own decay. His life has become, it seems, a
kind of purgatorial progress without the hope of salvation; he is chained
to one location ('I only know the city of my childhood' he says in 'The
Calmative'(*CSP* 62)), unable to move far from it, trapped in an endless
cycle of aimless motion, waiting and reflecting, hoping for release from
consciousness

But it's to me this evening that something has to happen, to my
old body as in myth and metamorphosis, this old body to which
nothing ever happened, or so little, which never met with anything,
loved anything, wished for anything, in its tarnished universe,
except for the mirrors to shatter, the plane, the curved, the magnify-
ing, the minifying, and to vanish in the havoc of its images.

(*CSP* 63)

The Beckett's hero's wish has not changed since *Murphy*: the havoc
of images into which the protagonist wishes to vanish is similar to the
'ceaseless unconditioned generation and passing away of line' (*M* 66)
in the innermost circle of Murphy's mind.

However, this escape is even less likely than it was for Murphy,
who at least died, once and for all, in his rocking chair. In the *nouvelles*,
speech continues after the apparent death of the body; the protagonist
still has to tell himself stories beyond the grave, because even there he
is unable to find the kind of transcendence that will allow him finally
to escape his physical self. In Beckett, even the traditionally fine and

quiet grave is simply a place where the body continues to sabotage the mind

> For I'm too frightened this evening to listen to myself rot, waiting for the great red lapses of the heart, the tearings at the caecal walls, and for the slow killings to finish in my skull, the assaults on unshakeable pillars, the fornications with corpses ...

> (*CSP* 61)

The *nouvelles* introduce us to the interior monologue form that Beckett will use throughout the trilogy; they also introduce us – or rather, they deepen our acquaintance – with the intellectual tramp figure who is forced to narrate the events of his life, in order to give them a meaningful pattern. Finally, they rehearse the progression of the trilogy; from a life conducted on the fringes of a world that has only the most dreamlike appearance to the narrator, to and past the moment of death, to a limbo where it is not possible to escape the need to speak and to create.

---

## iii: *The Trilogy*

---

The Trilogy **[30–4, 137, 190–91]** – *Molloy* **[127, 160, 162]**, *Malone Dies*, and *The Unnamable* – is without doubt Beckett's most successful work in prose, and one of the key prose works of the twentieth century. It was written relatively quickly; Beckett began the first novel in 1947, and finished the series in 1950. It begins in familiar territory; the tramp Molloy embarks on a desultory quest for his mother, on his bicycle and then on crutches, which, after various encounters and sidetracks, is unsuccessful. He ends his journey in a ditch, from which he cannot extricate himself; from there, he is taken (we presume) to his mother's room, where he has been instructed to write the story that we have just read. He tells his tale, some eighty pages long, in prose that seems to flood directly from his mind to the page: thoughts are written out, then contradicted or rendered more vague than they at first appear. He speaks, not only to describe himself, but at the behest of inner voices that speak to him of a world in infinite decline

> I listen and the voice is of a world collapsing endlessly, a frozen world, under a faint untroubled sky, enough to see by, yes, and frozen too. And I hear it murmur that all wilts and yields, as if loaded down but here there are no loads, and the ground too, unfit

for loads, and the light too, down towards an end it seems can
never come...

(T 40)

This phenomenon is not new in Beckett's fiction (Watt heard voices,
for example); but in the Trilogy and the works that follow it, the internal voice becomes steadily more and more insistent, until by *How It Is*
it all but drowns out the protagonist's own speech.

In *Molloy*'s second half, we are introduced to the comfortable French
bourgeois Jacques Moran, who spends his time hunting down indigents
such as Molloy for his immediate superior Gaber and their mutual boss
Youdi. In the past, it seems, he has performed similar searches for
Murphy, Watt, Yerk (the name that Beckett now gives to the protagonist of the *nouvelles*), Mercier and Camier. Ordered to track down
Molloy, he leaves his comfortable house in the company of his son,
Jacques junior. Moran's quest, though, is unsuccessful. While on the
journey, he finds that his legs are slowly becoming as useless as
Molloy's; he sends his son to buy a bicycle (again, in an unconscious
echo of Molloy's preferred mode of transport). Alone, he perhaps meets
Molloy, but does not recognise him; in a state of unconscious frenzy,
he kills a man (Molloy on his travels dealt with one encounter with
the same kind of abrupt violence). As he approaches Molloy's home
town, Gaber appears once more, to order him to return home. On his
return he finds his house deserted and derelict; he himself is lame and
dishevelled, a mirror image of the man he was sent to pursue. He
finishes his report with words that directly contradict its opening; he
is free of his obligations, but to what purpose he does not know. At the
novel's end, he prepares himself to leave, to take up a life that sounds
suspiciously like Molloy's, at the urging not of his superiors, but of a
voice that only he can hear

> I have spoken of a voice telling me things. I was getting to know it
> better now, to understand what it wanted. It did not use the words
> that Moran had been taught when he was little and that he in
> turn had taught to his little one... It told me to write the report.
> Does this mean that I am freer now than I was? I do not know. I
> shall learn. Then I went back into the house and wrote, It is
> midnight. The rain is beating on the windows. It was not midnight.
> It was not raining.
>
> (T 176)

And yet Moran has not simply become Molloy: rather, they have come to the same general location by differing routes.

Malone, in *Malone Dies*, seems to exist in the rubble of Molloy's and Moran's tales. He is bedridden, in a house whose precise location and function he does not know; he has a pile of possessions (in which there are, amongst other things, a bicycle bell and half a crutch-possessions that tie him directly to the characters in the previous novel). Like Molloy, he has no clear recollection of his arrival at his final location; like Molloy and Moran, he is driven to write, even though the resources on which he can draw to fuel his fiction are running low

> I began to play with what I saw. People and things ask nothing better than to play, certain animals too. All went well at first, they all came to me, pleased that someone should want to play with them. If I said, now I need a hunch-back, immediately one came running, proud as punch of his fine hunch that was going to perform ... But it was not long before I found myself alone, in the dark. That is why I gave up trying to play and took to myself for ever silence and speechlessness, incurious wondering, darkness, long stumbling with outstretched arms, hiding. Such is the earnestness from which, for nearly a century, I have been unable to depart. From now on it will be different, I shall never do anything any more from now on but play ... But perhaps I shall not succeed any better than hitherto I shall find myself abandoned, in the dark, without anything to play with. Then I shall play with myself ...
>
> (*T* 180–1)

Malone's life, he decides, will now be spent in the creation of stories ('One about a man, one about a woman, one about a thing and finally one about an animal, a bird probably'. (*T* 166). However, he does not get further than the end of the first of these tales; a tale about a boy called Sapo, to whom Malone gives the unwavering gull's eyes possessed by Murphy in Beckett's first novel, who grows into a man named Macmann, a passive indigent, who finds himself one day confined

> One day, much later, to judge by his appearance, Macmann came to again, once again, in a kind of asylum. At first he could not know it was one, being plunged within it, but he was told so as soon as he was in a condition to receive news. They said in substance, You are now in the House of Saint John of God... Fear nothing, you are among friends. Friends! Well well. Take no thought for anything, it is we shall think and act for you, from now forward ...
>
> (*T* 257)

In other words, Malone and his creation are beginning to merge, although not exactly (much as Molloy and Moran came to parallel each other). Even though at the beginning of the narrative Malone takes pleasure in a character who is nothing like his creator, in the telling of the story, the narrator finds that he cannot keep himself separate from the story he is telling. At the end of Macmann's tale, he and his fellow inmates drift off from the shore in a boat; they have been forced aboard by Lemuel, an orderly given to the same kind of irrational bouts of frenzied rage to which both Molloy and Moran surrendered. As his creations drift away, Malone himself drifts finally toward death

> Lemuel is in charge, he raises his hatchet on which the blood will never dry, but not to hit anyone, he will not hit anyone, he will not hit anyone any more, he will not touch anyone any more, either with it or with it or with it or with or
> or with it or with his hammer or with his stick or with his fist or in in dream I mean never he will never
> or with his pencil or with his stick or
> or light light I mean
> never there he will never
> never anything
> there
> any more
>
> (T 289)

At the end of *Malone Dies*, the subject (the 'I' of Malone's narrative) has dissolved; at the beginning of *the Unnamable*, that self is revived. However, this time we are not in the presence of a Molloy, a Moran or a Malone. The voice in *The Unnamable* cannot truly be termed a narrator; although it is driven to narrate and describe just as surely as its predecessors, it does not have the luxury of narrative distance. It only exists as long as it speaks

> Where now? Who now? When now? Unquestioning. I, say I. Unbelieving. Questions, hypotheses, call them that. Keep going, going on, call that going, call that on ...
>
> (T 293)

This short quotation neatly outlines the profoundly paradoxical nature of the Unnamable (both the character and the novel). Words create stories, as they do in *Molloy* and *Malone Dies*; but words also create the author of the story. The Unnamable does not have an 'I', until it says the word. It does not know that it should keep going, until it defines for itself what 'going on ' means. It is trapped inside a narrative over which it has only the most tenuous control: and, what is more, Beckett's other characters are trapped with it, in a setting which seems once more to evoke Dante's Purgatory

> Malone is there. Of his mortal liveliness little trace remains. He passes before me at doubtless regular intervals, unless it is I who pass before him. No, once and for all, I do not move ... He passes close by me, a few feet away, slowly, always in the same direction. I am almost sure it is he ... Sometimes I wonder if it is not Molloy. Perhaps it is Molloy, wearing Malone's hat ... To tell the truth I believe they are all here, at least from Murphy on, I believe we are all here, but so far I have only seen Malone ...
>
> (T 294–5)

But even this setting only exists because it is described; it is quickly abandoned because it no longer provides any useful illumination of The Unnamable's plight.

Its search is, in essence, a simple one. It wishes to reach the end of the stories that have previously held out the promise of self-definition and final silence. However, it soon finds that the lure of the story is still great, and begins to tell itself a tale about another indigent, even more decrepit than Molloy, Malone or Macmann. Once the Unnamable has invoked this character (named Mahood), it finds it impossible not to begin to image the world through Mahood's eyes: the 'I' of the Unnamable becomes the 'I' of Mahood. In a desperate attempt to pull itself back from this new fiction, the Unnamable invokes yet another creature, called Worm. For a moment, it seems as though Worm might be more suitable than any of the Unnamable's previous personas: Worm is as close to nothingness as a named character can possibly be

> Worm, to say he does not know what he is, where he is, what is happening, is to underestimate him. What he does not know is that there is anything to know. His senses tell him nothing, nothing about himself, nothing about the rest, and this distinction is beyond him ...
>
> (T 349)

But before long, the Unnamable realises that even Worm is useless; there is no way for the Unnamable to enter into such an unknowing

state (rather as Murphy found Mr Endon basically unfathomable, and
Watt never pierced the mystery of Mr Knott)

> ... Is there a single word of mine in what I say? No, I have no voice,
> in this matter I have none. That's one of the reasons why I confused
> myself with Worm. But I have no reason either, no reason, I'm like
> Worm, without voice or reason, I'm Worm, no, if I were Worm I
> wouldn't know it, I wouldn't say it, I wouldn't say anything I'd
> be Worm. But I don't say anything, I don't know anything, these
> voices are not mine, nor these thoughts, but the voices and the
> thoughts of the devils who beset me. Who makes me say that I
> can't be Worm, the unexpungable ... That since I couldn't be
> Mahood, as I might have been, I must be Worm, as I cannot be ...
>
> (T 350)

If fictional characters will not save it, the Unnamable's only recourse
is speech itself. The text of *The Unnamable* is gradually transformed by
the overpowering torrent of words that has become the Unnamable's
only possible route of escape; the novel eventually becomes one long
paragraph, filled with sentences punctuated (it seems) by the speaker's
desperate gasps for air. The Unnamable's goal is now simply silence,
the discursive fury of the novel's ending its attempt to break the barriers
imposed by language

> ... I'll wake, in the silence, and never sleep again, it will be I, or
> dream, dream again, dream of a silence, a dream silence, full of
> murmurs, I don't know, that's all words, never wake, all words,
> there's nothing else, you must go on, that's all I know, they're
> going to stop, I know that well, I can feel it, they're going to
> abandon me, it will be the silence, for a moment, a good few
> moments, or it will be mine, the lasting one, that didn't last, that
> still lasts, it will be I, you must go on, I can't go on, you must go
> on, I'll go on, you must say words, as long as there are any, until
> they find me, until they say me, strange pain, strange sin; you
> must go on, perhaps it's done already, perhaps they have said me
> already, perhaps they have carried me to the threshold of my story,
> before the door that opens on my own story, that would surprise
> me, if it opens, it will be I, it will be the silence, where I am, I don't
> know, I'll never know, in the silence you don't know, you must go
> on, I can't go on, I'll go on.
>
> (T 418)

In his early monograph on Proust, the young Beckett had outlined the direction that he felt any worthwhile contemporary artistic endeavour should take

> The only fertile research is excavatory, immersive, a contraction of the spirit, a descent. The artist is active, but negatively, shrinking from the nullity of extra-circumferential phenomena, drawn into the core of the eddy.
>
> (*PTD* 65–6)

It is tempting to read the trilogy as a whole in the light of this statement. It seems so neatly to describe the movement of the novels, from the relative light and movement of *Molloy* to the wordstorm of *The Unnamable*. We seem to have reached the source of all the stories that Beckett and his protagonists have told us, from 'Assumption' onwards; and we have discovered that the underlying motivation for these tales is the desperate attempt to break free of the need to tell tales. If, as Beckett maintains in *Proust*, the ideal route for the artist is one that takes him or her to the core of the self, then it is difficult to imagine any way forward, either for Beckett's characters or for the writer. However, it is neither that simple nor that conclusive. The compulsive need to shape experience felt by Molloy, Moran and Malone is still felt by the Unnamable, even when it has decided that stories are simply a distraction:

> ... it begins trying again, quick now before there is none left, no voice left, nothing left but the core of murmurs, distant cries, quick now and try again, with the words that remain, try what, I don't know, I've forgotten, it doesn't matter, I never knew, to have them carry me into my story, the words that remain, my old story, which I've forgotten far from here, through the noise, through the door, into the silence ...
>
> (*T* 417–8)

Even though the Unnamable hopes to be carried through to final silence, it still places its faith in the voices and the stories that have led it to create all of its fictional ur-selves, the Molloys, Morans and Malones whose tales only masked its own painful dilemma. There is no indication, at the end of the trilogy, that the Unnamable's goal has been reached; only that the voice will continue its desperate, paradoxical attempt to speak its way to the end of all speech.

## iv: *Eleutheria* and *Waiting for Godot*

The completion of the trilogy brought an end to the series of novels and stories that had preoccupied Beckett from the beginning of his writing life; in fact, it brought him perilously close to the boundaries of writing itself. What kind of fiction, after all, could survive such a determined attempt to destroy the foundations on which fiction is constructed? After *The Unnamable*, Beckett unsurprisingly found prose composition difficult; he was not to complete a prose work until *Comment C'est* (*How It Is*) in 1960. Instead, he turned increasingly to a new medium, one which had already proved to be something of a relief from the increasingly claustrophobic world of the Trilogy. Beckett had attempted to write for the stage before the war: but it was not until the late forties that he began to produce work that was finished, let alone stageable. His first attempt at a complete dramatic work, *Eleutheria*, was written quickly in early 1947, between the *nouvelles* and the Trilogy.

*Eleutheria*'s protagonist, Victor Krap, is like Murphy a young man trying to escape from the constraints of the physical world: his family, his acquaintances, his fiancee, and several incidental characters (including his landlady, a glazier come to fix a broken window in Victor's empty room, and in the final act an irate member of the audience) try to drag him back to real life, but they are ultimately unsuccessful. The play ends with Victor, lying alone in his room, 'turning his emaciated back on humanity' (*E* 170). The play contains some interesting elements, such as Beckett's rather self-conscious attempt to draw attention to the theatricality of the play

Spectator:   ... Actually, who wrote this rubbish? (*programme*) Beckett (*he says 'Beke'*), Samuel, Beke, Beke, he must be a cross between a Jew from Greenland and a peasant from the Auverge.

(*E* 136)

The stage set is also worth noting, split as it is between Victor's bare apartment and his family's crowded bourgeois drawing room in the first two acts, and wholly occupied by Victor's room in the third act, as though his room has pushed his parents' room from the stage. Victor's father, despairing of his place in the play and in the world, and the spectator, who finds that the longer he spends on stage the less clear his motives become, both prefigure characters in the later plays (Krapp in *Krapp's Last Tape*, the hesitations that afflict Vladimir, Estragon, and Pozzo in *Waiting For Godot*).

*Eleutheria* is *Dream of Fair to Middling Women* imagined for the stage (a first rehearsal of themes and preoccupations, more successfully incarnated in later work); Beckett's next play stands comparison with the Trilogy. *Waiting for Godot* **[34, 117, 143–4]** has become one of the key works of the twentieth century; and its central image – two tramps waiting by a tree in the open country, for Godot to come – has become one of the most famous images of the modern stage. It is a remarkably simple play; an early critic, Vivian Mercier, famously remarked that it was a play in which 'nothing happens, twice', and although this is not an adequate summary of the plot, it does indicate the spareness of Beckett's writing and stagecraft. *Godot* replaces the scrupulously imagined and realised worlds of most modern plays with a setting that seems as close to nowhere as it is possible to get; the set description is laconically brief (A country road. A tree. Evening (*CDW* 11): we learn of the stage's only other decoration, a low mound, during the first set of stage directions). In this bare location, the two tramps, Vladimir and Estragon, pass the time before Godot's expected arrival: in each act, they meet Pozzo, a landowner, and Lucky, his servant; and at the end of each act, after a boy has brought them a message from Godot, saying that he will meet them without fail on the following day, they decide to go, but do not move.

On this simple structure Beckett builds a piece of theatre out of the building-blocks of theatre itself. Any theatrical event can be thought of as a series of events, both physical and verbal, repeated night after night for as long as the play runs; a play is, therefore, an interval of time filled with action. In *Godot*, similarly, the tramps have to fill time with action; the only difference is that they are aware of this, and are also aware that the actions in themselves are directionless. In abandoning the purpose of action on stage, Beckett also abandons one of its usual qualities; its ability to create and sustain realistic characterisation. On stage, action creates character; in *Godot*, Beckett's use of purposeless activity to fill the time of performance leads inexorably to the blurring of distinctions between characters. The tramps are slightly differentiated (Vladimir the questioning intellectual, Estragon the instinctive, sometimes childish dependent) but even these distinctions are not fixed; the two form a pseudo-couple as surely as Mercier and Camier – a couple who periodically think and act as one. Pozzo and Lucky appear, at least on the first encounter, to be more dynamic than the tramps. They at least are going somewhere; Pozzo is taking Lucky, his decrepit servant, to market to sell him. But even Pozzo and Lucky are trapped: the next act sees them back passing along the road in the same direction, wheeling around the tramps as Malone wheeled about the Unnamable. All four characters have, it seems, no escape from this location or from these actions; the elements of theatre that would support a narrative have themselves become the narrative. The play is not about Godot; it is about waiting, and about the compulsive need for action, if only to pass the time.

In the first act, the tramps are able to support the burden of waiting relatively easily, even though some doubt is cast on the location and the time (Estragon in particular takes some delight in teasing Vladimir- '... what Saturday? And is it Saturday? Is it not rather Sunday? (*Pause.*) Or Monday? (*Pause.*) Or Friday? (*CDW* 16–17)). They engage in long dialogue exchanges that would not be out of place in a music-hall

Estragon: You're sure it was here?
Vladimir: What?
Estragon: That we were to wait.
Vladimir: He said by the tree. [*They look at the tree.*] Do you see any others?
Estragon: What is it?
Vladimir: I don't know. A willow.
Estragon: Where are the leaves?
Vladimir: It must be dead.
Estragon: No more weeping.

(*CDW* 15–16)

This back and forth style of dialogue, which reminded the play's first director and its first reviewers irresistibly of circus clowns or vaudeville comics, relies for its effectiveness on rhythm and repetition (as in the play's most frequent exchange- 'Let's go'. 'We can't'. 'Why not?' 'We're waiting for Godot', which recurs in the tramps' dialogue with the frequency of a song's chorus). In the second act, though, it is noticeably more difficult to keep the dialogue going; it is almost as though the tramps are beginning to exhaust the possibilities of speech and action ([*Long silence.*] Vladimir: Say something! Estragon: I'm trying. [*Long silence.*] (*CDW* 59)). Pozzo and Lucky undergo a similar, though more pronounced deterioration. In the first act, Pozzo is a tyrannical bully, given to moments of intense self-doubt and self-pity: Lucky is a decaying wreck, although still capable of action (he kicks Estragon, and dances when ordered) and thought (he delivers a long, garbled monologue about the fate of man caught between an indifferent God and an inhospitable nature). In the second act, Pozzo is blind, and Lucky dumb. Even the tree changes; in the second act it has sprouted some leaves. The second act is therefore, not simply a mirror of the first. Something has happened: the world has come a little closer to an end, but there is no indication of when that end might be, as there is no indication of Godot's arrival. Vladimir's monologue, delivered toward the play's end, neatly captures *Godot*'s central dilemma. Everything changes, and nothing does: all days blur into one day, but life itself is short, and passes quickly

Vladimir: Was I sleeping, while the others suffered? Am I sleeping now? When tomorrow comes, or I think it does, what shall I say of today? That with my friend, Estragon, at this place until the fall of night, I waited for Godot? That Pozzo passed, with his carrier, and that he spoke to us? Probably. But in all that what truth will there be? [*Estragon, having struggled with his boots in vain, is dozing off again. Vladimir stares at him.*] He'll know nothing. He'll tell me about the blows he's received and I'll give him a carrot. [*Pause.*] Astride of a grave and a difficult birth, down in the hole, lingeringly, the gravedigger puts on the forceps. We have time to grow old. The air is full of our cries. [*He listens.*] But habit is a great deadener. [*He looks again at Estragon.*] at me too someone is looking, of me too someone is saying, he is sleeping, he knows nothing, let him sleep on ...

(*CDW* 84–5)

---

### v: *Endgame*

---

*Godot* makes theatre from the need to act; Beckett's subsequent dramas place more and more limitations on the character's physical and mental ability, making the possibility of purposeful action increasingly remote. *Endgame*, **[36, 38–9, 125, 164]** his third play, and Beckett's own favourite text, imprisons its characters in a room which might be the only place on earth to house human life. Here Hamm, blind and confined to a wheelchair, tries to maintain his authority over his servant Clov (who cannot sit) and his parents, Nagg and Nell (whose legless bodies are stored in dustbins). Hamm's attempts to fill the time by telling stories, taking tours of his miniature kingdom, and monitoring via Clov the state of the outside world are either shown to be futile, or are undermined by his reluctant servant or his half-senile, half-dismissive father; Clov's answer to any request is that 'there's no more ...' of the article requested, and Nagg informs his son that when he cried as an infant, they moved him out of earshot. Hamm himself is uneasily aware that his life is now something between an act and a game; he talks of 'warming up for my last soliloquy', (*CDW* 130) and, when Clov asks 'What is there to keep me here?', Hamm sardonically answers 'the dialogue' (*CDW* 120–1). At the end of the play, Clov sees a small boy outside of the refuge; he prepares to leave, armed with a gaff, presumably to kill the child and therefore ensure that the whole sorry mess of human life will not restart itself. He prepares to leave: Hamm delivers his final soliloquy, and places his blood-soaked handkerchief over his face, unaware that Clov, dressed for the road, is watching him. The play closes on this final image: Clov intent on Hamm, as he was at the play's beginning; the chess pieces suggested by the title have moved back into their opening positions, much like those commanded by Mr Endon in *Murphy*. Yet, even here, Beckett adds considerable ambiguity to the repetition. The relation between Hamm and Clov has shifted: Nell is dead in her dustbin. As with Godot, *Endgame*'s world is both changing and changeless.

Many critics, noting that *Endgame*'s stage set calls for a bare, grey open space with only a few items of stage furniture, with two small windows placed high on the back wall, have assumed that Beckett has set the play inside a skull; others, following Beckett's own lead, have noted the implications of the name *Endgame*, and have assumed that the play mimics the last few moves of a hopeless chess match. The play, though, while it might support these and other readings, never confirms any of them; its power resides, at least partly, on the infinitely allusive nature of the setting and the text. For example, Hamm's story of the 'painter ... and engraver' might suggest that the play dramatises a purely personal, psychological holocaust

Hamm:     I once knew a madman who thought that the end of the world had come. He was a painter – and engraver. I had great fondness for him. I used to go and see him, in the asylum. I'd take him by the hand and drag him to the window. Look! There! All that rising corn! And there! Look! The sails of the herring fleet! All that loveliness! [*Pause.*] He'd snatch away his hand and go back into his corner. Appalled. All he had seen was ashes. [*Pause.*] He alone had been spared. [*Pause.*] Forgotten. [*Pause.*] It appears the case is ... was not so ... so unusual.

                                                              (*CDW* 133)

But even here, the ambiguities accumulate. Hamm's hesitation (is... was) makes a number of contrary readings eminently possible: either the madman's psychosis is now shared by the play's characters, or the madman saw the future, or, conversely, the madman simply saw and understood the true nature of the world beneath the superficial beauty that Hamm used to be able to see.

---

## vi: Post-*Endgame* drama

---

At the same time as he was writing *Endgame*, Beckett began to experiment with other theatrical, visual and aural forms. Both *Endgame* and *Godot* were inherently theatrical pieces, using the basic elements of performance (rhythm, silence, movement and stillness) in an increasingly precise and controlled fashion; Beckett further explored the possibilities inherent in the theatrical image in two mimes – *Acts Without Words I* and *II*. *All That Fall* **[36, 151–2]**, his first radio play, (which was written in English: from the mid-1950s onwards, Beckett used both languages interchangeably) played with the essentials of the form; to exist on radio one has to speak (Mrs Rooney: Do not imagine, because I am silent, that I am not present, and alive, to all that is going on. (*CDW* 185)). A summary of its plot might lead one to assume that *All That Fall* is something of a murder mystery. Mrs Rooney travels to Boghill station to meet her blind husband, whose train is unaccountably delayed. On the way home, he mentions that he has entertained thoughts of killing a child; at the play's end, despite her husband's protestations, Mrs Rooney learns that the train was delayed because a child fell from the carriage under the wheels. However, the play does not revolve around Mr Rooney's guilt or innocence; rather, the semi-rural Ireland imagined in the play is a land where decay, inertia and death are shown to be the norm. The Rooneys' own daughter, Maddy, died in infancy; Mrs Rooney passes a house whose female inhabitant plays Schubert's *Death and the Maiden*; no form of transport works as it should; on the way to the station, a chicken is run over and killed. In such a place, news of a sermon whose text is ' "The Lord upholdeth all that fall and raiseth up all those that be bound down" ' could only be greeted with 'wild laughter' (*CDW* 198). Beckett uses the blatant artificiality of the medium to suggest a world as bleak as *Endgame* or the Trilogy

Mrs Rooney: All is still. No living soul in sight. There is no one to ask.
The world is feeding. The wind – [*Brief wind.*] – scarcely
stirs the leaves and the birds – [*Brief chirp.*] – are tired

singing. The cows – [*Brief moo.*] – and sheep – [*Brief baa.*] – ruminate in silence. The dogs – [*Brief bark.*] – are hushed and the hens – [*Brief cackle.*] – sprawl torpid in the dust. We are alone. There is no one to ask. [*Silence.*]

(*CDW* 192)

Beckett's next stage play, *Krapp's Last Tape* **[37]**, again uses the technological possibilities of recorded speech; but this time to create a dramatic illusion – a monologue that is also a dialogue. Krapp, a '*wearish old man*' (according to the stage directions) records a tape each year on his birthday, in which he reflects on the year just past; he has also got into the habit of listening to a tape from a previous year. On the night of his sixty-ninth birthday, he listens to a tape made thirty years earlier, the year when his mother died, when he bade farewell to love (as the tape summary has it), and when he had a revelation that, he felt at the time, would help him create his 'opus magnum'. However, the sixty-nine year old Krapp has difficulty recognising his younger self, just as the thirty-nine year old Krapp could not understand the twenty-nine year old whose tape he in turn played ('Just been listening to that stupid bastard I took myself for thirty years ago, hard to believe I was ever as bad as that' (*CDW* 222)). Krapp has, it seems, removed himself from the world in order to nourish his own creative spark; but this has come to nothing (of the 'opus magnum', the old Krapp sourly remarks 'Seventeen copies sold, of which eleven at trade price to free circulating libraries beyond the seas. Getting known' (*CDW* 222)). To the old man, the only memory worth replaying is the moment when his younger self renounced love; he plays the tape once more from this point, and lets it run to the end, its closing words offering an ironic yet poignant contrast to the stage image

Tape:      … I said again I thought it was hopeless and no good going on and she agreed, without opening her eyes. [*Pause.*] I asked her to look at me and after a few moments – [*Pause.*] – after a few moments she did, but the eyes just slits, because of the glare. I bent over to get them in the shadow and they opened. [*Pause. Low.*] Let me in. [*Pause.*] We drifted in among the flags and stuck. The way they went down, sighing, before the stem! [*Pause.*] I lay down across her with my face in her breasts and my hand on her. We lay there without moving. But under us all moved, and moved us, gently, up and down, and from side to side.
[*Pause. Krapp's lips move. No sound.*]

Past midnight. Never knew such silence. The earth might
be uninhabited.
[*Pause.*]
Here I end this reel. Box – [*Pause.*] – three, spool – [*Pause.*] –
five. [*Pause.*] Perhaps my best years are gone. When there
was a chance of happiness. But I wouldn't want them back.
Not with the fire in me now. No, I wouldn't want them
back.
[Krapp *motionless staring before him. The tape runs on in silence.*]
(*CDW* 223)

In 1959, Beckett returned to radio drama. The short play *Embers*
**[37]** is set, apparently, by the sea; the central character, Henry, tells
himself stories and conjures up voices and sounds from his past life in
order to drown out the persistent sound of the sea sucking at the shore

> Today it's calm, but I often hear it above in the house and walking
> the roads and start talking, oh just loud enough to drown it, nobody
> notices.
>
> (*CDW* 254)

Henry is (unusually in Beckett's universe) a married man; he and
his wife Ada even have a child, Addie. However, although we hear
both their voices during the play, we hear them through the filter of
Henry's mind; he calls up the thought of his wife so that he will have
someone to talk to, and we hear Addie only when her father remembers
her failures. Finding no comfort in imagining his family, Henry returns
to the story he told himself at the play's beginning, in which a character
named Bolton pleads with a doctor, Holloway, for relief which is not
provided. The tale is uncompleted; rather, Henry's voice trails off,
leaving the listener with the sound of the sea that so troubled Henry
at the play's opening. Although the sea is never given an unambiguous
meaning, it is associated with death (Henry's father drowned himself);
in aural terms, the sound of the sea is also the sound made by a radio
tuned between stations. At the play's end, we are left with a sound
that evokes both absence and mortality.

---

### vii: Post-*Trilogy* prose and *How It Is*

---

During the 1950s, Beckett made various attempts to escape from the
impasse his prose had reached at *The Unnamable's* end; indeed, the
beginning of his next published prose work, the *Texts for Nothing* **[35,
134–5]**, seems to answer the conclusion of the previous work

Suddenly, no, at last, long last, I couldn't any more, I couldn't go on. Someone said, You can't stay here. I couldn't stay there and I couldn't go on ...

(CSP 100)

The *Texts for Nothing* have been somewhat ignored by many Beckett scholars, perhaps because of the apparently dismissive title that Beckett assigned to them. The title, though, is rather more interesting, and rather more indicative, than it might first appear. It is a musical term, meaning 'a bar's rest' – the moment when an instrument is silent, an interesting notion for a writer who has established silence as the goal of his narrator's endeavours. Secondly, it at least indicates the direction in which these short prose pieces tend – to nothing, the source Watt reaches in Knott's house, the goal of Murphy's meditations; and nothing, in Beckett's previous work, has been shown to have a dynamic, protean life of its own (one thinks of the endlessly changing Mr Knott, for example). The *Texts* themselves do not have a structure; rather, they have a series of recurring themes – fragmented memories of a past life; images of confinement, underground, in the narrator's skull, and in one of the texts, in a courtroom; and the recurring notion that the narrator is now split from the voice that seems to speak through and for it. The other published fragment, *From an Abandoned Work*, presents us with a narrator who does not have the rather sardonic, distanced tone of voice of Molloy or Malone; he is prone to moments of extreme rage that are unprovoked by anything in the narrative. These elements – the narrator with only a tenuous control over a narrative voice that occasionally seems to have its own agenda; a narrator who remembers flashes of his past life, but whose present life takes place underground; a narrator prone to violence – blend together more coherently in Beckett's last full-scale prose work, *How It Is* **[39, 135]**.

*How It Is* is a work that defies easy description. It is usually called a novel, not because it fits the usual idea of a novel, but because there is no other area to which it can be assigned. It is written in short bursts of unpunctuated prose, broken into paragraphs only by the narrator's pauses for breath

how it was I quote before Pim with Pim after Pim how it is
three parts I say it as I hear it
voice once without quaqua on all sides then in me when the
panting stops tell me again finish telling me invocation

past moments old dreams back again or fresh like those that
pass or things always and memories I say them as I hear them
murmur them in the mud
in me that were without when the panting stops scraps of an
ancient voice in me not mine

(*HII* 7)

From the novel's beginning we are aware of a paradox that is not
resolved until the novel's end. The voice we hear is and is not that of
the speaker (who comes to call itself Bom in the second section of the
novel); it is ' in me not mine', spoken by a narrator who seems not to
be in control of its words ('I say it as I hear it'). From the beginning of
the novel, therefore, the precise status of the information that we
receive is confused not only by its rather garbed delivery, but by the
fact that we are never sure of the truth of what we hear: is this Bom's
voice telling us of Bom's journey, or is it a voice that issues through
Bom, creating the speaker as the speaker creates the story? The simple
three part structure of the novel – a journey towards Pim, during which
Bom tells us of its world and tells us of the fragmentary memories of a
life above ground; the second section, where in a grotesque parody
both of sexual coupling and education, Bom tortures Pim, a mirror
image of himself, until Pim understands his torturer; and the third
section, in which Bom posits an endless cycle of torturers and tortured,
and prepares itself for its own encounter with a torturer- is built upon
this uncertain foundation. At the novel's end, Bom finds that the
arithmetic of torturer and tortured simply does not add up, and the
structure of never-ending journeys to and from torture is unsustainable;
it finally realises that the only voice it hears is its own, that there was
no Pim, no torture, nothing but its own inexorable progress through
the mud

alone in the mud yes the dark yes sure yes panting yes someone
hears me no no one hears me no murmuring sometimes yes when
the panting stops yes not at other times no in the mud yes to the
mud yes my voice yes mine yes not another's no mine alone yes
sure yes a few scraps yes that no one hears no but less and less no
answer LESS AND LESS yes

(*HII* 160)

## viii: *Happy Days*

In his last full-length drama, *Happy Days* **[40, 143, 181–2, 183–4]**, Beckett presents us with another confined central character who creates a world from the fragments of a previous existence. Winnie is sinking into the earth; in the first act, she is buried up to her waist, and can pass the time between the bell that wakes her up and the bell that ends her day by alternately engaging her husband Willie in conversation, indulging in memories of a previous life, telling herself stories, and rummaging amongst the possessions in her bag. If Bom is at the mercy of a voice which might not be its own, Winnie is at the mercy of a listener who might fail her

Winnie:     ... Ah yes, if only I could bear to be alone, I mean prattle away with not a soul to hear. [Pause] Not that I flatter myself that you hear much, no Willie, God forbid. [*Pause.*] But days too when you answer. [*Pause.*] So that I may say at all times, even when you do not answer and perhaps hear nothing, something of this is being heard, I am not merely talking to myself, that is in the wilderness, a thing I could never bear to do- for any length of time ...

                                                (*CDW* 145)

Bom rejects the possibility of a listener and in doing so, confirms its own existence in the present; Winnie needs the possibility of a listener to confirm her existence in the past. Even though Willie's responses are infrequent and rarely more than monosyllabic, they allow Winnie to speak, as she puts it, in 'the old style'; however, she is uneasily aware that at some point in the future '... words must fail'. In the second act she has come closer to this point; she is buried up to her neck, and is unable to use the routines she has developed around her last few possessions; Willie is now out of her sight, and as such cannot be the constant reference point of her speech. It is no wonder that she finds herself losing touch with the images and memories that had previously confirmed her sense of self

Winnie:     ... The sunshade you gave me ... that day ... [*Pause.*]... that day ... the lake ... the reeds. [*Eyes front. Pause.*] What day? [*Pause.*] What reeds? ...

                                                (*CDW* 162)

Ominously, the only possession that she can see clearly is the revolver that she used to carry in her bag. At the play's end, Willie reappears, 'dressed to kill'; his appearance, and his last word (a 'just audible' 'Win') provoke a last burst of 'the old style' from Winnie, who sings the *Merry Widow Waltz* to her husband. The glutinously romantic words of the song are in sharp contrast not only to the sheer strangeness of the final image, but also to its ambiguity. Willie might be in search of his wife; or he might be in search of the revolver, to be used either on Winnie or on himself. Either way, Beckett leaves us (as in *Endgame*) at the brink of an irrevocable change in the world of the play, but leaves the nature of that change unresolved. Whatever happens, though, the relation between Winne the speaker and Willie as her audience cannot be re-created; Winnie's existence cannot be confirmed in 'the old style' any more.

## Further Reading

Unsurprisingly, this period has come in for the most sustained attention from Beckett's critics. There are numerous study guides and edited collections on individual works (Birkett (1987), Cohn (1967 and 1987), Graver (1989) on *Waiting for Godot*: Bloom (1987) on *Godot* and (1988) on *Endgame*; Connor (1992) on *Godot* and *Endgame*; Worth (1990) on *Godot* and *Happy Days*; O'Hara (1970) on the Trilogy) and monographs both on individual texts and on the period as a whole (Cohn (1980), Esslin (1961), Webb (1972) on the drama; Fletcher (1964), Webb (1970), Moorjani (1982), Sherringham (1985), Hill (1990) and Watson (1991) on the prose). Cohn (1980), Kalb (1989) and Oppenheim (1994) provide valuable insights into the staging of Beckett's dramas.

## (c) THE LATER WORK: 1960–1989

The completion of *How It Is* and *Happy Days*, it might seem, had taken Beckett to an even more intractable impasse than he found himself in at the end of the trilogy. *How It Is* had finally dispensed with the need for narrative: *Happy Days* had thrown into question the relation between the actor and the audience. It might seem that there would be nowhere to go after these works: and yet Beckett continued to write, producing over the next decades work that was as striking, and in many cases even more radical, than the major texts that had made his reputation.

However, these works were on a different scale. Beckett had already reduced the prose narratives to fragmented monologue, and his theatrical pieces to simple images and clearly defined and described actions. From the early 1960s to his death, Beckett refined his style in both media (and in other media- film, television and radio), producing work which was minimalist in scope, but which made a virtue of the fact that it used so few elements. The titles that Beckett gave to the collections of work (the *Residua, Ends and Odds, Nohow On*) that he allowed to be published might seem to be as dismissive as the title *Texts for Nothing*; but, as with the earlier title, they are rather more evocative than might at first appear. They describe Beckett's explorations exactly; an approach to writing that made use of the fewest possible resources, that dealt in the discarded or overlooked elements of creative work. In prose, he explored the relation between word and image: in theatre, between speaker, image and audience; and in the electronic media, between the technology of the medium and the creation of character and narrative.

---

## i: Experiments in prose

Something of the nature of Beckett's experiments in prose **[39, 130, 137–8, 163–4]** can be gleaned from the first few sentences of the short piece *Imagination Dead Imagine*

> No trace anywhere of life, you say, pah no difficulty there, imagination not dead yet, yes, dead, imagination dead imagine. Islands, waters, azure, verdure, one glimpse and vanished, endlessly, omit. Till all white in the whiteness the rotunda. No way in, go in, measure. Diameter, three feet, three feet from ground to summit of the vault. Two diameters at right angles AB CD divide the white ground into two semicircles ACB BDA. Lying on the ground two white bodies, each in its semi-circle. White too the vault and the round wall eighteen inches high from which it springs. Go back out, a plain rotunda, all white in the whiteness, go back in, rap, solid throughout, a ring as in the imagination the ring of bone.
>
> (*CSP* 182)

The reader is asked to imagine the impossible; that imagination is dead. All the conventional images associated with imagination (Islands, azure, water ...) are summarily dismissed, and the reader is asked to contemplate what is left, which initially seems to be nothing (all white in the whiteness). But the imagination is persistent, and will fill this apparent emptiness with something; and, sure enough, Beckett finds that he and we are contemplating a simple image – a rotunda, on which two bodies are symmetrically arranged. However, simply describing the image does not solve Beckett's central dilemma; imagination is not dead yet, the impulse that drove the Unnamable to create endlessly is still in force, even though Beckett is at pains to deny it (No way in, go in ...). The language, which veers between the mathematical (two diameters at right angles AB CD ...) and the poetic (... a ring as in the imagination the ring of bone ...), is itself under strain; as so often in the late prose works, conventional linguistic structures are no longer adequate to describe the images encountered by the eye of the narrator. The late prose works are full of references to the eye and the gaze; it is as though the prose is engaged in an ultimately futile attempt to describe exactly what the eye sees – and when the eye's gaze is distracted (as it is momentarily at the end of *Imagination Dead Imagine*) the image ceases to exist

> ... Leave them there, sweating and icy, there is better elsewhere. No, life ends, and no, there is nothing elsewhere, and no question now of ever finding again that white speck lost in whiteness, to see if they still lie still in the stress of that storm, or of a worse storm, or in the black dark for good, or the great whiteness unchanging, or if not what they are doing.
>
> (*CSP* 185)

In some of the late prose pieces, the attempt to describe an image exactly places language under even more strain. In *Ping* and *Lessness* words and sentences are used almost as a composer would use variations of pitch and rhythm; Beckett employs repetition and neologism (the creation of new words) as much for sound and shape as for sense

> ... White walls each its trace grey blur signs no meaning light grey almost white. Light heat all known all white planes meeting invisible. Ping murmur only just almost never one second perhaps a meaning that much memory almost never. White feet toes joined like sewn heels together right angle ping elsewhere no sound. Hands hanging palms front legs joined like sewn. Head haught eyes holes light blue almost white only colour fixed front ...
>
> (*CSP* 194)

Ruins true refuge long last towards which so many false time out of mind. All sides endlessness earth sky as one no sound no stir. Grey face two pale blue little body heart beating only upright. Blacked out fallen open four walls over backwards true refuge issueless.

(*CSP* 197)

With patience, the reader can discern the images that Beckett describes in these works: in *Ping*, a little body enclosed in a white cube, its blue eyes simultaneously the only sign of colour and the only sign of life (a sign that seems to be associated with the abrupt intrusion of the word ping into the prose); in *Lessness*, a body fallen over in the middle of infinite space. The creation of these images is, however, an arduous task for the narrator, who cannot avoid lapsing into ambiguity and undecidability, no matter how rigorous the attempt to use only the most precise terms. The words, that seem so simple taken in groups of two or three, become increasingly unclear the longer the sentence goes on. For the Unnamable, stories were untrustworthy, because they could not describe the self; in these late works, Beckett seems to find the same problem, but this time in words themselves.

Some of the prose pieces (*All Strange Away*, most of the *Fizzles*) are clearly unfinished fragments; some, in particular the short pieces *Still*, *Sounds*, and *Still 3*, describe a single image caught at a moment of relative (and perhaps deceptive) calm – the seated figure described in *Still* is found on closer inspection to be trembling all over. Some late prose works approach conventional narrative; *Enough* tells of a couple (an old man and his young companion) who travel over a landscape that seems, in comparison to the worlds inhabited by Beckett's other characters, almost paradisial

I don't know what the weather is now. But in my life it was eternally mild. As if the earth had come to rest in spring ...

(*CSP* 191)

Yet even here there is ambiguity (it is not absolutely clear whether the speaker is male or female, for example); and the descriptions of the couple are suffused with a sense of loss (the narrator, now old, recalls imperfectly a time when he or she not alone). In *The Lost Ones*, the longest of these pieces, and the longest prose work between *How It Is* and *Company*, Beckett describes a confined world in which two hundred people search, with varying degrees of desperation, for their lost ones;

the location of their search (the cylinder, as Beckett calls it) is analysed, the behaviour of its inhabitants is minutely classified, the rules that govern their lives are described; and yet the precise nature of the search is never fully made clear. The impression is that all activity in the cylinder is issueless; not only is the goal of the search unknown, but the cylinder itself is running down. The narrative ends with all life in the cylinder apparently extinguished; the final paragraph describes the last encounter between a searcher and a woman (one of the vanquished, those inhabitants who have lapsed into complete stasis)

> There he opens then his eyes this last of all if a man and some time later threads his way to that first among the vanquished so often taken for a guide. On his knees he parts the heavy hair and raises the unresisting head. Once devoured the face thus laid bare the eyes at a touch of the thumbs open without demur. In those calm wastes he lets his wander till they are the first to close and the head falls back into its place. He himself after a pause impossible to time finds at last his place and pose whereupon dark descends and at the same instant the temperature comes to rest not far from freezing point. Hushed in the same breath the faint stridulence mentioned above whence suddenly such silence as to drown all the faint breathings put together ...
>
> (*CSP* 223)

As we have seen before, Beckett is drawn to the image of one person gazing into another's hesitant or unseeing eyes. Here, the encounter is, if anything, rendered more moving by the relative simplicity and hesitancy of the language; the usual implication of the image – that of a failure to communicate, or a farewell to communication – here becomes a poignant image of the final failure of a world.

---

## ii: Experiments in theatre

---

In the theatre during this period Beckett produced a number of works that in retrospect make *Godot* appear impossibly rich and complex **[41–7, 170–1]**. From *Play* onward, he refined the tendency established in his full-scale plays toward a single image; by the time he came to compose *Not I* and the plays that followed it, the stage image had been reduced to its simplest possible form (a figure pacing back and forth in *Footfalls*; a woman in a rocking chair in *Rockaby*; identical men, either engaged in cyclical acts of torture and confession in *What Where*, or split into a reader and a listener, in *Ohio Impromptu*; three identical women poised between the past and death in *Come and Go*; a spotlit mouth and a dimly visible hooded figure in *Not I*). Here, as in the late prose work, attention is focused as much on the means as on the end. For example, *Play* **[40]** presents its audience with a simple, if striking image: three faces ( a man and two women, identified as M, W1 and W2) protruding from three urns, each lit at first together, then in turn, by a spotlight. After an opening chorus in which all three speak together, the faces tell the audience in a delivery as quick and as uninflected as possible the banal details of a love triangle; then, after a brief reversion to choral speech, they meditate on their current plight. As the play progresses, the audience comes to realise that the light is as much of a character as the three speakers: it keys their words, flicking from face to face as a viewer flicks between television channels; they in turn talk to it, ascribing to it emotions and a purpose

W2:     When you go out – M and I go out. Some day you will tire of me and go out ... for good ...

W1:     Is it that I do not tell the truth, is that it, that some day I may tell the truth at last and then no more light at last, for the truth? ...

W2:     What do you do when you go out? Sift?

(*CDW* 312, 313, 315)

The inescapably cyclical nature of both the speakers and the light's situation is made clear in a stage instruction buried near the end of the text: *Repeat play* (*CDW* 317).

Beckett here calls our attention to a feature of theatre that, most of the time, is supposed to escape our notice; here, light tortures and interrogates as much as it illuminates. He also draws attention to another aspect of theatre that an audience does not normally consider; its repeatability. A play will be performed night after night; the same actions will happen in the same order in the same place at the same time, no matter what. By truncating the time between performances, Beckett converts a normal part of the theatrical process into a telling image of confinement and obsession.

From *Play* onwards, Beckett's theatre increasingly exhibits strengths more usually associated with sculpture, dance or musical composition. The images are presented simply, most usually against a black background; movement is tightly choreographed, so that each gesture comes to have a significance far in excess of its physical scope (even the opening and closing of the actor's eyes are timed and described); and the text is built on the same principles as the later prose, although with due care given to the actor's need to speak the words. Where there is conversation, it is fragmented; dialogue exchanges follow a pattern, as in *Come and Go*, a play that consists of three near identical dialogue exchanges. Monologues are also based on repetition; and, where possible, the personal pronoun is to be strenuously avoided

*Mouth:*   ... out ... into this world ... this world ... tiny little thing ... before its time ... in a godfor- ... what? girl? ... yes ... tiny little girl ... into this ... out into this ... before her time ... godforsaken hole ... godforsaken hole called ... called ... no matter ... parents unknown ... unheard of ... he having vanished ... thin air ... no sooner buttoned up his breeches ... she similarly ... eight months later ... almost to the tick ... so no love ... spared that ... no love such as normally vented on the ... speechless infant ... in the home ... no ... nor indeed for that matter any of any kind ... no love of any kind ... at any subsequent stage ... so typical affair ... nothing of any note till coming up to sixty when– ... what? ... seventy? ... good God!... coming up to seventy ... wandering in a field ... looking aimlessly for cowslips ... to make a ball ... a few steps then stop ... stare into space ... then on ... a few more ... stop and stare again ... so on ... drifting around ... when suddenly ... gradually ... all went out ... all that early April morning light and she found herself in the– ... what? ... who? ... no! ... she! ...

(*CDW* 376–7)

Mouth, in *Not I* **[43–4, 184–5]**, cannot bring herself to acknowledge that the memories she recounts are hers; more than this, it also seems as though she is prompted while speaking by a voice that only she can hear ('sixty when– ... what? ... seventy? ...'). Like Bom in *How It Is*, she speaks at the insistence of a voice that is 'in me not mine'; the particularly Beckettian dilemma of the split self trying to resolve its existence through compulsive speech has been given a striking physical shape. Most of the impact of *Not I* in performance comes from the sheer strangeness of the stage image; a mouth, closely spotlit, gabbling furiously in the darkness, seemingly divorced from the rest of the body, somewhere between a purely mechanical conduit for the text and a small writhing animal. This pattern is reversed in *That Time* **[44]**. Here the split between the voice and the self is more pronounced; a spotlit head listens while three voices, coming from the darkness on both sides and above, describe events from a life increasingly devoid of human contact. According to the stage directions, the voices belong to the face that we see; but in performance the arrangement of the voices around the head gives the impression that the voices emanate not from his subconscious but from somewhere outside him. The self is split, just as surely as it is in *Not I*. In *Ohio Impromptu* **[47]**, an old man listens, as he has apparently done every night for many years, to a reader reading out a narrative based on his life; but listener and reader have over the years grown identical, becoming perhaps halves of the one self. In *A Piece of Monologue* **[47]**, the speaker is divorced not only from the person whose life he narrates, but the location and the movements that he describes.

Beckett's interest in mime and movement finds expression in *Footfalls*, *Rockaby*, *Catastrophe* and *What Where* **[44, 47]**; each one presents a character or characters trapped, willingly or unwillingly, in repetitive cycles of movement. In *Footfalls*, a woman paces back and forth along a dimly lighted strip; her footsteps are clearly audible, as is the count that keeps her pacing exact. In the first of the play's four short scenes, she talks to her mother, whose voice we hear coming from offstage; in the second section, the mother describes the process that led her daughter to the state we see

V:      I say the floor here, now bare, this strip of floor, once was carpeted, a deep pile. Till one night, while still little more than a child, she called her mother and said, Mother, this is not enough. The mother: Not enough? May- the child's given name- May: Not enough. The mother: What do you mean, May, not enough, what can you possibly mean, May, not enough? May: I mean, Mother, that I must hear the feet, however faint they fall. The mother: The motion alone is not enough? May: No, Mother, the motion alone is not enough, I must hear the feet, however faint they fall.
(*CDW* 401)

In the last section, May herself recasts her story into the third person, distancing herself from the narrative in the way already chosen by Mouth in *Not I*; in the fourth section, she has vanished from the strip, her story and her relentless pacing seemingly done. In *Rockaby*, a woman sits in her mother's rocking chair, listening to a voice whose words are timed to the chair's rock; the text, delivered in the toneless, rhythmic style Beckett employed in his late drama, become a haunting and unsettling lullaby, lulling the woman toward death

V:       so in the end
         close of a long day
         went down
         in the end went down
         down the steep stair
         let down the blind and down
         right down
         into the old rocker
         mother rocker
         where mother rocked
         all the years
         all in black
         best black
         sat and rocked
         rocked
         till her end came
         in the end came ...

                                              (*CDW* 440)

The gentle repeated movement (prompted by the seated figure, who asks for 'more' when the rocking ceases) and the soft, incantatory delivery give *Rockaby* in performance a surprisingly comforting quality, despite the oddness of the setting; so much so, that the words 'fuck life', spoken in the play's closing moments, come as something of a shock. The gentle movement toward death is, it seems, more determined and more painful than we realised. In *Catastrophe*, a director and his assistant try to create an archetyphally Beckettian image; an old man, spotlit, his head passively bowed. At the play's end, once the image has been set, the director asks for a run-through

D:       Now ... let 'em have it. [*Fade-out of general light. Pause. Fade-out of light on body. Light on head alone. Long pause.*] Terrific! He'll have them on their feet. I can hear it from here. [*Pause. Distant storm of applause. P raises his head, fixes the audience. The applause falters, dies ...*]

                                              (*CDW* 461)

One can see why the play has generally been thought of as a political statement: P's raised head is a memorable image of resistance, a denial of the role forced upon him. In *What Where,* Beckett stages a cycle of torture and confession that is nearing its end, not because the truth is about to be revealed, but because the number of participants has shrunk to almost nothing. The information that is required (the 'what where' of the play's title) will never be revealed; instead, the process will end with the chief interrogator, Bam, standing alone on stage. Beckett stages this inexorable progression as a series of entrances and exits; Bam is presented twice, as a participant in the choreographed action, and as a disembodied voice, coming from a speaker to one side of the playing area. This voice seems to be distanced from the action, able to place it in time and to organise it (switching it on and off, as the voice informs us). However, the aspect of Bam that reflects on the action cannot illuminate it for us

> [*BAM enters at w, halts at 3 head bowed.*]
> V: Good.
> I am alone.
> In the present as were I still.
> It is winter.
> Without journey.
> Time passes.
> That is all.
> Make sense who may.
> I switch off.

(*CDW* 476)

---

### iii: Experiments in radio, film and television

The experiments in other media, begun in the 1950s with the radio plays *All That Fall* and *Embers*, continued through the next three decades until Beckett's death. The various plays he wrote for radio and television, and his one excursion in to film, all share an understanding of the peculiar constraints that each form imposes. In *Words and Music* and *Cascando* [41], written for radio in the 1960s, Beckett took advantage of the determining role played by speech and sound in establishing character. In both plays, a conductor (Croak in *Words and Music*, Opener in *Cascando*) invokes and attempts to orchestrate both words and music; in both the two forces work, separately and together, in the creation of a text. In both, though, the text created is not satisfactory. In *Words and Music* Croak is overwhelmed by the memories the text invokes; in *Cascando*, the story is unfinished at the play's end. In Beckett's only work for the cinema, *Film* [41–2], a man flees the intrusive gaze of the camera; once apparently safe in his room, he tries to destroy or remove all of his possessions that either have or whose shape suggests eyes. However, he cannot escape the camera completely; in the film's final moments he stares directly into the lens, and a reverse shot from his point of view reveals that the pursuing camera is in fact himself The film is a gloss on Bishop Berkeley's dictum, *esse est percepi* (to be is to be perceived); it suggests that there is no escape from perception, because the self always perceives itself – that is, we regard ourselves both as subjects and objects.

In television, Beckett characteristically paid close attention to the positioning of the camera and the framing of the image. In *Eh Joe* [41, 152], his first TV play, a camera draws inexorably closer to a man's face, as a woman's voice interrogates him. In later television work (*Ghost Trio, ... but the clouds ...,* and *Nacht und Traume*) Beckett uses the camera's ability to capture and replay movement. In each one of these plays, the camera records an action which is then repeated, either at the behest of an offscreen voice, or with the camera closer to the event, able to record it in more detail. In the TV piece, *Quad*, Beckett creates something akin to a visual sculpture. Four cowled figures pace in a pre-set pattern around a square, avoiding the centre; in the play's second movement, the pace is slower and colour has been drained from the image, as though the same movements have continued unchanged, save for a slow entropic decline, to an unguessable moment in the far future.

---

### iv: *Company, Ill Seen Ill Said, Worstward Ho* and *Stirrings Still*

---

Beckett's last substantial prose works, *Company, Ill Seen Ill Said*, and *Worstward Ho* [46–7], stand as a summary of the elements found in his prose from *How It Is* onwards; the fragmented images of a previous life; an image simultaneously created and effaced by a narrator unable to sustain it; the tendency in the prose towards neologism and compression. In *Company*, a figure on his back in the dark hears a voice telling him of his current situation and his past life; the voice is described as toneless and repetitive, coming from various positions in the dark around the listener (the similarities between this voice and the memories dramatised in *That Time* are striking). The voice is, as it says, 'devised for company', but it does not provide much obvious comfort. For one thing, it refuses the first person; for another, the voice is periodically contrasted with another voice, this time using the third person, that comments on the ambiguity and futility of the whole enterprise

> Use of the second person marks the voice. That of the third that cantankerous other. Could he speak to and of whom the voice

speaks there would be a first. But he cannot. He shall not. You cannot. You shall not.

(*C* 29)

The listener is driven, it seems, by a desire to accommodate the voice, if not by converting it into the first person, that at least by personalising it; or by positing the existence of others in the same situation. His impulse seems to be that described by Hamm in *Endgame*; '... the solitary child who turns himself into children, two, three, so as to be together, and whisper together, in the dark ...' (*CDW* 126). In the end, though, such attempts are doomed to failure

> ... But with face upturned for good labour in vain at your fable. Till finally you hear how words are coming to an end. With every inane word a little nearer to the last. And how the fable too. The fable of one with you in the dark. The fable of one fabling with you in the dark. And how better in the end labour lost and silence. And you as you always were.
> Alone.
>
> (*C* 88–9)

This failure is further explored in *Ill Seen Ill Said*. As the title suggests, the narrator attempts to describe a simple scene (an old woman, living in a cabin in a bare stony plain) but its ability to see and say what it sees is poor. No matter how hard it tries, it cannot prevent the images from diminishing

> She is vanishing. With the rest. The already ill seen bedimmed and ill seen again annulled. The mind betrays the treacherous eyes and the treacherous word their treacheries. Haze sole certitude. The same that reigns beyond the pastures. It gains them already. It will gain the zone of stones. Then the dwelling through all its chinks. The eye will close in vain. To see but haze. How can it ever be said? ...
>
> (*ISIS* 48)

As in *Company*, the attempt is abandoned; the narrator decides to 'say farewell' to the image, and looks forward to the 'void' that will replace it

> Decision no sooner reached or rather long after than what is the wrong word? For the last time at last for to end yet again what the wrong word? Than revoked. No but slowly dispelled a little

like the last wisps of day when the curtain closes. Of itself by slow
millimetres or drawn by a phantom hand. Farewell to farewell.
Then in that perfect dark foreknell darling sound pip for end begun.
First last moment. Grant only enough remain to devour all.
Moment by glutton moment. Sky earth the whole kit and boodle.
Not another crumb of carrion left. Lick chops and basta. No. One
moment more. Grace to breathe that void. Know happiness.

(ISIS 59)

*Company* dealt with the progressive failure of memory and of the
ability to create; *Ill Seen Ill Said* dealt with the failure of perception;
*Worstward Ho* deals with the failure of language. From the beginning,
we are in territory that can only be described by warping the sense of
the words that are used

On. Say on. Be said on. Somehow on. Till nohow on. Said nohow
on.
Say for be said. Missaid. From now say for be missaid.
Say a body. Where none. No mind. Where none. That at least. A
place. Where none. For the body. To be in. Move in. Out of. Back
into. No. No out. No back. Only in. Stay in. On in. Still.
All of old. Nothing else ever. Ever tried. Ever failed. No matter. Try
again. Fail again. Fail better.

(WH 7)

It is hard to imagine a more inhospitable environment for a narrator
than one in which every verb signifies its opposite and every image is
both present and absent ('Say a body. Where none'). And yet, through
an exercise in sheer creative will, the voice manages to conjure three
images out of nothingness; a skull; the bowed back of a woman; and a
couple, an old man and child, plodding on through the void. The images
are fragile, though, and difficult to sustain; the effort is finally too
much for the narrator, and the images suddenly disappear

Enough. Sudden enough. Sudden all far. No move and sudden all
far. All least. Three pins. One pinhole. In dimmost void. Vasts apart.
At bounds of boundless void. Whence no farther. Best worse no
farther. Nohow less. Nohow worse. Nohow naught. Nohow on.
Said nohow on.

(WH 46–7)

This ending echoes that of *The Unnamable,* though in compressed form; the contradiction between the futility and necessity of expression is now contained in the two-word formulation nohow on. These three works, taken together, represent Beckett's last sustained attempt to create an art out of the knowledge that creation itself is fundamentally impossible; to speak is to misspeak, because language itself is both seductive and poisonous, luring the narrator with the promise of expression only to distort that expression. All art is failure; all one can do is to attempt it in the hope that one might fail better.

And, true to the paradoxical nature of his art, it was no surprise that, after such a determined summary of his work, Beckett should try again. His last prose work, *Stirrings Still* **[47]**, revisits the territory already explored in *Company;* this time, though, the narrative is more distanced, calmer, more resigned

> ... but soon weary of vainly delving in these remains he moved on through the long hoar grass resigned to not knowing where he was or how he got there or where he was going or how to get back to whence he knew not where he came. So on unknowing and no end in sight. Unknowing and what is more no wish to know nor indeed any wish of any kind nor therefore any sorrow save that he would have wished the strokes to cease and the cries for good and was sorry that they did not ...
>
> (*CSP* 263)

*Stirrings Still* finishes on a phrase that seems half invocation, half prayer: 'Oh all to end' (*CSP* 265). It is tempting to read this as Beckett's final farewell to the artistic endeavour that had sustained him for nearly sixty years; however, such a reading must always be doubtful when it is used of an artist who made compelling use of the idea of ending and failure in his work. *Stirrings Still* might seem like a conclusion; but as the title reminds us, the creative urge has not yet been extinguished. As long as the artist perceives the world, he or she will try to give memorable expression to that perception, no matter how worn out and inadequate to the task are all the old tools of language and culture.

---

## Further Reading

As an introduction to this area of Beckett's work, Knowlson and Pilling (1979) is still useful (although it is neccesarily limited to the shorter work produced in the 1960s and 70s). Beckett's late prose is analysed in Brienza (1987), Locatelli (1990), and Brater (1994): his late dramatic works in Brater (1987) and McMullan (1993).

## (d) BECKETT THE POET

Beckett's poetry has not received anything like the acclaim accorded to his work in other forms. It is true that his early poetry can be (and frequently is) as intimidatingly erudite as his early prose: the reader, encountering the poems of the 1920s and early 30s, can find him or herself adrift in a sea of references, with no sign of landfall

> Faulhaber, Beeckman and Peter the Red,
> come now in the cloudy avalanche or Gassendi's sun-red crystally cloud
> and I'll pebble you all your hen-and-a-half ones
> *or* I'll pebble a lens under the quilt in the midst of day.
>
> (*CP* 1)

This from *Whoroscope* **[15, 105–6, 150]**, Beckett's first non-academic publication: a poem on the life of Descartes, for which Beckett provided footnotes of dubious helpfulness (the note for these lines reads 'He solved problems submitted by these mathematicians' (*CP* 5)). With patience, the early poems can be decoded; they are full of autobiographical references (Beckett's intimate knowledge of Dublin and London are reflected in the wanderings described in *Saines 1* and *Serena 1*); they display the young Beckett's intimate knowledge of other poetic forms (the associative free verse employed by contemporary French poets; medieval troubadour poetry, after whose forms many of the poems are named). Some show an embryonic gift for lyrical expression ('Alba', the poem written for Ethna McCarthy; 'Da Tagte Es', the poem written after his father's death); but, in others, this gift is all but stifled by the self-conscious obscurity that also marred Beckett's first experiments in prose.

After some more sporadic attempts to write poetry in English ('Cascando', 'Ooftish') Beckett used the medium for his first attempts at literature in French. The French poems, written between 1937 and 1939 **[26]**, display a greater control over structure and language than the English poems; in some, Beckett is able to create short, lyrical images whose effectiveness is increased by the relative simplicity of their language

'Dieppe'
again the last ebb
the dead shingle
the turning then the steps
towards the lights of old.

(CP 49)

After another group of poems, written between 1947 and 1949, Beckett seems to have abandoned poetry for the next two decades. He returned to the form after the experiments in prose and drama of the 1960s and early 1970s; his late poetry also displays something of the extreme compression, and resulting ambiguity, also found in his work for other media

'Roundelay'
On all that strand
at end of day
steps sole sound
long sole sound
until unbidden stay
then no sound
on all that strand
long no sound
until unbidden go
steps sole sound
long sole sound
on all that strand
at end of day

(CP 35)

These poems display the same concern with rhythm and linguistic precision that Beckett employed elsewhere in his work. Fundamentally, they betray the same impulse as the later prose and drama; a search for the simplest possible means of expression, the word that will summarise the events of a life. It is oddly fitting that Beckett's final piece of writing in any medium should be a poem (given that his work had, for many years, displayed characteristics more normally associated with poetry) and oddly fitting, given Beckett's love and mistrust of language, that it should be called *what is the word*.

## Further Reading

To date, the only dedicated study of Beckett's poetry remains Harvey (1970).

# PART III

# CRITICISM

Beckett has become one of the most discussed literary figures, not only of the twentieth century, but of any era; as the compilers of a recent survey of Beckett criticism put it

> The sheer volume of criticism in Beckett's mother tongue is indeed formidable (it has been projected that by the end of the century it will equal the literature devoted to Napoleon and Wagner).
> (Murphy, Haber, Bruer and Schell 1994: 3)

Given Beckett's habitual concerns, this is perhaps unsurprising. He wrote, in prose, drama, and other media, works that questioned the basic structures of literature and drama; as an artist, he had undertaken an ontological investigation of the nature of writing (a study of first principles; in this case, a study of the assumptions underlying any piece of fiction). Furthermore, he refused (by and large) to explain his work, leaving the field relatively open for academics intrigued by such an enigmatic author. Beckett's works cried out for explication, and he was unwilling to supply the necessary analytical tools; and so, from the first, this vacuum was filled by a steadily increasing stream of articles, special journal editions, specialised journals, essay collections and books.

Critical interest in Beckett has also coincided with a wider re-evaluation of the nature of literary criticism itself. It is something of a simplification to say that an approach to texts that was basically humanist (that is, concerned with the literary text's ability to teach the reader about the essential nature of humanity) has been challenged, and in some cases superseded, by approaches that are more concerned with the way in which a literary text uses language (these approaches – structuralist, post-structuralist, feminist, psychoanalytical – will be discussed later in this survey). However, although the practice of Beckett criticism has been rather more complex than this simple model implies, it is true to say that, especially in the last fifteen years, his work has become a battleground on which literary critics have contested their various positions. It is a commonplace of Beckett criticism that the work raises fundamental questions; precisely what those fundamental questions are, has tended to depend on the particular tradition from which the individual critic writes.

Beckett criticism has gone through four main stages: the initial stage, in which the perameters for much of the following debates were established, which coincided roughly with the period between the first publication of the trilogy and the awarding of the Nobel prize in 1969: a second period, in which the arguments established in the first period were further expanded, studies began to appear on specific aspects of

Beckett's work and the orthodoxy of Beckett criticism up to this point came under increasing scrutiny; a third period, from the 1980s to the mid-1990s, in which Beckett's work was subject to multiple and conflicting readings that were themselves influenced by the theoretical debates that had become common currency in the academic study of literature; and a fourth period, from the mid-1990s to the present, in which the availabitily of new biographical information began to influence the field. Such divisions are, of course, not exact, and always exist as much for the convenience of a particular writer (and a particular reader) as they do in reality; however, they should provide a useful introduction to what can be, at first glance, an intimidatingly large and complex body of critical work.

Beckett himself, in a letter to Alan Schneider, famously disclaimed all responsibility for the critical readings that proliferated around his art

> But when it comes to journalists, I feel the only line is to refuse to be involved in exegesis of any kind ... And if that's not enough for them, and it obviously isn't, it's plenty for us, and we have no elucidations to offer of mysteries that are all of their making, My work is a matter of fundamental sounds... made as fully as possible, and I accept responsibility for nothing else. If people want to have headaches among the overtones, let them. And provide their own aspirin.
>
> (Bair 1978: 397)

In an attempt to prevent as many headaches as possible for the interested reader, I will be limiting my study of Beckett criticism in two ways. First, I will deal with criticism published in English: second, I will deal with book-length studies. This will, I hope, narrow the field enough to enable its complexity to be understood: it will also deal with those texts that are more widely available to the average student. This is not to say that journals and periodicals should be ignored: *The Journal of Beckett Studies* (first published in 1976) has provided a forum for the various debates surrounding the author; more recently, the bilingual journal *Samuel Beckett Today/Aujourd'hui* has run a number of issues on specific aspects of Beckett's work; debates about Beckett have been conducted in great depth in the pages of *Modern Drama* and *Modern Fiction Studies*; and important analyses of Beckett's theatrical working methods appeared in the journal *Theatre Quarterly* in the 1970s. Indeed, a strong case could be made that modern Beckett criticism in English was itself started by a journal (the special issue of *Perspective* devoted to Beckett's work that was published under Ruby Cohn's editorship in 1959). Similarly, in focusing on criticism in English, I do not deny the importance of Beckett criticism in other languages, particularly French and German; and some of the most influential contributions from these languages (Theodor Adorno's essay on *Endgame*, Alan Robbe-Grillett's article on 'presence' in Beckett's theatre) have been widely available in English for quite some time.

## (a) BECKETT THE CARTESIAN: 1959–1969

Beckett criticism in English began in earnest in 1959, when Ruby Cohn edited a special issue of the journal *Perspective* devoted to Beckett's work (*Perspective* 11.3). Beforehand, Edith Kern had published an article on *Godot* in 1954, and Beckett's work had featured in Henri Peyre's study, *The Contemporary French Novel*, in 1955; however, most Beckett criticism in the 1950s was, unsurprisingly, in French. The *Perspective* issue identified Beckett as an important figure in English Literature; and, moreover, it introduced the notion that the Beckettian universe was governed by rules that were, at bottom, philosophical. This note had already been sounded in French criticism: early studies had noted Beckett's relationship to the then current philosophical fashion for existentialism; English criticism in the 1960s linked Beckett not only to existentialism, but to Schopenhauer, Kierkegaard, Wittgenstein, and, most decisively of all, to the work of the seventeenth-century French philosopher René Descartes and his philosophical disciples.

The link to philosophy was legitimated, first of all, by Beckett himself; in a letter to the critic Sighle Kennedy, he said

> If I were in the unenviable position of having to study my work my points of departure would be the 'naught is more real ...' and the '*Ubi nihil vales ...*' both already in *Murphy* and neither very rational.
>
> (Kennedy 1971: 300)

References to Descartes, Arnold Geulincx, and Nicolas Malebranche recurred in his work; and (it was soon discovered) Beckett's first published piece, *Whoroscope*, had been a poetic meditation on Descartes' life and thought **[14, 98]**. Cartesian philosophy (the term given to Descartes' work) seemed comprehensively to explain Beckett's universe. In the *Meditations*, Descartes had sought to establish a secure foundation for his knowledge of the world; in doing so, he had (as a point of philosophical principle) cast doubt on the certainty of the physical world around him (even though the physical world included his own body). Even though he perceived the external world as real, his perceptions were liable to error; the only thing that such a radical doubt left intact was the mind that doubted; and the only way to reach this certainty was to turn away from all the manifestations of an apparent reality

> I shall now close my eyes, stop up my ears, turn away all my senses, even efface from my thought all images of corporeal things, or at least, because this can hardly be done, I shall consider them as being vain and false; and this communing only with myself, and examining my inner self, I shall try to make myself, little by little, better known and more familiar to myself. I am a thing which thinks, that is to say, which doubts, affirms, denies, knows a few things, is ignorant of many, which loves, hates, wills, does not will, which also imagines, and which perceives. For, as I noted above, although the things I perceive and imagine are perhaps nothing at all outside me and in themselves, I am nevertheless assured that those modes of thought, certainly reside in and are found in me ...
> (Descartes, René, *Discourse on Method/The Meditations*,
> Harmondsworth: Penguin 1968: 113)

This central insight, that only the mind could be identified as the true location of the self, is usually termed the Cartesian *cogito* (after the Latin phrase, used by Descartes in the *Discourse on Method*, *cogito, ergo sum* – I think, therefore I am). It posited a radical split between the mind and the body; and, as can be seen from the above quote, it required the individual to turn inward, to study the mind's experience of the world. The parallels between this practice and Beckett's writing were, for his early critics, irresistible.

Descartes did leave room for a physiological connection between the mind and the external world. However, even this tenuous link was too much for some of Descartes' followers. The Occasionalist philosophers (in his work, Beckett refers specifically to two – Arnold Geulincx and Nicolas Malebranche) believed in an even more radical split between the mind and the body. For them, the world and the self were only connected by God; the mind and the world (including the body) run on parallel paths. In fact, for Geulincx, there was no causal connection between the mental and the physical; any apparent interaction was in fact nothing more than a series of coincidences arranged by God. Given this, the best way to deal with a world that one could not influence was simply to regard it, calmly, from the only secure territory that the individual could claim; the mind. As Geulincx put it, *ubi nihil valis, ubi nihil velis*: Where I am worth nothing, I should want nothing (this phrase was quoted by Beckett in his letter to Sighle Kennedy: see above).

In early Beckett criticism, then, the Cartesian worldview was identified as a strong influence on the author's work, but with one decisive difference: the absence of a God converted the quietly optimistic philosophy of Descartes into a fundamentally pessimistic view of the world. There was no longer any confirmation of the reality of the external world; nothing to anchor the self in any secure relation to its surroundings. In adopting this viewpoint, Beckett seemed to his early critics to align himself with Existentialism, a philosophical trend which flourished in mainland Europe (and especially in France) immediately after the Second World War. Existentialism began from a point similar to that of Cartesian philosophy; a position of radical doubt as to the relation between the self and the world. In other ways, however, it reversed the implied hierarchy of Cartesian thought. For Descartes, the thinking self existed independently of the external world; for the existentialists, the existence of the individual predated the existence of the self. One only became oneself through an encounter with the world; the individual could not lay claim to any abstract truths, and only knew what he or she knew from his or her subjective experience of the world. Given that no rules existed independently of human activity, the existential individual carried ultimate responsibility for his or her actions. For many existentialists, there was something inherently noble about the human being's struggle to understand the burden of existence. Albert Camus, for example, recreated the classical figure of Sisyphus as an existential hero; condemned in Hell to push a boulder up to the top of a slope, he was doomed never to complete his task (the boulder would always prove too heavy, and would roll back to the bottom of the hill, compelling him to begin once more). For Camus, Sisyphus became heroic when he accepted this meaningless task, while knowing it to be meaningless; existential man, too, became heroic when he decided to shoulder the burdens of existence, even though he knew that his existence had no ultimate meaning. To exist in the world, for Camus, the individual had always to face the absurdity of everyday life

> At certain moments of lucidity, the mechanical aspect of [human] gestures, their meaningless pantomime make silly everything that surrounds them. A man is talking behind a glass partition; you cannot see him but you can hear his incomprehensible dumb-show; you wonder why he is alive. This discomfort in the face of man's

own humanity, this incalculable tumble before the image of what we are, this 'nausea', as a writer of today puts it, is ... the absurd.
(Camus, Albert, *The Myth of Sisyphus*,
Harmondsworth: Penguin 1955: 18–19)

In the early days of Beckett criticism, the variety of existentialism most commonly evoked was that of the contemporary French philosophers Sartre and Camus; other varieties, however, were to prove equally fruitful. Soren Kierkegaard (an important precursor of existentialist thought) provided a model of human life that stressed the ever-changing nature of existence; human beings were trapped in an endless flux of events in which the truths established at one moment were proved false the next. For Kierkegaard, any individual who committed himself to thinking about human existence was involved in a quest both comic and pathetic: this was because

> Existence itself, the act of existing, is a striving, and is both comic and pathetic in the same degree. It is pathetic because the striving is infinite; that is, it is directed towards the infinite, being an actualization of infinitude, a transformation which involves the highest pathos. It is comic, because such a striving involves a self-contradiction. Viewed pathetically, a single second has infinite value; viewed comically, ten thousand years are but a trifle ...
> (Kierkegaard, Soren *Concluding Unscientific Postscript*,
> Princeton: Princeton University Press 1941: 84–5)

Early critics also came to note the pervasive influence of Arthur Schopenhauer **[14]** on Beckett's writing. Schopenhauer (mentioned by name in *Proust* and in the early poem 'Dortmunder') opposed the world as it appeared to the individual (the 'representation') to the world as it actually was (the expression of 'will' – the world as blind force, existing beyond the control of the mind). In other words, the external world (including the body) existed outside the mind's control; any order that seemed to exist in the external world only existed in the mind of the individual perceiving subject. Given that, for Schopenhauer, to exist was to suffer, the only course for the suffering individual was to deny his or her 'will to life' (the blind striving force that united the body with the rest of the world)

> Then, instead of the restless pressure and effort; instead of the constant transition from desire to apprehension and from joy to sorrow; instead of the never satisfied and never-dying hope that

constitutes the life-dream of the man who wills, we see that peace that is higher than all reason, that ocean-like calmness of the spirit, that deep tranquillity, that unshakeable confidence and serenity, whose mere reflection in the countenance ... is a complete and certain gospel. Only knowledge remains; the will has vanished.

(Quoted in Janaway, Christopher, *Schopenhauer*, Oxford: Oxford University Press 1994: 92)

For Schopenhauer, art – and especially music – was the activity of will-less contemplation; of the mind working independently of the 'restless pressure and effort' of the will-to-live.

The similarities between these philosophical traditions are clear: each one begins from the idea that the self and the world are split; each one places great emphasis on the mind's ability to form the world; and each one places the development of the self at the heart of the human condition. The drama played out in every human being is essentially internal; and there is something heroic (if, in some cases, rather comic) about the individual's attempts to describe the reality of the self as completely and as honestly as is possible. Finally, each one is, if not openly pessimistic, then at least unable to admit easy comfort for the individual. Even Cartesianism has its bleaker implications; once God – the ultimate guarantor of the self's place in the world – is removed, the self is left alone, fundamentally isolated, in a world which cannot be connected to the impressions, ideas and feelings experienced by the mind.

It is not that early Beckett criticism used these philosophical models to the exclusion of everything else; to the names mentioned above, one could add Bishop Berkeley (who claimed that the external world was an illusion): Bergson (whose theories of laughter and comedy form an important part of Ruby Cohn's early study, *Samuel Beckett: The Comic Gamut*) Fritz Mauther (who argued that language was itself fundamentally untrustworthy); and the pre-Socratic philosopher Democritus, who suggested that every attempt to describe the world foundered on the paradox of nothingness; the external world, apparently real, in practice defies adequate analysis (Democritus' paradox, 'nothing is more real than nothing' was a phrase that Beckett admitted lay behind the creation of *Murphy*).

For Beckett's first academic interpreters, the greatest literary influence on his work came from the poet whose work he had studied while at Trinity, under the tutelage of Madame Esposito. Dante's influence on Beckett was held, by the early critics (and by many of the late ones) to be all-encompassing. There was a great deal of justification for this;

the *Divine Comedy* **[9]** proved to be perhaps the single most influential text in Beckett's writing life. He returned to it many times, finding particular inspiration in the poem's first two sections; the *Inferno* (where the souls of the damned suffer an eternal punishment appropriate to the sins they committed while alive) and the *Purgatorio* (where souls atone for errors in their lives before attaining salvation). The *Paradiso* proved less compelling; 'Dante and the Lobster' **[56–7]** opens with Beckett's protagonist 'stuck in the first of the canti of the moon'. (*MPTK* 9) – a particularly intractable passage in Dante's third book. The hero of the early fiction is named after a character from the *Purgatorio* (Belacqua, a Florentine lutemaker noted for his indolence) **[53–7]**; in an unexpectedly lyrical passage, Murphy **[57–60]** imagines himself blissfully waiting out the time of his earthly life, as Dante's Belacqua does, on the slopes of Mount Purgatory

> [Looking] down at dawn across the reeds to the trembling of the austral sea and the sun obliquing to the north as it rose, immune from expiation until he should have dreamed it through again, with the downright dreaming of an infant, all the way from the spermarium to the crematorium ... [He] would have a long time lying there dreaming, watching the dayspring run through its zodiac, before the toil up hill to Paradise ...
>
> This he called his Belacqua fantasy and perhaps the most highly systematised of the whole collection. It belonged to those that lay just beyond the frontiers of suffering, it was the first landscape of freedom.
>
> (*M* 48)

In *Molloy* **[66–8]**, Molloy observes the meeting of two men, A. and C., from a similar vantage-point, this time located not on Mount Purgatory but in countryside whose topography suggests the landscape around Dublin

> ... He [C] gazed around as if to engrave the landmarks on his memory and must have seen the rock in the shadow of which I crouched like Belacqua, or Sordello, I forget ...
>
> (*T* 12)

In the radio play *All That Fall* **[36, 78–9]**, Maddy Rooney imagines herself and her husband walking backwards down the long road home from Boghill station

Or you forwards and I backwards. The perfect pair. Like Dante's damned, with their faces arsey-versey. Our tears will water our bottoms.

(*CDW* 191)

Pim in *How It Is* **[81–2]**, the trio trapped in urns in *Play* **[89]**, the population of the cylinder in *The Lost Ones* **[87–8]**, either sedentary, vanquished or frantically in search of an exit, all echo the powerful images of stasis, entrapment, and cyclical suffering and atonement in Dante's visions of Hell and Purgatory, with one crucial difference. Dante's universe is structured around the idea of salvation; all of the punishments he describes are justifiable, because they are designed by a benevolent God. Beckett's universe is godless, and the punishments his characters endure are for less personal crimes; as Beckett noted in *Proust*, tragedy is the expiation of the sin of being born.

The influence of Marcel Proust (the subject of Beckett's early mono-graph **[15–16, 72]**) was also noted; in Proust's massive novel sequence *Remembrance of Things Past*, the narrator Marcel recreated his life from childhood not as a conventional narrative, but as a demonstration of the influence of time on human life, and of the role of memory in the individual's idea of himself and of his world. Marcel's world is a curi-ously fluid place; in addition to the conventional idea of memory (which provides a stable background of images against which the individual measures him or herself) he is also at the mercy of involuntary memory (a strongly imagined set of associations called up by an unexpected encounter with an object whose significance has been forgotten). For example, in the first novel of the sequence, Marcel is only able to re-create his childhood in detail because of the associations called up when he tastes a cake dipped in tea, a taste that he has come to associate with his earliest memories. The similarities between the Proustian narrator (to an extent at the mercy of the world and of his own past) and the Beckettian narrator similarly adrift, were quickly noted; and critics also discerned an interesting similarity in the two writers' styles. Proust's sentences were long and involved, an attempt to render into prose the associations and memories that passed through Marcel's consciousness. The prose in Beckett's mature work was similarly loose, and seemed also to describe the moment by moment workings of his protagonists' minds. However, as was noted by Steven Rosen and Nicholas Zubrigg, there were profound differences between the two authors. Proust's style aimed to describe the workings of a coherently imagined consciousness, while Beckett's aimed to show that consciousness disintegrating; and Proust's cycle of novels was, if not optimistic, then at least guardedly positive about human life and art a comment that could not be made of Beckett's work.

While Beckett was a Trinity undergraduate, the Abbey revived the plays of John Synge **[9–10]**. Beckett later credited Synge as the greatest influence on his theatrical work, and it is easy to see why; Synge favoured a simple, yet striking visual and verbal style, and wrote plays that mixed humour, pathos, tragedy and bleak farce in unpredictable amounts. Beckett's knowledge and love of the French dramatist Jean Racine, whose plays followed the prescription (derived from a reading of Aristotle) that all plays must conform to the three unities of time, space and action, might have inspired the enclosed, entropic world of the mature drama, at least in part; but the tone, half comic, half despairing, the bleak simplicity of the settings, and the rhythmic, patterned dialogues are undoubtedly taken from Synge.

Other writers associated with Beckett's work at this point included, naturally, Joyce (the stream of consciousness monologue, in which the self seems to speak without the intervention of the author; **[12–13]**); Swift (the satirical descriptions of human behaviour, and the entrenched disgust at the sheer physicality of the human body); Sterne (the uncertain, playful narrator, only tangentially in charge of the tale he tells); Rabelais (the parade of useless erudition; the exaggerated, comic descriptions of basic human activities – sexual, excremental, and so on). Taken all together, the general view of Beckett's work that emerged in the first decade of Beckett criticism took the general philosophical model suggested by the combination of Cartesianism, Occasionalism, Existentialism, and Schopenhauerian pessimism, and created a composite image for the Beckettian universe: a universe in which the isolated self, split from the world and from his own physical existence, attempted to come to terms with the absence of any meaning, or indeed of any fragments of meaning, in a cold, inhospitable, grotesque, absurd and damaging world. This allowed early critics to form Beckett's work into a narrative, that described the direction taken by Beckettian man, from the external world to the world of the self; this was generally described as an existential quest, a search for meaning (however futile) in a meaningless cosmos, and, as such, as a fundamentally heroic enterprise.

The first full length studies of Beckett's work began to appear in 1961, with the publication of Hugh Kenner's *Samuel Beckett: A Critical Study*; in the same year, Martin Esslin published the first edition of *The Theatre of the Absurd*. Both books helped to establish the idea of Beckett the Cartesian/existential artist. Kenner's study, in particular, described the Beckettian hero as a Cartesian clown; a man split from his body, essentially solitary, concerned with the life of the mind, but at the same time prone to the tragicomic indignities of existence; and doomed to failure

> The clown exploits impotence, to be sure, when he allows to bubble up into sustained mimetic coherence his own inability to walk a tightrope, missing his footing, misplacing but never dropping his bowler hat (which catches on a button behind his collar and, obeying immutable mechanical laws, is carried round out of reach as he turns to clutch at the space where it was) collapsing in an arc which carries his hands exactly to a graspable stanchion, retarding his pace to zero for long reflection, crowding six desperate acrobatics into a split second. He does not imitate the acrobat; it is plain that he could not; he offers us directly, his personal incapacity, an intricate artform. The man who imitates is the acrobat himself (all ropewalkers are alike), adding to what we have already seen before in other circuses some new minuscule difficulty overcome, moving on felt-shod feet a little further along the dreary road of the possible.
>
> (Kenner 1961: 33–4)

For Kenner, the Beckettian clown was most uniquely individual, most truly himself, at the moment when he failed; to succeed was to ally oneself with the purely mechanical world of the acrobat, whose activities only emphasised his lack of individuality.

Kenner argued strongly that a developing Cartesian split between the mind and body was central to the development of Beckett's work: as Beckett progressed, the divisions between mind and body became greater (the body became more mechanical, less amenable to the mind's control, and the mind increasingly isolated, forced to turn in on itself). In a striking metaphor for this transformation, Kenner noted the prevalence of bicycles in Beckett's fictional world. The man in the bicycle was a metaphor for smoothly functioning Cartesian man. Together, they formed a composite being that Kenner described as the Cartesian Centaur; the mind (the rider) in charge of a fully functioning machine (the bicycle). By the time Beckett reached *The Unnamable*

> The bicycle is long gone, the Centaur dismembered; of the exhilaration of the cyclist's progress in the days when he was lord of the things that move, nothing remains but the ineradicable habit of persisting like a machine. The serene confidence of the lordly Cogito

... is similarly dissociated, in this last phase of the dream of Cartesian man, into a garrulity, vestigially logical, which is perhaps piped to him by other beings ...

(Kenner 1961: 131) **[69–71]**

And yet Beckett's work was not fundamentally miserable: rather, the impulse behind it was fundamentally comic, albeit comedy of a rather specialised kind. The humour in Beckett came from the characters' unshakeable commitment to expression

Beckett's work ... is far from being a by-product of hopeless misery. It is the unassimilable by-product of a set of operations with words, very word of which retains its meaning and every operation its vitality. And the work leaps from end to end with comic invention...

(Kenner 1961: 202)

Kenner's study contained a chapter on the drama, which claimed (notably, in the light of future discussions) that Beckett's theatre operated on the boundaries of theatricality. This theme was expanded on in Martin Esslin's *The Theatre of the Absurd*, the first text to attempt to fit Beckett into a contemporary artistic trend. However, to say that Absurdist Theatre was a coherent movement, with clearly defined aims and goals, was to simplify what was in practice a rather disparate collection of plays and playwrights, united (apparently) only by a common rejection of a world run on rational principles. Esslin's analysis of these writers was heavily influenced by the then-current philosophy of existentialism; he took the term 'the Absurd' from the writings of Albert Camus (see above). Absurdist playwrights saw man cast adrift in a world that does not make sense; that obeyed uncontrollable mechanical principles; a world in which personality was fluid, and the individual was always at the mercy of an obscurely threatening outside world. Esslin noted the similarity between Beckett's worldview and that of the existentialists; but he introduced an important caveat against a simple equation between the two

If, for Beckett as for Sartre, man has the duty of facing the human condition as a recognition that at the heart of our being there is nothingness, liberty, and the need of constantly creating ourselves in a succession of choices, then Godot might well become an image of what Sartre calls 'bad faith' – 'The first act of bad faith consists in evading what one cannot evade, in evading what one is' (*Being and Nothingness*, Gallimard, 1943: 111). While these parallels may be illuminating, we must not go too far in trying to identify Beckett's vision with any school of philosophy. It is the peculiar richness of a play like Waiting for Godot that it opens vistas on so many different perspectives. It is open to philosophical, religious, and psychological interpretations, yet above all it is a poem on time, evanescence, and the mysteriousness of existence, the paradox of change and stability, necessity and absurdity ...

(Esslin 1961: 61-2)

In noting that *Godot* was more poem than philosophical demonstration, Esslin, like Kenner, began to edge his discussion of Beckett's drama toward the idea of metatheatre (that is, a theatrical event that does not require an external justification for its meaning, but that creates its effects, as a poem does, by the careful use of the form itself).

These two studies were followed in quick succession by Frederick Hoffman's *Samuel Beckett: The Language of the Self* and Ruby Cohn's first substantial piece of Beckett criticism, *Samuel Beckett: The Comic Gamut* (both 1962). Hoffman placed Beckett in a tradition that also included Dostoievsky and Kafka; all three authors dramatised the slow decline of rational thought in western society. Beckett stood at the end of this tradition: his characters took the tendency toward nihilism found in these earlier authors to its logical conclusion. In line with Kenner, Hoffman saw Beckett's essential worldview as both Cartesian and tragicomic; the plays and novels were painfully funny descriptions of minds divorced from bodies, and from any defining system. These descriptions lent themselves more naturally to prose than to the theatre, where the form of drama itself gave them too concrete an existence

Beckett's selves are, to begin with, persons without God, or (Murphy and Watt) persons with God imperfectly within them. As they proceed (chiefly from novel to play to comic interlude or sketch), their deliberations are fixed upon the fragments both of a rational order and of a once well-established and defended armour-propre. As confidence in either system declines, the rhetoric becomes disengaged, runs off on its own. Only in the plays does the result come within scope and order: and this because the requirements of the theatre, however ignored or adapted to his tastes, do make for a more than occasional comprehension of Beckett's dispositions. Yet the theatre also oversimplifies: and, as the Textes pour Rein prove, the 'pure rhetoric' of Beckett's 'residual Cartesianism' is limited and impeded by dramatic necessities ...

(Hoffman 1962: 160–1)

Ruby Cohn's first book on Beckett, *Samuel Beckett: the Comic Gamut*, ranks alongside Kenner's as one of the most influential, and one of the most cited, of the early studies; it also established Cohn firmly in the forefront of Beckett scholarship (a position that she had already begun to mark out in 1959, with the special edition of *Perspective* devoted to the author's work). Although Cohn herself later expressed doubts about the work, it played an important part in early discussions of Beckett as a writer of particularly grim comedy, the master of the illiberal jest

> The illiberal jest lies at the root of the corrective theory of comedy – the leading theory of comedy of the Western cultural tradition. By laughing at the comic defect in the victim, the laugher exercises that defect from his own makeup. More recently, comedy has been interpreted as social consolation, to which laughter is irrelevant. In the latter view, the comic hero is integrated ... into his society, whereas the tragic hero is isolated from his.
>
> Since this study will be concerned with Beckett's treatment of the comic, it must be stressed that neither of the two major themes of comedy is applicable to his work. So ambiguous are Beckett's comic heroes that we scarcely know why we laugh, and whether we laugh at or with. So asocial are Beckett's heroes that they appear to exist in tragic isolation rather than comic consolation. But can a work be labelled tragic when the isolation of the hero from his society is conveyed by recourse to various comic tricks of a literary or theatrical heritage? If tragicomedy can be defined as 'a play mainly of tragic character, but with a happy ending', perhaps Beckett's works should be called comitragedy.
>
> (Cohn 1962: 8)

Cohn discerned a development in Beckett's comic art, from the rhetorical complexities of the early work (discussed with reference to the categories established by the French philosopher, Henri Bergson, in his analysis of the comic techniques of language) to the work from *Watt* onwards; with *Watt* Beckett decisively entered the comitragic world of the mature prose and drama. The trilogy was an ironic reflection of man's life in a meaningless cosmos, a life that could only be given a shape through literature: but the process of writing itself falsified the existence it described

> Beckett's motif ... is that words are thoughts are emotions, that fiction is our only knowledge, and all knowledge a fiction written in a foreign tongue ... All Beckett's fictions merge, finally, into the

unique, suffering artist-human, ironically probing the meaning of fiction, and the fiction of meaning. This is Beckett's unique achievement, uniquely achieved.

(Cohn 1962: 167–8)

Nor was the world of Beckett's drama any more comforting: a text such as *Waiting for Godot* (described by Beckett himself, as Cohn pointed out, as a tragicomedy) dramatised the same conflict as the prose in explicitly theatrical terms

> ... In Godot's continued absence, man becomes a king of shreds and patches, of blindness and dumbness, fit only to play the clown and feed the worms 'with neither decencie nor discretion'. Fallen too low to be a subject for 'right Tragedy', feeling too much anguish to be capable of 'right Comedy. Beckett's man, while waiting for Godot, plays a part in a tragicomedy – a slapstick part of victim in a world that he did not make, and that resists his efforts to make sense of it.
>
> (Cohn 1962: 225) **[74–6]**

Cohn's conclusion prefigured many of the staple elements of Beckett criticism over the next three decades: Beckett's writing was concerned, in part, with the structure of writing of the particular artforms that he used; Beckett the writer was always aware of the sheer untrustworthiness of words; and Beckett's art undermined, not only literature, but also the metaphysical system on which the idea of art in Western culture was based

> Dramatic or fictional, Beckett's work paints an ironic portrait of man, Everyman, as artist – liar. He paints in words – in the words that his heroes revile and unravel, in the words he weaves into one of the masterly prose styles of our time ...
> Within each literary genre, Beckett undermines that very genre – fictional formulae in the fiction and dramatic conventions in the drama. By making the literary form within that form, Beckett questions the boundary between art and life, between fiction and fact. Such interrogations is part of the traditional stock in trade of the fool, and Beckett plays it for all its farcical, metaphysical worth. He pommels existence with the questions of his characters, or with their frenzied affirmations immediately followed by more frenzied negation. These questions slap at life as well as art; for any interpretation of life as a construction, a game, a work of art. Bordering on

a reality that is necessarily unknown, unknowable, and frustratingly seductive.

(Cohn 1962: 298–9)

In 1963, Lionel Abel provided the first discussion of Beckett's drama as metatheatre, in *Metatheater: A New View of Dramatic Form*. The following year saw no fewer than four studies of Beckett's work: Richard Coe's and William Tindall's studies, both titled *Samuel Beckett*; John Fletcher's *The Novels of Samuel Beckett;* and Josephine Jacobsen and William R. Mueller's *the Testament of Samuel Beckett*. Tindall's short essay, published as part of the Colombia modern writers series, contained a brief biographical study, before an analysis of the work that drew heavily on the view of Beckett already well-established in the work of Esslin, Cohn, Kenner and Hoffman. Coe's study discussed Beckett's writing as a constant striving toward nothingness, which was doomed to failure because it was impossible to speak of silence. He also identified time as one of the great themes of Beckett's writing. Beckett, for Coe, viewed human existence as both time-bound and timeless. In discussing the dramatic works, Coe stressed the unfinishable nature of Beckett's dramatic world, which was tied to the characters dual existence both inside and outside of time; things happened, but life (and therefore suffering) was endless. John Fletcher's discussion of the novels up to *How It Is* split the development of Beckett's fictional universe into three main stages, each one identified with the relation of the self to the world: the hero as citizen ('Assumption' to *Murphy*); the hero as outcast (*Watt* to *Malone Dies*); and, finally, the hero as voice. He argued that, as the Beckett hero moved further away from the real world, he took on an almost mythic dimension

> As a novelist of such revolutionary significance, Beckett cannot be ignored, nor passed over in a sentence. He is there, looming large and inescapable on the literary landscape; the games which he has been playing with words for over thirty years have gradually become matters of immediate relevancy to us. His extraordinary hero roams about in our consciousness, a haunting and troublesome shadow. The croak of Molloy's voice, his ragged clothes, his limping gait, his festering sores, live on in our memory. We have, in Beckett's novels, new heroes, unfamiliar gods, a whole modern mythology. These fictions tell us simply but insistently the story of a fragile voice – a human voice – which refuses stubbornly to die, which flickers on, somehow resisting submersion and assimilation ...

(Fletcher 1964: 233)

Jacobson and Mueller went further than previous critics in insisting on the fundamental unity of Beckett's work: they collapsed all of his writing into one text

> The whole of Beckett's monstrous, unified, circular time – that temps enormee to which he refers in *Comment C'Est* (*How It Is*) – is by genus a bitter, funny, and terrible poem ...
>
> (Jacobson and Mueller 1964: 20)

This single work had a single hero, identified in the study by the initial Q, which stands for a quidam (or an unknown figure: the name is shared by the anonymous diarist in Kierkegaard's *Scenes from Life's Way*)

> All of Beckett's work can be divided – as Q (the quidam figure) is torn – between two forces: the lusting after nothingness and the voice, distant, unintelligible, pitiless, which prevents him sinking into the void so desperately desired. The epicentre of this endless, ludicrous, violent struggle is the monstrous figure of Q ... Now and again we are allowed to catch a glimpse of this giant figure, a figure both agonized and onerous, impossible to place in space and time, since it advances and retreats almost in a single motion, impossible to define satisfactorily, since ambiguity is its very essence ...
>
> (Jacobson and Mueller 1964: 23)

This figure is unfixed and ambiguous because the world in which it moves is unfixed and ambiguous. Its progress through this world contained, for Jacobsen and Mueller, strong echoes of the Passion of Christ; they noted that this did not mean that Beckett placed any faith in the idea of salvation, either for the individual or for the species as a whole (that is, a writer fundamentally concerned with analysing and ameliorating human life), noting that Beckett did not find any hope in humanity. However, this did not mean that Beckett's work was unconcerned with the value of human existence; they, like Kenner, found that Beckett's humour was the key to understanding his attitude to human life

> It is no good trying to isolate Beckett from values; if he has been unable to establish them for others, for himself, it is to their hypothetical postulation that he dedicates the full force of his work. He directs his laughter, he says, against that which is not good, against that which is not true, against that which mocks suffering.

119

That laughter is his testament – his legacy to that which is good, to that which is true, that which is compassionate

(Jacobson and Mueller 1964: 174)

In 1965, Martin Esslin edited the first volume of critical essays in English devoted to Beckett's work. The collection included a translation of 'Three Dialogues with Georges Duthuit' (the first time this key work had been made widely available in English), brought together some of the most influential Beckett critics, and reprinted some of the articles that had helped to set the agenda for Beckett criticism in the 1960s. The collection included Maurice Nadeau's early essay, 'Samuel Beckett: Humour and the Void'; A.J. Leventhal's 'The Beckett Hero' (an important early discussion of Beckett's debt to Dante, and to the figure of Beclacqua); Jacqueline Hoefer's essay on *Watt*, which allied the linguistic strategies of the novel to Wittgenstein's *Tractatus Logico Philosophicus* (in the *Tractatus*, Wittgenstein explored the limits of a logical analysis of the world; the work's final statement, 'whereof one cannot speak, therefore one must be silent', seemed neatly to describe Watt's encounter with the uncontainable complexity of Knott's house **[60–2]**). Martin Esslin's introductory essay established Beckett as an existential artist, struggling with the ultimate emptiness of human existence; it treated Beckett's work, not as the recreation of the individual's experience of a meaningless world, but as a direct transcription of that experience

How is it that this vision of the ultimate void in all its grotesque derision and despair should be capable of producing an effect akin to the catharsis of great tragedy?

Here we find the ultimate confirmation of our initial contention that it is not the content of the work, not *what* is said, that matters in a writer of Beckett's stamp, but the *quality of the experience* that is communicated. To be in communication with a mind of such uncompromising determination to face the stark reality of the human situation and to confront the worst without even being in danger of yielding to any of the superficial consolations that have clouded man's self-awareness in the past; to be in contact with a human being so free of self-pity, utterly oblivious to the pitfalls of vanity and of self-glorification, even that most venial complacency of all, the illusion of being able to lighten one's load by sharing it with others; to see a lone figure, without hope of comfort, facing the great emptiness of space and time without the possibility of miraculous rescue or salvation, in dignity, resolved to fulfil its obligation to express its own predicament – to partake of such courage and noble stoicism, however, remotely, cannot but evoke a refilling of emotional excitement, exhilaration.

(Esslin 1965: 14)

In the same year, Raymond Federman published the first study of Beckett's early fiction. The study followed what was by now becoming a standard pattern in Beckett criticism; his work was all of a piece, and the development of his thought could be traced from work to work, with each succeeding novel building on (or, more correctly, dismantling) the previous text. Federman began, out of sequence, by studying the later novel *How It Is* as an exercise in an almost completely disintegrated text: having established *How It Is* as an endpoint, he returned to the earliest work (in this case *More Pricks than Kicks*) to trace the Beckett character's gradual removal from the real world. Federman identified the key themes in Beckett's writing as

... Human loneliness, physical disintegration, mental alienation, intellectual fiasco, creative failure, and above all the unavoidable dualism of mind and body, reality and fiction ...

(Federman 1965: 57)

– a list that recapitulated the common themes of Beckett criticism up to (and after) the mid-1960s. In describing Beckett's work, up to *Mercier and Camier* and the *Nouvelles*, as demonstrations of the artist's failure to express, Federman reached a conclusion that coincided neatly with Esslin's: the Beckettian universe was one in which characters struggled endlessly, but heroically, with the intractable problem of being

Placed on the periphery of human life, reduced to nondescript identities, these subhuman creatures represent the evolution of mankind from the ape to the mystery of its future condition. In his French works Beckett no longer satirises, as he did in his English fiction, the mediocrity of certain types of people, of certain social institutions; instead he confronts the reader with the crude image of *being* – the image of a creature stripped of all human attributes, who, while crawling naked like a worm in the mud, reveals the secret of the creative process as well as the agony of the process of life, whether real or fictitious.

(Federman 1965: 204–5)

121

In 1967 John Calder published a tribute volume (*Beckett at Sixty: A Festschrift*); and Ruby Cohn edited the first collection of writing on a specific text (*A Casebook on Waiting for Godot*). Cohn's volume drew together critical work on the text (from G.S. Fraser, Sue-Ellen Case, Lawrence Harvey, Herbert Blau and Colin Duckworth) and articles and essays that dealt with the initial impact of the play; it included some of the first reviews (in particular, the French novelist Alain Robbe-Grillet's first reaction to the performance of *Godot*) and contributions from actors involved in Beckett productions (Peter Bull, the first English Pozzo, contributed an interesting account of an actor's first response to what initially seemed an impossible play).

John Fletcher's companion volume to *The Novels of Samuel Beckett*, *Samuel Beckett's Art* (1967) dealt with the features of Beckett's writing that Fletcher had left undiscussed in his earlier study. It contained a chapter, previously published in Esslin's 1965 collection, on Beckett's poetry, one of the earliest analyses of this area of Beckett's work to appear in English. The study also included analyses of Beckett's criticism and a discussion of his approach to the French language. He provided a comprehensive analysis of Beckett's debt to Dante, the philosophical dimension of the texts, and the literary influences that might be surmised from a study of Beckett's work. Fletcher placed Beckett in a tradition of literary eccentrics, writers who used the conventional forms of prose narrative for their own unconventional ends (Fletcher listed Sterne, Swift, Cervantes, Rabelais and Voltaire as writers whose concern either with the cruelty or the inherent formlessness of human experience found expression in texts that self-consciously invoked the fictional process). However, the Beckett protagonist was, for Fletcher as for Esslin, essentially heroic

> ... If Beckett is gloomy about life, he retains a sort of faith in man; not the faith that can be expressed in the accents of a time that knew no Passchendale or Auschwitz, for they would now no longer ring true, but a faith that he expresses in his own way, by setting up against the tyrants his heroes, who battle on defiantly against all efforts to subdue them. His bravest and most dogged hero remains the Unnamable, fighting to reach the 'real silence' that he knows he will never attain. This may only constitute a modest affirmation, but it is an affirmation for all that ...
>
> (Fletcher 1967: 14)

Ihab Hassan, in *The Literature of Silence: Henry Miller and Samuel Beckett* (1967) proposed a radically different interpretation of the Beckettian universe. Hassan was one of the first critics whose view of literature could be classed as post-modern (for a discussion of this term, see section c below). He took the then-current idea that Beckett's work dealt with a fundamentally absurd universe, and broadened its implications. Beckett did not describe meaninglessness; rather, the words that he habitually employed themselves came close to meaninglessness. Beckett, like Henry Miller, was therefore a practitioner of what could only be termed 'anti-literature', a literary style that developed, paradoxically, by pulling itself apart. Language no longer conveyed meaning: language was itself a game – and the end result of the game was the ultimate exhaustion of the possibilities of speech and writing

> ... Knowing that art cannot be art these days unless it is wrested from impossibility, he comes close to reducing literature to a mathematical tautology. The syllogism of Beckett assumes that history has spent itself; we are merely playing an endgame. The syllogism can be relentless. Language has become void; therefore words can only demonstrate their emptiness. Certainty in knowledge is no longer possible; therefore epistemology must become parody. Religion and metaphysics have lost their authority; therefore we shall wait for Godot in vain. Human relations are at bottom cruel; therefore love is a disguise of power and power a disguise of solitude. Decaying matter remains forever alien to the mind; therefore mind and crippled body can have no union. In this Cartesian nightmare, Beckett leaves only one thing intact; the capacity of human consciousness to reflect on itself and to entertain its own end. Thus literature becomes the inaudible game of a solipsist ... in this rigorous fidelity to failure, he also reveals the secret tendency of literature to silence. Despite the monstrous endurance of his characters and the deadly skill of his words, Samuel Beckett may be considered the author who wants to seal the lips of the muse. Yet his silence, despite its grim, satiric note, has something in common with the silence of holy men who, after knowing pain and outrage, reach for a peace beyond human understanding ...
>
> (Hassan 1967: 30–1)

Ronald Hayman, in a short study of the plays published in 1968, put forward something of a dissenting view: Beckett had created an undoubted masterpiece in *Waiting for Godot*, but his subsequent work had overstrained the boundaries of what was permissible in the theatre

> In the theatre, Beckett's achievement is ... limited. He's achieved two outstanding coups. He managed to invert the normal stage suspense into the suspended time of *Godot*. And in *Krapp* he turned

the tape-recorder into a time-machine that could carry the solitary voice backwards into the past. He has also evolved an individual style and an extraordinarily individual vocabulary for translating his vision into concrete stage terms. The decrepit old men and the dustbins have become almost a cliché but they had a considerable impact at the beginning. The trouble is that Beckett has shown very little interest in exploiting the potentialities of the medium, tending latterly to make his stage plays aspire to the condition of radio. His dictatorial stage directions leave very little freedom to the directors and actors, with their detailed specifications about timing and staging, and not content with immobilising his actors, he has come more and more to insist on expressionless faces and expressionless voices ... This of course is Beckett's intention, but theatrically it's self-destructive.

(Hayman 1968: 78)

The question of Beckett's theatricality became an important part of critical debates over his dramatic work in the 1970s and 1980s: in time, the same questions would be asked of Beckett's use of the technical resources in other performing media (radio, film and television). Indeed, in the same year as Hayman's study, Alec Reid produced a short text, *All I Can Manage, More Than I Could*, that dealt with precisely this question. For Reid, Beckett created work that was specifically designed for performance

The first point to be established is that Beckett has deliberately designed his plays to be performed by actors for an audience sitting in a theatre or beside a radio. He means them to be experienced immediately, as the sounds come at us across the footlights or out of the loudspeaker: they are not intended to be read from the silent, immobile page, and least of all are they ... commentaries on Beckett's novels. They are pieces of theatre, needing to be performed if they are to make their full impact, as a symphony needs to be played or a ballet to be staged ...

(Reid 1968: 19)

To make his case, Reid drew not only on the texts but on actors' comments and on contemporary reviews. He argued that Beckett's work had the same effect as classical tragedy (catharsis, or the purging of emotion), but that this effect was created not by the lessons that the text demonstrated but by the experience of the text itself in performance.

In 1969 *Endgame* was the subject of a volume in the twentieth century views series: the editor, Bell Chevigny, drew together commentaries from Martin Esslin, Ruby Cohn and Hugh Kenner (commentaries that had already appeared in *the Theatre of the Absurd, Samuel Beckett: The Comic Gamut* and *Samuel Beckett: A Critical Study*) and essays from Richard Goldman (on *Endgame* as an entropic drama, running down to nothingness), Anthony Easthope (who argued that *Endgame* was a dialectic between the 'pursuit of meaning and the indifference to meaning' (p 70) and Ross Chambers (who analysed the play as a performance text). The collection also included a translation of 'Towards an Understanding of Endgame' by the German philosopher and critic Theodor Adorno **[36, 38, 76–8]**. Adorno rooted the play firmly in its historical context

> After the Second World War, everything, including a resurrected culture, was destroyed, although without its knowledge. In the wake of events which even the survivors cannot survive, mankind vegetates, crawling forward on a pile of rubble, denied even the awareness of its own ruin.
>
> (Chevigny 1969: 85)

– and argued that, in such a world, there was no clear division between hope and death; the resources for escape were simply unavailable to the protagonists, and so they were forced to contemplate their own extinction in a world shorn of distractions

> The final absurdity is that the repose of nothingness and that of reconciliation cannot be distinguished. Hope crawls out of a world in which it is no better safeguarded than pap or candy, back to where it started: to death ... Consciousness makes ready to look its own end in the face as though it sought to survive it ...
>
> (Chevigny 1969: 114)

## (b) THE BECKETT INDUSTRY: 1970–1980

The awarding of the Nobel Prize for literature to Beckett in 1969 provided further impetus to critical discussion of his work; as can be easily seen from the above section, his work did not lack commentators, but after the Nobel, however, the number of scholars engaged in Beckett studies increased exponentially. In the main, most of these critics did not stray too far from the terms and arguments established in the 1960s. The picture of Beckett formed in the previous decade, however, was influenced (and began to alter) in the light of the work that Beckett himself continued to produce; the Cartesian comic of the earliest studies did not seem to be an apt description for the author of the austere prose and theatre works that appeared in the following decade. Also, as the critical industry surrounding Beckett moved into high gear, an increasing number of studies and monographs began to appear, both on individual works and on specific aspects of Beckett's art. Although this had begun to happen in the previous decade, it is true to say that the 1970s marked the period in which the main channel of Beckett studies began to branch out into a variety of tributaries.

---

## i: General studies

The new decade began in a flurry of activity. In 1970, the first bibliography of Beckett criticism (a sure indication of an intense scholarly fascination with Beckett's work) was complied by Raymond Federman and John Fletcher (*Samuel Beckett: His Works and His Critics*). Patrick Murray's *The Tragic Comedian: A Study of Samuel Beckett* (also 1970) discussed Beckett's work along lines established by Cohn and Kenner in the 1960s, as a series of despairing yet heroic tragicomedies about the human condition. Melvin Friedman edited a collection of essays (largely translated from a volume first published in French in 1964) entitled *Samuel Beckett Now* (1970): Friedman intended the new collection to be a re-examination of Beckett's work, and a critical re-evaluation of the approaches adopted in the previous decade. The work contained essays on previous discussion of Beckett's work: Bruce Morrisette re-examined Robbe-Grillet's claim that Beckett's plays exhibited 'presence', that is, a style of characterisation that did not employ a realistic psychology or sociology requiring nothing more than the existence of a character at a specific space and time. John Fletcher's essay re-examined *Molloy* **[66–8]** as a quest for psychological fulfilment

> [The] image of the mother dominates this novel as fruitfully as it does Camus' *L'Etranger* [*The Outsider*]. Both Moran and Molloy are happy to take up a uterine position, and Molloy's hat is of course a figure for the caul. Erich Fromm has said that one of the deepest longings in everybody is to keep the tie to mother. It is this aspiration which gives Molloy Its profoundly disturbing quality and makes of this great novel its author's masterpiece: a masterpiece of satisfying unity in that a sadist-type, sent in search of a

masochist-type, is imperceptibly transformed into the type sought. The circularity of the work thus lies deeper than in form alone. It is the circularity of psychological tensions resolved; as such it brings comfort. *Molloy* is therefore a novel not of mental sickness, but of an arduously won, and therefore doubly precious, mental health.

(Friedman 1970: 170)

Michael Robinson's *The Long Sonata of the Dead* (1970) treated Beckett's work, once more, as an existential quest: however, Beckett's quest was conducted not simply in the face of absurdity (as Kenner or Esslin had argued in the previous decade), but against the corporeal existence of the individual human being

[Beckett's] writing ... does not make any ultimate pretensions for our existence or attempt to provide a final answer. Instead he speaks of the heroic absurdity of human endeavour in the face of death, a subject which always leads to his most sustained passages of poetic prose filled with a basic imagery and emotion yet all the more powerful for their constraint within a form that is classical in its precision. This revolt, which begins in Watt, is against the intolerable imprisonment of man within the determination of cause and effect, of beginning and ending, of being obliged to end because something else is beginning, or begin because something else is ending ... At its most basic it is a revolt against the meaningless limitations and compulsions of birth and death, and the universe which imposes such conditions on man can never be accepted ...

(Robinson 1970: 32)

Robinson identified Molloy **[66–8]** as the archetypal Beckett hero; Molloy was a man whose existence was a mobile protest against the conditions of human life, and whose ultimate form remained unfixed throughout his narrative, enabling him to escape, at least in part, the 'determinations of cause and effect' described above. Given Robinson's strong emphasis on the heroic rebelliousness of Beckett's central characters, it was not surprising to find that, for him, Camus' *The Myth of Sisyphus* provided an important model for Beckett's writing

... The man who, like Beckett, continues to create ... is, as Camus writes in *The Myth of Sisyphus*, 'the most absurd character'. The conflict between the world's irrationality and man's hopeless desire for unity is most acute in the artist who, having once believed in his near omnipotence, is now forced to recognise his almost total impotence. Yet there remains ... the right to fail. Creating, or not creating, changes nothing, and the words which are written will remain, at best, only a hesitant approximation of those finer words that, if they do exist, continue to elude his need. But if he persists in this endeavour which he knows to be futile he will have sustained his consciousness in the face of the universe and its absurdity ...

(Robinson 1970: 301)

It is hard to find a stronger endorsement of the existential heroism of Beckett's art than this.

Francis Doherty's *Samuel Beckett* (1971) did not cover Beckett's earliest work (neither *Dream* nor *More Pricks Than Kicks*) but concentrated on those works readily available to the interested reader; the discussions of the novels followed a familiar pattern (both *Murphy* and *Watt* were examples of a growing Cartesian divide between the body and the mind), and the drama described a world caught in an irreversible entropic decline, in which the conventional signs of human life were fading away. On the Trilogy, though, Doherty raised a point that was to become, with a slightly different critical perspective, the theme of much of the Beckett criticism of the 1980s

... By choosing characters who all try to pursue a meaning for their existence, and who can be seen in progressive states of decay and asylum from the ordinary world, Beckett more and more closely approaches the problem of the writer who uses writing in order to avoid the inevitable task of facing himself ...

The Trilogy is a gradual approach towards the problem of the nature of the self, the nature of language, and the nature of creation ...

(Doherty 1971: 20)

For Robinson (and for most of the critics who saw Beckett as a heroic existentialist) Beckett's work represented a struggle to express the essential self in an absurd world: even though the struggle was lost before it was begun, hope resided in the struggle itself. Doherty indicated that writing in the Trilogy was a way of escaping the self, and that language was itself a problematic expression of the writer's selfhood. This emphasis on the problematic nature of language in Beckett's work would become a staple of post-modern and deconstructionist readings of the texts.

Al Alvarez's *Beckett* (1973) was published as part of the Fontana Modern Masters series; it dealt with Beckett's work up to (and in a postscript including) *Not I*. Alvarez saw Beckett as a writer of undoubted quality, but with an almost wilful desire to abandon the territory more normally occupied by the writer

> ... it is as though the whole of Beckett's writing career were a search for an adequate artistic expression for his depression and his distaste for art, a slow but inevitable progress from manic high style through obsessionality to the latest minimal works, which are as close to silence as a man can decently get while still remaining a practising author ...
>
> (Alvarez 1973: 17)

He characterised Beckett's development as a despairing recoil from the conventional artist's imaginative recreation of the world, toward work which conveyed nothing

> The narrowness of Beckett's range, the way the same themes are repeated, transfigured, from work to work until the whole thing seems like a single block of marble – smooth, white, but with intricate veins of colour connecting each area with all the others – is unusual in a writer of his stature. His unassailable reputation among both experts and the general public is, I think, a tribute to his continual search for a special kind of perfection, a perfection manifest in his unfailing stylistic control and economy of language, his remorseless stripping away of superfluities. It is also an acknowledgement of the persistency with which he has been true to his own black lights: he began depressed, worked his way through to an art that expressed that depression poignantly and in a multitude of ways, and has rarely deviated from his logic of denial. He is like a painter whose distaste for the excesses of style and the claims of the imagination make him end with a blank canvas ...
>
> (Alvarez 1973: 123)

Ruby Cohn's *Back to Beckett* (1973) promised to return to the texts themselves, and to ignore (as far as possible) the extensive secondary literature that had built up around the author. This included her own work; in a foreword, she remarked that she 'cringed' (Cohn 1973: 5) at the over-systematisation of her earlier (1962) study. For Cohn in 1973 Beckett's work was the exploration of a series of idea-feelings; that is, a perception of the world that was both intellectual and emotional, both thought and felt by Beckett and his protagonists. The key to

Beckett's work was now his over-riding concern with mortality; he confronted

> ... the outrageous fact of death. Beckett knows that other men have been haunted by mortality, and we occasionally hear their echoes in his work ... Though mortality has been Beckett's familiar for over half a century, he dwells also with other idea-feelings. 1: Since man is mortal, he lives in time, and the tricks of time fill Beckett's fiction and drama. 2: Mortal man, as Descartes insisted, is split between body and mind. The mind alone is rich and graceful, adds Geulincx, but it is fastened to a dying animal. 3: The mind expresses itself in words, at once a compulsion and a curse. 4: The mind knows that it is limited to and by words, which falsify whatever they approach ...
>
> Words have been mistaken as the only subject of Beckett's own words. Beckett writes so large and small about words, that they seem to be reflexive. But Beckett is not a metalinguist [that is, a writer concerned with the structure of language]... he is a speleologist [a word which means, strictly, one who explores caves] of human essence – call it being, self, identity. The essence defies verbalisation, and Beckett defiantly tries to verbalise it. As human beings, most of us investigate ourselves and our worlds with words. As a writer, Beckett can dig only with words.
>
> (Cohn 1973: 5–6)

Cohn, therefore, examined Beckett's language, tracing its development from the early work to the late, short prose pieces; in a discussion that had strong similarities to Brian Finney's analysis of the shorter fiction, Cohn described Beckett's post-*How It Is* fiction **[39, 85–8]** as a set of 'lyrics' – short, poetic evocations of nothingness. Her conclusion linked the excavatory nature of Beckett's artistic practice back to the author himself

> Beckett himself occasionally speaks of his oeuvre as though it has taken place in his absence; or as though he were a resonator for works that speak through rather than from him. He feels that the root of each of his works lies in a previous work, and he is sometimes puzzled by the order in which the works come to him ... What he sketches is a variant of the artist as seer. And yet, it is not into his works but into himself that Beckett sinks in order to write – a self that cannot be divested of its experience, nor of words that, willy-nilly, recall experience.
>
> (Cohn 1973: 270–1)

Hugh Kenner's *A Reader's Guide to Samuel Beckett* (1973) also represented something of a revision of previous work. In part, this was due to the readership toward whom the guide was aimed: the study was chronological rather than thematic, and Kenner kept the philosophical discussion of Beckett's work to a minimum. The study represented a pared down, rather more historically and biographically specific analysis of Beckett's work. The experience of the tramps in *Waiting for Godot* was likened to the experience of refugees during the war (with Pozzo as the type of the Gestapo bully); the spotlight in *Play* was identified as interrogative, the kind of tool that authoritarian forces habitually employed.

In other ways, Kenner's study presented a view of Beckett that was less complex than the image contained in his earlier study. Beckett's works no longer demonstrated a distinct philosophy; rather, they were essentially self-sufficient poetic or musical meditations

> ... Like music, Beckett's language is shaped into phrases, orchestrated, cunningly repeated. The statements it makes have torque within the work's content and only there, while the form, the symmetry, ministers to the form of the work, its uniqueness ... It is that structure shaped, sometimes self-cancelling if it pleases him, that he has laboured to perfect, draft after draft ... After years of familiarity with his work, I find no sign that it has ambitions to enunciate a philosophy of life. Nor had Stan Laurel.
> (Kenner 1973: 37–8)

However, this concern with the purely formal constituents of his work did not mean that Beckett had abandoned the artist's moral obligation to reflect (and to reflect on) the world. For Kenner, Beckett's pared down style reflected an almost religious devotion to the structure and texture of language. In the conclusion, Kenner explored this idea by comparing Beckett's writing to the work of T. S. Eliot, whose explicit devotion to Christianity was expressed in a poetic style as measured and as spare as Beckett's

> How trivial – that is a lesson that Eliot taught us – the religion of art was finally; how provincial, how unhistorical, how impoverished. His explicit profession of Christianity ... was in part a way to make this point ... In making no declaration of faith, Beckett has established that a like quality of devotion to the word not only need not be a writer's substitute religion, but need not encroach on a reader's religious impulses. He believes in the cadence, the comma, the bite of word on reality, whatever else he believes, and his devotion to them, he makes clear, is a sufficient focus for a

reader's attention. In the modern history of literature at least he is a unique moral figure, not a dreamer of rose-gardens [an image that occurs in Eliot's late poetry] but a cultivator of what will grow in the waste land, who can make us see the exhilarating design that thorns and yucca share with whatever will grow anywhere.

(Kenner 1973: 193–4)

The essay collection *Beckett the Shape Changer* (1975), edited by Katherine Worth was, on the other hand, concerned not so much with Beckett the poet of man's heroic suffering as with Beckett the formal innovator, stretching the boundaries of the genres within which he worked

It is as an artist of the protean kind that Beckett has appealed to the contributors of this volume. The transformation process is our subject: how Beckett renews and reshapes himself from one form, language, genre, medium to another: how the characters take us into the pains, terrors, and jokes of the reshaping, the Unnamable panting 'If I could be like Worm',, the voice is Cascando stretching itself to 'get' Woburn, say him, know him and change him; above al, how the illusion draws its strength from being exposed, handled, turned round for us to see how it is done, until finally there is no distinguishing how it is done from how it is ...

(Worth 1975: 3)

The collection included essays from John Chalker in the 'anti-structure' of *Watt*; from Barbara Hardy ('The Dubious Consolations in Beckett's Fiction: Art, Love and Nature'); from Worth herself, on the physicality of Beckett's theatre; and from Harry Cockerham, who contributed an essay on the largely undiscussed topic of Beckett's bilingualism [33]. For Cockerham, Beckett's decision to write in French was the inevitable consequence of his abiding interest in the structures of language itself

... What seems to attract him about French is the very fact that it is less second-nature to him than is English, that his relationship to it is different and makes him more able to manipulate it consciously. Any writer is a student of language, but one operating in a foreign language is so in a very special sense. One is constantly aware of Beckett in his plays, not as a litterateur striving after fine writing, as the final justification for the work, but rather as a student of the French language, and thence of language itself, listening patiently to his characters and consciously registering all.

(Worth 1975: 156)

Ruby Cohn's *Samuel Beckett: A Collection of Criticism* (1975) included essays by John Fletcher on the poetry (Fletcher, in common with Harvey, saw Beckett's early poetry as containing, in essence, the themes and concerns that would come to dominate his writing in later years); and an essay by Dougald MacMillan on the relation between Beckett's work and visual art.

John Pilling's *Samuel Beckett* (1976) contained perhaps the most comprehensive discussion of actual and potential influences, both literary and philosophical, that had appeared in Beckett criticism to this point. He also included useful sections on the intellectual, cultural and literary background to Beckett's writing; this meant, necessarily, that Pilling's study contained a useful summary of Beckett's life, alongside discussions of the prose, poetry, drama and criticism. Some of the themes that Pilling uncovered in Beckett's work were already well-established by the time of the study's publication; the prose, for example, was an attempt to provide structure for a random universe

Despite the fact that there are no things but nameless things, no names but thingless names', no bodytight mind, no mindtight body, one must have the absurd but dauntless quest after such things. And the quest will take many forms. Malone is, in the end, absolutely right: 'the forms are many in which the unchanging seeks relief from its formlessness'. And in the process, life becomes art.

(Pilling 1976: 66)

Beckett's drama was a concrete demonstration of the problems inherent in all attempts at communication

... It is as if Beckett's own creativity has come under scrutiny; the necessary liberation to compose one's narrative ... is ousted by the remorseless repetition of event – what the Proust book calls 'habit' – to which passing time commits us all. As the plays become more and more elemental there is less and less time for the narratives to tell themselves; but our fictions have their revenge by taking on independent life, and compelling us to go on telling them.

(Pilling 1976: 109)

However, for Pilling, Beckett's work was not an existential response to the position of man in an uncaring world; rather, it was a rejection of the idea that man can actively oppose such a world, and a defence, in the last instance, of the artist's basic need to express (even if, for Beckett, the artist should not be seen as the 'inventor' of a self-contained fictional world, because, in doing so, he necessarily presents a false image of the real world). To reinforce his argument, Pilling returned (as many critics, before and since, have also done) to the 'Three Dialogues with Georges Duthuit' **[31]**

> [Beckett] rejects unequivocally, symbolism, satire, Promethianism, misanthropy, sensationalism and pot-boiling, and rests his case on a qualified humanism. This humanism has been variously described as 'defensive', 'quietist', and 'graveyard' and should at all time be distinguished from the tragic variety exemplified by Camus. It is, nevertheless, determinedly humanistic because Beckett's aim is a literature that is 'the passive receptacle for a self entirely independent of literary 'inventiveness'. He realises that it is impossible of attainment. 'You realise the absurdity of what you advance?' says Duthuit. To which Beckett replies, 'I hope I do'.
>
> (Pilling 1976: 24)

In 1979, Richard Admussen published a study of Beckett manuscripts (*the Samuel Beckett Manuscripts*); Robin J. Davis produced a checklist to Beckett's later work (*Samuel Beckett: Checklist and Index of His Published Works, 1967–76*); J.A. Edwards compiled an index to Reading University's Beckett collection (*The Samuel Beckett Collection: A Catalogue*). and Lawrence Graver and Raymond Federman co-edited *Samuel Beckett: The Critical Heritage*, a collection of responses to Beckett's work from the late 1920s to the 1970s. This collection included, in addition to reviews of Beckett publications and performances, the interviews that Beckett gave to Israel Shenker and Tom Driver in 1961, and to E.M. Cioran in 1975.

James Knowlson and John Pilling's *Frescoes of the Skull: The Later Prose and Drama of Samuel Beckett* (1979) dealt with all of Beckett's work from the *Texts for Nothing* onward; the study began, though, by addressing those early works that had not yet been published (*Dream of Fair to Middling Women; Eleutheria*). Pilling's discussion of the late prose identified the *Texts* **[35, 80–1]** as the link between the earlier and later writing; in the *Texts*, Beckett was for the first time able to dispense with the need for a narrating character (the *Texts* describe the progressive dismemberment of such a figure), and came as close as he had yet done to the paradoxical aim of letting silence speak. In *How It Is* [**39, 81–2**]

... Beckett is moving away from the visual and towards the verbal, which is why the 'images' have to cease: he becomes less concerned with 'seeing' how it is and more concerned with 'saying' how it is.

(Knowlson and Pilling 1979: 63)

In line with these developments, Pilling argued that Beckett's late prose was concerned with the need to establish, through language, a point of silence and rest; he took the late text *Still* as perhaps the closest that Beckett had yet come to this paradoxical conclusion. Knowlson's study of the drama from *Krapp's Last Tape* onwards noted Beckett's gradual progress toward a dramatic language that gradually stripped itself of all but the simplest elements. This sometimes strained the boundaries of the form; but it did not necessarily lead to the production of a less ambiguous play

Beckett has focused more recently on simple, stark fraught situations, on an extreme concentration and economy, and on a musical style of patterning of motifs. Reduction in the number of characters, reduction of the human body to a part rather than the whole, and reduction in other elements involved has not meant a similar reduction in density or emotional power. In the miniatures of the seventies, indeed, this density and power derives partly from the juxtaposition or confrontation of different time states, and partly again from establishing an unusual relationship between the material of the play and the audience watching... Exactly how successful as pieces of theatre these miniatures will eventually be judged to be is difficult to predict ... Yet, although the canvas is smaller than in *Waiting for Godot* and *Endgame, Not I,* and *Footfalls* seem to possess some of the resonance of the earlier plays as well as having their own sources of dramatic interest and strength.

(Knowlson and Pilling 1979: 234)

The study also included three appendixes; one on the criticism, one on Beckett's debt to J.M. Synge, and one on the relation between Beckett's theatre and that described in Kleist's essay 'On The Marionette Theatre'. Kleist had argued for a style of theatre that relied on the automatic, non-intellectual response of the actor (who should respond to the demands of the text in the automatic, unconsidering way that a puppet reacted to the puppet master); Knowlson drew a parallel between the puppet figure in Kleist's essay and the puppet-like characters in Beckett's plays, similarly enjoined to react as unthinkingly to external forces.

## ii: Prose

At the beginning of the decade, J.D. O'Hara edited a volume on the Trilogy (*Twentieth Century Interpretations of 'Molloy', 'Malone Dies'* and *'The Unnamable'* (1970)) that included a notable essay, written by the volume's editor, on the structure of *Malone Dies*. In *Samuel Beckett: A Study of His Novels* (published in the same year as O'Hara's volume), Eugene Webb argued that Beckett's intellectual approach was governed by his reaction to Dante, Descartes and Proust; however, Webb went on to argue that Beckett's art was not a reflection of, but rather an engagement with, their work. Unlike Dante, Beckett's heroes inhabited a godless universe, where there was no evidence of an overall design to existence; unlike Descartes, Beckett saw the human being not as a dual creature, composed of mind and body, but as a completely fragmented being, unable to establish any secure connection with the world or with the idea of a rational mind. Proust was, of the three, the most congenial to Beckett's artistic concerns: he developed an implicit strand of Proust's work into a governing principle in his characters' lives

> The idea that each individual is composed of a temporal series of distinct selves does not have to mean that the successive selves do not involve a certain continuity. In the thought of both Proust and Beckett the personalities that make up the successive stages of one's life tend to be only too similar. Since they are all subject to the human condition, they all share the same limitations and a tendency to make the same mistakes over and over again. In the case of Beckett, this view of human nature led him to the development of one of his most important themes, that of cyclical time. The idea that time goes through repetitious patterns is implicit in Proust, but in Beckett it is quite elaborately developed. Watt, on leaving Knott's house, has learned that there is no certain knowledge of reality, but nothing can prevent his 'for ever falling' into the same 'old error', the mistake of trying to understand the unintelligible. The Unnamable is the most lucid of Beckett's characters, the most aware that all attempts to explain reality are futile, but his very lucidity makes him the more frustrated at his inability to stop trying to devise explanations.
>
> (Webb 1970: 30–1)

Webb discussed each of the prose works in turn, beginning with 'Assumption' (leaving out the unpublished *Dream of fair to Middling Women*); the Trilogy **[66–72]** came in for the most detailed analysis, as the fullest illustration of the nature of a Beckettian universe populated by creatures aware that they are trapped in meaningless, cyclical time

> As the characters of the trilogy come to find themselves trapped in an endless necessity to keep going on, moving or thinking or both, they come to see time as an 'enormous prison' (*Unnamable*, p. 171). The earlier characters, who still retain some hope that time is moving toward a goal, do not fully realise that there is no escape. As this realisation dawns on them and becomes fully conscious in the Unnamable, time ceases to appear to have a direction; it is seen finally as either a monotonous repetition of the same patterns or simply an eternal present, the reality of which can only be described as hell.
>
> (Webb 1970: 130)

The first book dedicated to a specific Beckett text, Sighe Kennedy's discussion of the sources behind the creation of *Murphy* **[23–4, 57–60]** (*Murphy's Bed: A Study of Real Sources and Sur-real Associations in Samuel Beckett's First Novel*) appeared in 1971: it contained useful information on the philosophical background to the novel (particularly on Beckett's debt to Democritus). Kennedy also provided a detailed analysis of the potential significance of *Murphy*'s detailed chronology

> Murphy's calendar presents, in terms of dates, the same patterns as that composed by the personae of the novel – an outline of the outstanding points in the history of man's conception of time. Its dates commemorate the first 'messages' man received from the beams of the stars; from the sun's varied rising, and setting, and turning ...
>
> (Kennedy 1971: 115)

Brian Finney's pamphlet *Since How It Is: A Study of Samuel Beckett's Later Fiction* (1972) **[39, 85–8]** attempted to site the later, more experimental fiction within the same worldview that had produced the novels from *Murphy* onwards. Finney argued that what had changed was the scope of Beckett's art and the nature of the narrating voice

> ... 'Residua', says the Oxford Dictionary, is 'what is left or remains over': these prose pieces are in other words the distillation of

Beckett's artistic exploration of the human condition, the insistent voice of the narrators between *Molloy* and *How It Is* reduced to at most a murmur. With the partial exception of *Enough*, the presence of a first person narrator obsessed with his own self-exploration has been replaced by an impersonal pseudo-objective tone in these later pieces. The approaching end of consciousness, the immanence of death, continues to provide Beckett in these five pieces [The texts Finney discusses are *Imagination Dead Imagine*, *The Lost Ones*, *Ping*, *Lessness* and *Enough*] with his most effective measure of life, as it did in most of his novels. But the variety of artistic modes employed in these later pieces testifies to an ever more rigorous attempt on his part to find an appropriately chaotic form to suit the chaotic nature of his subject.

(Finney 1972: 10)

H. Porter Abbot in *The Fiction Of Samuel Beckett: Form and Effect* (1973) saw Beckett's developing prose style as an innovative solution to the novelist's dilemma; how to create a fictional universe that would capture and hold the attention of the reader. Abbot argued that there had been two tendencies in Beckett criticism thus far: Beckett had been regarded either as an allegorist, creating philosophical fables for his audience, or as a formalist, concerned with questions of artistic structure and shape. Against these two readings, Abbot proposed a third; Beckett as a practitioner of 'imitative form'; his writing

... is neither an empirical Balzacian universe nor [does it convey] a sense of philosophical truth. It is the immediate experience of a variety of mysteries. Thus, when we speak of 'imitation' we refer not so much to a notion of reflection or representation as we to a generation in the reader of the experiences that are at the same time the subject of the work. Through imitative form, in other words, the reader is forced into a relationship with the book, which imitates the central figure's relationship with the world... His work is at once about and creative of what Beckett calls 'true experience'. And his double ends are effected through the subtle manipulation of a host of formal components: the archetypal pattern, the narrator, the report, the two-part form, storytelling, the tale of espionage, syntax.

(Abbot 1973: 7–8)

For Abbot, this meant that Beckett's prose fiction moved away from the conventional structures of the novel. A traditional novel 'achieve[d]

closure' – came to an end with the narrative threads neatly sewn together; Beckett's work (with the exception of *Murphy*) moved away from the idea of closure, replacing it with narratives that seemed to hold out the promise of pattern and structure, only to let those patterns and structures collapse, leaving the reader to sift through the wreckage of the narrative. Abbot's emphasis on the reader's experience of the text, although relatively new in studies of Beckett's prose, bore a striking similarity to a common theme found in discussions of Beckett's dramas; the novels were imitations of the experience of reading, in much the same way as Beckett's theatre pieces were imitations of the experience of theatre (see, for example, the discussion of Fletcher and Spurling below). Abbot's model, however, broke down (as he himself admitted) when it was applied to *How It Is*, a work that despite the confusion inherent in its language, had at least a strong central structure that moved (albeit paradoxically) toward closure in the manner of a conventional narrative.

Philip Solomon's monograph, *The Life After Birth: Imagery in Samuel Beckett's Trilogy* (1975) attempted to uncover the underlying structural principles of the trilogy, discussing the novels in relation to five categories of imagery: space, movement, softness, light, and animals.

## iii: Drama/theatre

As the decade progressed, critics began to pay an increasing amount of attention to Beckett's theatrical work (perhaps because his plays were beginning to feature heavily on undergraduate reading lists). John Fletcher and John Spurling's introductory work *Beckett: A Study of His Plays* (1972) set out to demonstrate the inherently theatrical nature of Beckett's dramas

> What I hope to show is that the Beckettian demonstration is a thoroughly dramatic one; that, in other words, though he set out as poet and novelist and was quoted ... as seeing himself as a novelist who also writes plays, the point at which his public found him and he found his public was the right one. Samuel Beckett was waiting for the theatre as the theatre was waiting for Samuel Beckett.
>
> (Fletcher and Spurling 1972: 15)

The inherent theatricality in Beckett's work came from his revisioning of the central tension in the theatrical event between the stage and the auditorium. For Fletcher and Spurling, Beckett himself recreated this central tension in the structure and style of his plays: he envisaged the plays as a series of dialogues between himself as author and himself as audience

> ... The truth is that [his theatre] is intended in the first place to satisfy himself, himself as sole audience ... Beckett's theatre is neither humane nor friendly, for the simple reason that it is addressed to himself ...
>
> What is on the stage is not only the occasion for the content of the dialogue with the audience, it is also a metaphor, an image of the dialogue between the author and himself as audience, between the member of the audience and himself as narrator.
>
> (Fletcher and Spurling 1972: 37–8)

Fletcher and Spurling placed Beckett in a non-naturalistic theatrical tradition (that is, a theatrical tradition that did not believe that it was possible to represent and analyse human society on stage), because, for them, Beckett's work was paradoxically too real: it caught human beings as they engaged in activities designed to provide a distraction from, and a pattern for, their otherwise unstructured and meaningless lives. Fletcher and Spurling noted Beckett's debt to twentieth century Irish theatre; their discussion of *Waiting For Godot* placed the play alongside the work of Strindberg, Vitrac, Alfred Jarry's *Ubu* cycle of plays, and the films of Charlie Chaplin, but also acknowledged Beckett's debt to Synge and Yeats. They noted also the importance of repetition and reflection in the plays (the discussion of *Endgame,* in particular, dealt with the almost musical nature of the play's structure); and they discussed the ways in which Beckett's works for theatre, radio, film and television exploited the peculiar technical restraints of each form (although, on the whole, they were less impressed by Beckett's work for media other than theatre: *All That Fall* was successful, but *Eh Joe* was too simple to be effective). They made the general point that Beckett's work was less successful when he abandoned the spoken word; the mimes and *Film* were too explicit for a writer who needed words to communicate incommunicability. The study concluded with a chapter on the performance of Beckett's theatre (and the response to those performances) that stretched from *Le Kid* (the Pelorson skit, attributed here, as was commonly assumed by many critics, to Beckett) to *Breath.*

The theme of Beckett's theatrical effectiveness was explored in another study in the same year: Colin Duckworth's *Angels of Darkness: Dramatic Effect in Beckett with Special Reference to Eugene Ionesco* (1972). Duckworth's image of Beckett the playwright was of a man concerned with the isolated human consciousness reacting to a world that seemed to have no structure; man was 'imprisoned' (p 22) by eternity and infinity. The study, though, was as concerned with the effect that the plays had on an audience as it was with the meaning of the plays themselves. To this end, Duckworth submitted questionnaires to audiences who had seen productions of *Godot* and *Endgame* at the Young Vic in London, and a second production of *Godot* at Nottingham Playhouse. The results of these questionnaires led Duckworth to the conclusion that Beckett's drama was not the product of an entirely personal despair; compared to the work of the Absurd dramatist Eugene Ionesco, Beckett's dramas were, at least, more compassionate, even at their bleakest

> ... Human solidarity and mutual help, so beautifully parodied in the second act of *Waiting for Godot*, are nothing so pretentious as an ideal for Beckett, but he does recognise them as a basic need of our mutual dependence. Ionesco's fear of massification, on the other hand, leads him to stress a more strongly marked dicotomy between the individual and society. Hence, Beckett seems a more compassionate writer than Ionesco ... Beckett's work is as self-centred as Ionesco's. But it is less egocentric. If he is a sounding board for suffering, it is not just his own suffering. He paints a picture, not recognised by all but responded to by most, of man in solitude imprisoned within the time and space of a silent and unresponsive universe. Only the very brash or complacent can fail to react to that.
>
> (Duckworth 1972: 104)

James Knowlson's short text, *Light and Darkness in the Plays of Samuel Beckett* (1972) concentrated on *Krapp's Last Tape;* it examined the dialectic in Beckett's writing between the conventional symbolic meaning of light (usually associated with reason) and dark (conventionally treated as a representation of the soul or spirit). Knowlson noted that Beckett's characters inhabited a universe that was predominantly grey (that is, caught between light and darkness) and the temptation felt by many of the characters in Beckett's prose and theatre to turn towards the darkness was an ambiguous one

> But to understand both the fundamental nature of light and darkness and their ambivalence in Beckett's world, one needs to see them in relation of one of the major preoccupations of his fiction, indeed of all his writing since *Murphy*. This is that search for some

credible reality that might conceivably be found when all the layers of illusion have been striped away. For, from Murphy onwards, all Beckett's people are, in the most profound sense, exiles, excluded from some inner reality of the self which, if it exists at all, and they feel, in spite of everything, that it does, or, at the very least, that it *should*, would lie outside the dimensions of time and space, somewhere in the huge inner world that Murphy was already seeking to plumb in his willing acquiescence to the darkness with its 'chaos of forms', so that he might become 'a mote in the darkness of absolute freedom ...

... [This] ending seems at once unattainable and unbearable, if it should ever be attained. Darkness is then understandably to be feared as well as earnestly desired ...

(Knowlson 1972: 32, 35)

Eugene Webb's *The Plays of Samuel Beckett* (1972) was a companion piece to his earlier study of the novels; like the earlier study, the volume on the plays began by placing Beckett's work in familiar critical territory – this time, in the philosophical tradition of the absurd

Man in our age is the heir to centuries of analysis which have left experience in fragments and man a stranger in an unintelligible universe. The literature of the absurd is an expression of the state of mind to which this situation gives rise. We are impelled by our nature to seek understanding, but reason, the only instrument we have with which to seek it, has proven a clumsy and a fragile tool. Beckett's Unnamable speaks for many when he describes the frustration of having to try forever to understand the unintelligible: 'That the impossible should be asked of me, good, what else could be asked of me? But the absurd! Of me whom they have reduced to reason'.

(Webb 1972: 15)

From here, Webb once more treated the work in sequence, ending with *Eh Joe*: he argued that the essential difference between Beckett's prose and drama was that the drama worked within a concrete situation, and was not so immediately concerned with the philosophical itches felt by the protagonists in the novels

... The novels tend to focus on man's need to know and on the inevitable frustration of this need due to the failure of the philosophical systems he relies on for its satisfaction ...

The plays also give attention to man's need to know, and in some plays – *Waiting for Godot*, for example – it is almost the whole idea, but as a group they do not take this as their main concern. This is probably why Beckett said in Berlin in 1967 that the way to understand his plays is to talk 'not about philosophy, but about situations'. The plays are explorations into the meaning of human life as it is in its full reality, and this meaning is not an abstract idea of the kind that can be known objectively with the intellect, but a mystery that is lived in with the whole self. Consequently although they are concerned in part with philosophical problems, they are concerned even more broadly with the psychology – using this term in a very broad sense – of concrete individuals ...

(Webb 1972: 131–2)

James Eliopulis' *Samuel Beckett's Dramatic Language* (1975) analysed the construction of a specifically theatrical discourse in Beckett's drama. S.E. Gontarski's detailed examination of the various manuscript versions of *Happy Days* **[40, 83–4]** (*Beckett's Happy Days: A Manuscript Study* (1977)) revealed the development of a complex interaction between speech and movement in the play, and drew attention to Beckett's use of allusion in the playtext. James Knowlson published a bilingual edition of *Happy Days* (*Happy days/Oh Les Beaux Jours*) in 1978; in the same year, Beryl Fletcher, John Fletcher, Barry Smith and Walter Bachem collaborated on *A Student's Guide to the Plays of Samuel Beckett* (1978), a study that aimed to give as much help as possible to the student reader. The study dealt with Beckett's work in relation to the absurd, and included a section on the particular problems of interpretation posed by Beckett's plays. The body of the study dealt with each of the major plays in turn, giving details of the text, an indication of the play's initial reception, and notes on the play's decor, language and dramaturgical technique.

Bert O. States' study of *Waiting for Godot* (*The Shape of Paradox: An Essay on 'Waiting for Godot'* (1978)) **[34, 74–6]** tackled the play's relation to conventional dramatic practice

What impresses one about *Godot* (in contrast to *Hamlet*) is the linguistic spareness of its world. Whereas in *Hamlet* a single image is apt to get lost in a crowded universe of images and to become insignificant, or thematic through frequent variation and repetition, in *Godot* the image achieves an instant significance by virtue of occurring – and then only once – in an empty space, or one in which it obtrudes suddenly from a language texture composed of seemingly random or diversionary conversation. It is that quality of randomness that creates the paradoxical impression of an unplanned design ...

(States 1978: 5–6)

States was particularly fascinated by the operation of elements in the play that he termed 'figural', a figure in this context being a deceptive sign of something else (an example given by States is that of Estragon doing the tree in the play's second act; this could be read as a figura of Christ on the cross). This method governed the whole play, giving it a mythic dimension without requiring the viewer to construct a consistent allegory from the few elements that Beckett provided. Rather, the play's mythic status is constantly reinforced by the very instability of its figural elements

> ... [The] play derives a mythic tension from the constant 'oscillation' of background and foreground, elsewhere and here, a coming in and going out of focus of what are often contradictory loadings of the same shape ... the reading of the play ... is thus a constant effort at translation: trivial to profound, comic to serious, temporal to essential, etc. and vice versa. This is not properly an act of translation ... but an interrupted movement toward; an instability which may be likened to a mild though aesthetically absorbing frustration of the synapse.
>
> (States 1978: 29–30)

---

## iv: Philosophical/theoretical studies

In contrast to the next decade (see below), theoretical studies of Beckett in the 1970s tended to stay within the perameters established in the 1960s. There were exceptions to this, however; G.C. Barnard's *Samuel Beckett: A New Approach* (1970) was the first psychoanalytic study of Beckett's work. Barnard argued that Beckett's texts could be seen as a literary equivalent of schizophrenia (a condition in which the sufferers's sense of self fragmented; another feature of the condition manifested itself in voices that seemed to emanate from outside the subject but that only the subject could hear).

David Hesla's *The Shape of Chaos: An Interpretation of the Art of Samuel Beckett* (1971) was the first study entirely dedicated to the philosophical analysis of Beckett's work. According to Hesla, Beckett's work was, at its root, ontological (that is, concerned with questions of origin, of essential being). Hesla discussed Beckett's work in relation to those philosophers already identified by other critics (and for some, in Beckett's work itself) as providing important clues to the meaning of Beckett's art : the pre-Socratics (including Democritus), the seventeenth and eighteenth century rationalists (including Descartes), Schopenhauer, Bergson, Mauther, Hegel, Kierkegaard, Heidegger, Sartre, and Husserl. Once more, Hesla saw Beckett's work as an encounter with the absurd

> What is absurd is human existence. Why is it absurd? Because being human and existing are mutually contradictory. One could be a human being if one did not have to exist, and one could not exist, though not as a human being. But one cannot exist, and be a human being, in the same place, at the same time ...
> In other words, man is not contiguous with the conditions – the only conditions – provided for his existence ...
>
> (Hesla 1971: 8)

Where Hesla's study marked a distinct advance on previous analyses of the role of philosophy in Beckett's work was in the sheer scope and detail of the discussion. For example, *Murphy* was discussed through the thought of Descartes and Geulincx (an unsurprising coupling, given previous discussions of the text); Hesla's study, however, provided a more detailed gloss on the importance of Occasionalist philosophy in understanding the novel

> ... The being of the I is restricted to the art of thinking, and here it is radically free, for not even God can cause me to think or alter what I think or how I think. But the I does not enter into the world of matter or extension, not even in its own body. Indeed, with regard to its own body the I is merely the spectator. But since nothing of the I is invested in the *res extensa* [the external world], and since it can do nothing by itself to alter what happens in that realm, the I should set no value on it. The world of things does not affect and is not affected by the I so it is worth nothing to the I if the world is worth nothing, it is not worth being desired. *Ubi nihil vales, ubi nihil velis*.
>
> (Hesla 1971: 38)

Hesla, like many other commentators (John Fletcher and Michael Robinson, for example), saw *Watt* as the bridge between the external world and the internal world; after *Watt*, the Beckett character was trapped in a fruitless search for the final expression of the self. For Hesla, this search was impossible: the self cannot be spoken of, and cannot be written down. To support this point, he made the interesting suggestion that the Trilogy was cyclical: the next step for the *Unnamable*, after it decided that it had no option but to go on, was to return to the beginning of *Molloy*, and try once more to come to the end of speech. In contrast, Beckett's theatre, for Hesla, was concerned not so much with the search for the self but with the question of man's existence in time, an existence that had no structure beyond that which the character could create for him or herself through action, no matter how meaningless.

Hannah Case Copeland's *Art and Artist in the Works of Samuel Beckett* (1975) examined the image of the self-conscious artist in Beckett's writing; Steven Rosen's *Samuel Beckett and the Pessimistic Tradition* (1976) explored the philosophical position adopted in Beckett's own work. For Rosen, Beckett's universe was populated by a succession of failed sages, whose inability to describe the world and account for their actions in that world had something of the heroic about it

> ... [On] a larger plane, Beckett's allusions to philosophers comment on the failure of philosophical tradition, the futile repetition of philosophical activity. This commentary authorises his own pessimism; but at the same time, the evocation of the sage tradition lends dignity and weight to the preoccupations of Beckett's heroes – thoughts usually fleeting and trivial in themselves. All of his writings can be regarded as successive versions of Lucky's speech in *Waiting for Godot*, a testament to the futility of philosophical labours; but while this testament is pathetic and nearly incoherent, it does not lower Lucky in the audience's estimation. There is something awesome in the persistence of his consciousness.
>
> (Rosen 1976: 118)

In the second half of the study, Rosen searched for the roots of Beckett's pessimism and found them neatly encapsulated in the early study of Marcel Proust [15–16, 72]; however, as Rosen pointed out, the innate pessimism that Beckett discovered in Proust was not necessarily a reliable judgement of the French author's work. Beckett's Proust was filtered through Schopenhauer

> Since Proust's thought, in fact, provided insufficient basis for the rigorous pessimism formulated by Beckett, the latter required some other authority; in this function, Schopenhauer served him perfect-

ly. That modern sage is mentioned four times in Beckett's brief text; in comparison, Descartes and Dostoievsky, also linked to Proust as predecessors, are named only twice. At that, Beckett fails to indicate the extent to which he relies on Schopenhauer, translating Proust consistently into that philosopher's terms. In consequence it has been noticed that Beckett's analysis depends not only on Schopenhauer's main ideas, but also on details of that philosopher's thought, even on his literary allusions and examples ... Nor are Schopenhauer's ideas and learning the only elements of interest here; the tone of his writing suggests a sensibility midway between Beckett's rage and Proust's tolerant resignation. Accordingly, the philosopher can be thought of as the link between Proust and Beckett; he seems to help make the one accessible to the other.

(Rosen 1976: 145)

The collection edited by Edouard Morot-Sir, Howard Harper and Dougald MacMillan (*Samuel Beckett: the Art of Rhetoric* (1976)) contained an interesting essay by Lori Hall Burghart on the female figures in Beckett's early poetry (an early anticipation of the debates over Beckett's portrayal of female characters: see below). It's main interest lay, however, in an essay by Morot-Sir, ('Samuel Beckett and Cartesian Emblems'), which reviewed the history of Cartesian analysis in Beckett criticism, and asserted that the role of the philosopher had been fatally misinterpreted by most critics. Descartes was not a role model for Beckettian man: neither was he a symbol for the failure of rationality. Rather, Descartes was the first in the line of Beckett's literary anti-heroes

The Descartes of *Whoroscope* is temperamental, with alterations of violence and tenderness; he has on the whole a strong and self-contained emotional power, but with bursts of anger; he is self-centred and aggressive; he thinks of others only in relation to his own experiences or desires; to the very end, even when addressing Weulles, the Queen's doctor, he maintains a challenging attitude, always retaining his superiority; he is constantly reckless, insecure, without poise, and suffering a very real and deep anguish which turns to bitter pessimism ... In my opinion, Descartes as he appears in *Whoroscope* is, for Beckett, the image of man and the image of the writer. All such characters as Murphy, Watt, Molloy, Moran, Malone, Macmann, Mahood are direct inheritors of Descartes. Their likeness is striking. This does not mean that Beckett's works are simply variations of the *Whoroscope* tragedy. Each work has its own problems and corresponds to a specific movement in Beckett's personal literary adventure. But these movements are always referred to a basic human character.

(Morot-Sir, Harper, McMillan 1976: 63–4) **[15, 98]**

Kenneth and Alice Hamilton's *Condemned to Life: The World of Samuel Beckett* (1976) started from the assumption that Beckett's work was largely self-explanatory

> The thesis of our study is that the misery of the human condition is not only the most obvious theme in Beckett, but also the best clue to interpreting his works. Once this theme is made central, then the contours of the imagination reveal themselves and the pattern of his authorship takes on a constant shape ...
>
> (Hamilton and Hamilton 1976: 9–10)

Therefore, Beckett, even though he used philosophy, was not tied to any particular system. His view of the world could be simply stated in a number of self-evident propositions; that life was suffering in a godless universe; that birth was a sin, because it expelled the individual into a world filled with suffering; and that humour was an instinctive response to the horrors of the world

> Beckett's works ask us to see the outlines of a universe beyond redemption; of a human condition bedevilled by suffering and even more bedevilled by the illusion of hope; of man's destiny to endure the meaningless activity within a purgatory allowing him no rest. Perhaps, infinitely slowly, the whole process in which man is trapped is grinding to a halt. Perhaps it will reach a final state of darkness and silence when the last word shall cease. Perhaps the prospect of an end is not merely a tantalising illusion built into the process, tempting man to torment himself still further. It really makes no difference, for it is present endurance that counts, not multiplying theories about this or that. The imagination can conceive as many worlds as it wishes – world without end. But, for Beckett, the believer's affirmation, 'World without end, Amen!' is the ultimate terror and the final surrender.
>
> (Hamilton and Hamilton 1976: 196)

The Irish critic Vivian Mercier's *Beckett/Beckett* (1977) was an attempt to describe Beckett's art through a set of dialectical oppositions (that is, as a developing argument shaped by the opposition of two contrasting terms or ideas). Mercier noted that David Hesla (in *The Shape of Chaos* (Harvey 1970: 65)) had covered much the same territory in his study; however, whereas Hesla saw the unresolvable dialectic of Beckett's works from a primarily philosophical standpoint, Mercier sought to broaden the discussion to all aspects of Beckett's life and art. He described the structure of the book thus

> The aim of the chapters that follow, as their titles imply, is to focus attention on certain aspects of this all-pervasive dialectic. They do this, I hope, in three different ways. First of all, the chapters entitled 'Ireland/The World' and 'Artist/Philosopher' deal with areas in which critics have by now agreed that a dialectic is present ... At least three other chapters – 'Gentleman/Tramp', 'Classicism/ Absurdism', 'Eye/Ear' – were written in the belief that Beckett criticism, while somewhat aware of each dialectic, tends to empha- sise one of its poles to the almost total neglect of the other. In the chapter headings, to emphasise this neglect, I have put what might be considered the antithesis [the subordinate term] before the too- familiar thesis. The chapter 'Painting/Music' falls into yet a third category, being concerned with a dialectic that, so far as I can dis- cover, Beckett criticism has not previously recognised. Finally, to which of my three categories should I assign 'Woman/Man'? ...
> (Mercier 1977: 11–12)

For Mercier, these oppositions could be thought of as part of a wider dialectical opposition between intellect and emotion; the tension between these opposing terms could not finally be reconciled. If Beckett's work contained flaws, then, in Mercier's opinion, they were not to be found in the rigorous structures of the Beckettian dialectic: rather, they were failures in tone. The plight of the Beckettian prota- gonist, seen by other critics as a prime example of existential heroism, was seen by Mercier as, in some of its manifestations at least, a kind of lofty self-pity

> Nevertheless, my own severest criticism of Beckett's oeuvre is based not on its pessimism but on its proneness to self-pity, even though that self-pity is of a very special kind, expressed by his characters on behalf of the human race ... *Footfalls* provides yet another example of this nagging pity. When May asks her mother, 'Would you like me to inject you again? ... Dress your sores? ... Sponge you down? ... Moisten your poor lips? ... Pray with you? ... For you?', human suffering is being compared with that of Christ. One is left

wondering why so few of Beckett's characters carry their distaste for life to its logical conclusion in self-destruction ...

(Mercier 1977: 237–8)

---
## v: Poetry/media/other studies
---

Laurence Harvey's *Samuel Beckett: Poet and Critic* (1970) remains the only full-length discussion of Beckett's poetry, and as such is indispensable for any reader interested in this rather neglected area of Beckett's work. It was also written with the aid of Beckett himself, who was able to furnish Harvey with a great deal of detail about the nature, imagery and style of the poems. The study contained a long exegesis of *Whoroscope* **[15, 98]** linking the poem in detail to Descartes' life and thought, although, for Harvey, the poem was interesting mainly for the light it shed on Beckett's future development; it was the first example in Beckett's work of a disintegrating text

> The mind of the narrator, as death approaches, tries to hold together the fragments of his life, soon to be scattered for ever: against it is pitted another force, working toward dissolution. The author, as though divided against himself, plays both roles, that of man struggling to survive and that of a disjoining destiny. On the plane of his art, he executes the latter imperative whenever he dissolves the cohesive elements joining the two parts of his poem; by his notes, by interrupting the poem with the egg motif, by questioning the fiction itself through irony and the comic ... when the centrifugal force of personality begins to fail, the little worlds of a human lifetime are in danger of whirling off into the void.

(Harvey 1970: 65)

Harvey linked the poems of *Echoes Bones* to Ovid, Rimbaud, Dante, the Bible, Schopenhauer and the troubadour tradition; he argued that the poems written in French before the Second World War demonstrated that Beckett's poetry was evolving toward the *'pure lyric'* (Harvey 1970: 223), the simplest, most compressed expression of the poet's concerns. The second section of Harvey's book was something of a mixture: it contained discussions of the criticism, of the previously uncollected poems, and of Beckett's use of material from *Echoes Bones* in the composition of *Dream of Fair to Middling Women* (Harvey's study was the first to quote extensively from this as-yet unpublished text). A chapter on *Watt* **[28, 60–2]** argued that the novel dealt with middle age as a time in the individual's life when both birth and death seemed equally remote: in a paragraph near the beginning of this chapter, Harvey came as close as he ever did to providing a summary of the study

> Beckett evolves toward spareness according to the Schopenhauer prescription. The inevitable physical asceticism of ageing may be thought of as metaphor, for it parallels a progressive spiritual disengagement. The early fiction and poetry are 'impure' in the sense that its heroes are caught up in the struggle of will and practical reason ... Beckett's early style, as well, is 'impure', for the author sometimes fails to repress his weakness for gratuitous wordplay and erudite allusions. Even while he condemns technique and structure as artistic heresy perpetrated by intellect, the intellectualism of the young artist is everywhere apparent ... Watt's trajectory from society to the house of Mr Knott to the asylum – from action to enquiry to recollection, from will to intellect to apperceptive meditation – is a figure of the evolution not only from young man to old but from citizen of the macrocosm [the external world] to poet of the microcosm [the self], an evolution that in the case of Murphy and Belacqua was incomplete. Beckett's writing taken as a whole is the image of such an evolution and in this sense the story of his life ...
>
> (Harvey 1970: 401)

Kathleen McGrory and John Unterecker's edited volume *Yeats, Joyce and Beckett: New Light on Three Modern Irish Writers* (1976) related Beckett's work to twentieth century Irish literature; this study was complemented over the following years by Katherine Worth's *The Irish Drama of Europe from Yeats to Beckett* (1978), which linked Beckett to an emergent Irish theatrical tradition, and by Barbara Gluck's re-examination of the relationship between Beckett and Joyce (*Beckett and Joyce: Friendship and Fiction* (1979)).

Claus Zilliacus' study of Beckett's radio and television plays (*Beckett and Broadcasting: A Study of the Works of Samuel Beckett for and in Radio and Television* (1976)) is, to date, the only full length study of this area of Beckett's work. Zilliacus discussed the plays both as autonomous artworks and in relation to the development of public service broadcasting (especially in Britain: he provided, for example, a breakdown of audience responses to the broadcasting of *All That Fall* and *Embers*). For Zilliacus, Beckett's work for radio (Zilliacus' study predated most of the television plays) was marked by a narrowing of focus, from the relatively spacious and conventional *All That Fall* to the later, more austere works

It has been suggested, by John Spurling [in *Beckett: A Study of His Plays*] that whenever Beckett makes the test of a new medium, he always seems to take a few steps backward in the direction of conventional realism. Then he moves forward again, probing, abstracting. There is a gradual , consistent development from *All That Fall* onward. *All that Fall* tells a story; Embers portrayed a storyteller; *Words and Music* and the *Equisses* [the roughs for Radio] still have remnants of character and milieu; these are discarded in *Cascando* which, instead of focusing on a story, focuses on the story-telling condition ...

(Zilliacus 1976: 143)

Zilliacus spent most time on *All That Fall* **[36, 78–9]** he followed the play's development through various manuscript stages, noting the increased stylisation of the dialogue in successive drafts. In a discussion of *Eh Joe*, **[41, 94]** he argued that the play's formal complexity is revealed through Beckett's use of the camera

... The camera is a registering device, as the voice is not; it also serves to intensify, by degrees, the effect exerted by the voice on the face when it registers. It is both subjective and objective, external and internal ...

(Zilliacus 1976: 186–7)

Zilliacus argued that the tendency of Beckett's work in radio and television was toward silence and absence (which could be achieved in radio more succinctly than it could in prose; in radio, not to speak is literally not to exist). In a discussion of the role of pauses and silence in the radio work, Zilliacus identified a conventional radio term that described the goal to which Beckett's radio work aspired; in radio, an interval without speech is known as 'dead air'.

## (c) THEORETICAL BECKETT: 1980–1995

By the end of the 1970s, Beckett criticism had explored every avenue open to the traditional literary critic. His work had been exhaustively mined for its philosophical and literary import; the challenge that it mounted to conventional ideas of the literary and dramatic text had been explored, and something of a general critical consensus had emerged. Beckett's work was, if anything, more 'real' than the conventional text. It examined human existence on a fundamental level; it sought to establish a metaphysical response to the innate problem of human existence in the meaningless chaos of the world; and it did so by exposing the flaws in conventional realism, which was far too organised to convey both the ungovernable flux of the world, and the individual's inherently unfixed, subjective response to that world. It seemed that the only role left to Beckett critics was excavatory: the critical terms under which his work should be studied had been established, and the critic could do nothing more than explore, in ever more minute details, the implications of this paradigm.

This did not happen: indeed, during the 1980s and 90s, Beckett's work became one of the sites of battle between more traditional literary critics and those whose work sought to establish new paradigms, not simply for the study of Beckett but for the study of literature generally. Beckett's work was caught up in a wider debate about the meaning, structure and form of literature, between the defenders of a conventional notion of the literary and dramatic text, and those who worked under the influence of a new set of paradigms – structuralism, post-structuralism, feminist criticism, psychoanalytic and Jungian criticism, and so on. These developments are usually grouped together, under the general term Theory: this blanket term gives recent developments in literary studies more coherence than they perhaps merit, but it does, at least, signal one of the characteristic assumptions made by the new generation of literary critics, one that marked them off sharply from the critics that preceded them. For the new theorists, the literary text itself was not a self-contained repository of meanings for the critic to uncover: the literary text was only part of a wider network of texts, signs, and structures, that did not automatically convey a coherent, self-evident meaning. The reader helped to create the text in the act of reading, and this creation was influenced by his or her position in the world; the text itself relied on a structure of interpretation established not only in literature but in the social world outside the text; the text mirrored, in some form or other, the deep structures of human thought; or the text itself could not be relied upon to convey a stable meaning, but was itself open to contrasting, fragmented and contradictory readings.

And so the direction of Beckett studies changed, as the influence of these new theories and methods spread through the academic community; the divisions that had emerged in the previous decade between the various forms that Beckett adopted throughout his writing life were to a large extent superseded by new divisions, along the faultlines established by the growth of Theory in the study of literature.

## i: Structuralism, post-structuralism and post-modernism

The first of the new theories to have an impact on the study of literature in the English speaking world were those associated with structuralism and post-structuralism. The roots of these approaches went back to the beginning of the twentieth century, to the work of the Swiss linguist Ferdinand Saussure. Saussure was interested in the structure of language; how did the individual know that a word had a definite meaning, in a particular linguistic context? For Saussure, the answer could not lie in a simple link between the word and the object that it described: after all, the word changed from language to language, while the object remained stubbornly the same (a French person and an English person would both recognise a dog if they saw one; even though the French person would call the dog 'un chien'). For Saussure, the only explanation was that the link between the word and the object was completely arbitrary; there was nothing in a dog itself to suggest the word dog, and the word itself was only used in English to describe a dog because it did not sound quite like any other word in the language. The word was, therefore, simply a sign for the object in the external world, and had no direct, unchanging relationship to that object; it could only be defined in relation to the English language as a whole (dog means dog, only because the arrangement of letters in dog is different from that in log, fog, hog, or cog). The linguistic sign had two parts; the *signifier* (the arrangement of letters in the word) and the *signified* (the socially determined object that this arrangement of letters indicated). From here, it was a relatively short step to the idea that all meaning in the world was socially determined; and that it was possible to analyse the world as though it were a giant text, containing those meanings that a particular society had determined for its individual components, singly and collectively, at any given moment (an approach adopted, for example, by the theorist Roland Barthes: see *Mythologies* (1957)). Saussure's insight into the arbitrary connection between the linguistic sign and the external world led those critics that followed him into the study of the formal and structural attributes of the literary text; if the world (and the language used to describe that world) was organised around those structures that produced meaning for a particular society, then the critic's role was to uncover and expound on those structures. Paradoxically, this led structuralists (as these critics came to be known) back into territory previously occupied by the more traditional type of critic. To uncover the underlying structure of a text, one had to engage in a close reading of that text; in doing so, the structuralist critic had to treat the text as a self-contained, coherent assemblage of meanings.

Structuralism itself did not have much of an impact on Beckett studies; the idea that Beckett's work utilised archetypal literary structures (in particular the quest narrative in its various forms) was already well established (see, for example, Robinson (1970)). Beckett's use of these structures might be idiosyncratic; it might veer on the side of parody; but it was an accepted part of his work. Similarly, the term 'metatheatre' (a form of theatre that explored theatre as a form) had been used to describe Beckett's dramatic work as early as 1963. Structuralism did, however pave the way for a type of analysis that mounted a determined challenge to the idea of the coherent, self-contained literary text. If the link between the linguistic sign and the object it described was arbitrary, then it was also true that the connection between the sign and the object could change, and that the connection might not be as self-evident as it might at first appear (for example, a pun used a sign to convey two separate meanings simultaneously, exposing a weakness or confusion in the link between word and object). Similarly, the structure of the text itself was not always completely secure, and could, through careful analysis, be shown to lead to a variety of different readings, some of which directly contradicted the ostensible meaning of the text. No text could be relied upon to convey a simple, direct truth; all texts contained moments in which the structure that seemed to sustain them came under strain. The critic had to respond to these moments, and to explore the new perspectives on the text that they opened up. More than this, the critic had to be alive to the unfinalisable nature of the text itself. If the linguistic sign could not be relied upon always to exist in a stable relationship with the object, the critic had to develop an analytical style that could continually draw the reader's attention to that instability.

This analytical style was given the title Deconstruction, and was first associated with the work of the French philosopher Jacques Derrida. Derrida applied the analytical method first of all to philosophical texts, showing the various ways in which a philosophical argument was sabotaged by the philosopher's reliance on literary methods (metaphor, rhetoric, and so on). In doing so, he attempted to demonstrate that a philosophical text could make no claim to absolute, self-evident truth, that would be obvious to any reader who took the time to study it; in Derrida's phrase, he sought to attack the idea that a philosophical text could lay claim to a *metaphysics of presence* (that is, to an underlying assumption that a philosophical text could be cleared of literary flourishes, and could speak clearly for itself). To effect such an analysis,

Derrida engaged in a double reading of the text. First, the text was subjected to a close reading at those points where its structure was under the greatest strain; the critic, in doing so, established that the text was not saying what it was supposed to say, and was, in fact, contradicting or confusing the argument that the philosopher hoped to present. Second, the critic used the insight gained from this first analysis and applied it to the text as a whole, reconstituting the text on the grounds established by his first analysis. In other words, the critic first analysed the text to and past the point of its destruction; and then reconstructed it along new lines that demonstrated the inherently contradictory nature of the text as a whole. The double movement, from destruction to reconstruction, was collapsed into one term; 'deconstruction'.

For the deconstructor (or the post-structuralist – the two terms became interchangeable) the text was not the clear indication of the author's intention: the author had no control over the way in which the text upset any stable interpretation. The phrase, 'the death of the author' became a staple in post-structuralist criticism; by this, the critics did not mean that the idea of an individual, creating a text for consumption by readers, could now be abandoned: rather, they argued that this was no longer of primary importance in analysing a text. The author had no authority: neither did the text, because, under careful scrutiny, it could be shown to sabotage itself. All that was left for the critic was the active process of interpretation, which was never-ending, because it could not reach a conclusion in a definite, finally established truth. Derrida, like the structuralists, had therefore to assume that the meanings to be uncovered in the text could be uncovered because the language of the text itself contained them; there could be no recourse to facts and meanings outside the text (because they, in their turn, could be treated as a text, and could be subjected to a deconstructive analysis).

The turn from structuralism to post-structuralism coincided with the development of a set of theories that are loosely grouped under the general term post-modernism. Post-modernism must be one of the most confusing terms in critical and cultural discourse; it sometimes seems as though there are as many post-modernisms as there are critics writing about the area. For the purposes of textual study, though, there are certain common features to the phenomenon that proved of interest to the generation of Beckett scholars who came to prominence in the 1980s. First, there was the idea, adopted from post-structuralism, that the author had no ultimate authority over the text; a text was no longer the direct expression of the author's worldview, but could be shown to be an infinitely complex subversion of the writer's initial intentions. Second, the post-modern text, unlike its predecessors, did not even lay claim to being self-contained and self-explanatory; it was by its very nature fragmented, untrustworthy, composed of elements that parodied or pastiched other texts. It was a text that proceeded by questioning the foundations on which texts themselves were created; a text which foregrounded the fact that it was written; and a text that did not come to a neat, once and for all conclusion.

An interesting anticipation of the debates that would come to dominate Beckett criticism in the 80s and 90s was provided in Eric Levy's *Beckett and the Voice of Species: A Study of the Prose Fiction* (1980) Levy sought to move Beckett criticism on from the usual territory, marked out, for Levy, by the twin discourses of the existential and the absurd

> Like the artists and philosophers before him, he asks the question 'What does it mean to be human?' The answer he gets is disturbing: to be human is to seek endlessly for an identity and a universe in which to enjoy it. This is the plight of our species. Moreover, this position should in no way be constructed as a brand of Existentialism or a doctrine of Absurdity. While these two other schools both address what they see as the fundamental ambiguity and perplexity of human experience, they nevertheless have no difficulty elaborately constructing the two poles, subjective or objective, of that experience. The doctrine of Absurdity, for example, puts man in a meaningless universe but does not hesitate to enumerate the characteristics of that universe nor to suggest ways for man to cope with life in it... In contrast, the questioning in Beckett's fiction no longer concerns merely the objective pole of experience ... but now addresses the very process of structuring experience into the poles of subject and object ... Human experience is an experience of Nothing: the only reality it knows is the inability to interpret its own structure.
>
> (Levy 1980: 3–4)

In contrast, Beckett's narrators were 'pure narrators'; that is, they were concerned with nothing else than the act of storytelling, and had no resources to fall back on if the story should fail them (as it undoubtedly would). This analysis gestured toward deconstruction; the collapsing of binary oppositions and predetermining structures in Beckett's writing was an example of a wider malaise in Western thought and culture

Thus, in the pure narrator and his experience of Nothing, Beckett expresses the impasse reached by the great enterprise of western Humanism. With Beckett, as throughout this tradition, the ultimate task of self-consciousness is to know oneself qua man; that is, to decipher in the contours of personal experience the trace of species in us all. Interpretations of this trace have never been constant, and more theological eras have seen it as rooted to an absolute or participating in God. For Beckett, the trace of species appears in the need to structure experience and fix the poles of self and world. The real Fall occurred not in Eden but in our century. After the accumulation of too much history, we have lost the innocence required to believe in any more explanations. The only certainties left are the falseness of all interpretative structures and the radical unintelligibility of human experience without them.

(Levy 1980: 10)

In 1982 Judith Dearlove's *Accommodating the Chaos: Samuel Beckett's Nonrelational Art* argued that Beckett's work was a full-scale assault on the metaphysical system that underpinned Western thought. The comforting illusion that sustained the West was that the world could be described and understood; that there existed a relation between the external world, the words used to describe that world, and the mind of the person who attempted the description. For Dearlove, Beckett's art set out to disrupt these connections; as such, it was allied to a more general sense of cultural and social uncertainty

... Physicists, astronomers, geologists reveal how much we con not know about our universe. Psychiatrists, psychologists, sociologists display how little we can know ourselves. But it is the artist, according to Beckett, who must tell us, not of the uncertainty of universe or individual, but rather of the 'incoercible absence of relation' [*Three Dialogues with Georges Duthiut*] itself. In questioning the validity, adequacy and existence of a relationship between the artist and his occasion Beckett is questioning the metaphysical traditions which assert that there is a rational and harmonious system but also that it is knowable and imitable. Art is denied the justifications and significations provided by external orders ...

(Dearlove 1982: 5)

However, this was not to say that Beckett was content to leave his writing in such a state: the quest for a non-relational art was in itself paradoxical and doomed to ultimate failure, because the art produced would always stand in some relation to the world in which it was produced, even if that relation was difficult to describe. Dearlove discerned a change in Beckett's work in this regard from *How It Is* onwards

> ... Instead of belabouring the lack of associations between a speaker and his world, Beckett explores the possibilities of a voice unrelated to any world and hence unrestricted. Instead of focusing attention upon the divorce of the mind from the external world, he explores the internal, arbitrary and self-appointed worlds the mind creates. The interior focus in turn makes possible the highly self – conscious and arbitrary constructions of the 'residua' in which artifice and intricacy themselves suggest a more fundamental absence of order. Structure works in opposition to content. In the most recent fictions, rather than attempting to deny, explode, implode, ignore, or controvert the metaphysics of a relational art, Beckett permits the elements of traditional narrative to commingle with those of a non-relational narrative. It is no longer necessary to isolate or exacerbate either realm. The pieces reconcile, but do not reunite, an impotent speaker with an unknowable world. Beckett accepts both the impossibility of a non-relational art and the improbability of a relational one, and in doing so he finds yet another shape for the ambiguity, fluidity and uncertainty of the human condition.
>
> (Dearlove 1982: 5)

Dearlove's analysis was, fundamentally, in line with deconstructive theory (although she did not use the term): she examined the failure of language in Beckett to describe the world, and the extent to which language itself created the things it set out to describe.

The first overt attempt to place Beckett's work in relation to the new critical approaches outlined above was made in Angela Moorjani's *Abysmal Games in the Novels of Samuel Beckett* (1982). Moorjani argued that Beckett's fiction deconstructed not only itself but the conventional means of creating narrative. Where most texts proceeded in a linear fashion, moving from beginning to end, Beckett's novels were structured around an open-ended process of echoes and duplications. This, in a favourite deconstructive phrase, was an example of *mise en abyme*: the text rendered itself undecidable, because it constantly cast doubt on its own rhetorical strategies, and, by extension, on the conventional rhetorical strategies that all novels employed

> In light of the unknowable, the unrepresentable, Beckett's novels from *Watt* onward, staging but a few moments along the infinite

159

chain, teasingly manipulate and undermine the classic project of the novel to mirror inner and outer reality ...

(Moorjani 1982: 45)

This undermining process took two main forms: internal reduplication (as Beckett's texts mirrored themselves and each other) and the simultaneous echoing and deconstruction of narratives from outside the text. For example, Moorjani noted that Molloy's **[66–8]** monologue echoed one of the classical narratives of Freudian analysis (the Oedipus myth), but Molloy's reshaping of the myth did not serve to explain either the structure of the novel or the ultimate nature of the character

> From an examination of Molloy's narrative ... it appears that the components of the Oedipus myth are inscribed in duplicate. The Louisse episode condenses the entire drama into a dreamlike emblem in the middle of the narrative which, since it stages embedded inner journeys to the mother, traces Molloy's movements through regions that evoke the mother and the unconscious: the walled city of his birth, the seashore, the dark forest, and the central garden of Louisse. The quest, as we have seen, is both commanded and forbidden by multiple embodiments of a paradoxical law: maternal voices that order and forbid, paternal figures that obstruct and goad, sphinxes both male and female. The violence against the father, of which there are two versions, and the union with the mother figures, however, fail to lead anywhere. Indeed, rather than Oedipus, Molloy is an anti-Oedipus, for instead of solving the riddle of the sphinx and attaining sovereignty, Molloy in a regressive movement recedes from his mother's room via the sphinx to the killing of the stranger at the crossroads to the final crawling on all fours out of the forest and into the bowels of the earth.

(Moorjani 1982: 106)

S.E. Gontarski's *the Intent of 'Undoing' in Samuel Beckett's Dramatic Texts* (1985) sought to establish a common methodology behind the construction of the plays. Gontarski argued that the play texts were, at first, rooted in Beckett's own experience, and betrayed more of the author's mindset and concerns than did the finished versions. As Beckett revised the text, he removed or 'vaguened' (Beckett's own term) these references, and along with them the conventional narrative and dramatic structures that might, for another author, have supported the work. In other words, for Gontarski, Beckett proceeded by undoing the narrative, as it existed in the first manuscript drafts

... One invariably finds in Beckett's undoing a movement towards simplicity, toward the essential, toward the universal ... Such an artistic preoccupation in Beckett's texts might be anticipated given the sparse, often minimalist nature of the drama and late prose especially ... what is surprising, however, is how rooted and dependent that work is on its more traditional and realistic sources. Often the early drafts of Beckett's work are more realistic, the action more traditionally motivated, the world more familiar and recognisable, the work as a whole more conventional than the final. Revision is often toward a patterned disconnection, as motifs are organised not by causality but by some form of recurrence and (near) symmetry. This process often entails the conscious destruction of logical relations, the abandonment of linear argument, and the substitution of more abstract patterns of numbers, music, and so forth, to shape a work. It is finally a consciously literary process, which results in what the Russian formalists might call 'defamiliarisation', or what Brecht, in *A Short Organum for the Theatre*, termed estrangement.

(Gontarski 1985: 3–4)

Like Butler, Gontarski argued that Beckett's work is motivated by a rejection of the rational. Beckett, from his earliest works, rejected mimesis (the reflection of reality); however this did not lead him towards the creation of fundamental parables. Rather, his work was an attempt to find a form of expression that was patterned, but not mimetic

From his earliest artistic years, Beckett struggled to reject mimesis, based as it is on a fundamental empiricism, as an art of surfaces. The perfection of the illusion of reality interested him little. A flirtation with naturalistic film in the 1930s notwithstanding, his most strongly and frequently expressed aesthetics was antinaturalistic, anti any system that makes of art finally another set of conventions by imposing an artificial order a phrase that, for the young Beckett, at least, is redundant). On existence, on the self. Beckett's continuing artistic struggles are to discover or develop accurate, pleasing, formal substitutes for the logic and causality that he rejected by repudiating naturalism or psychological realism. The aesthetic danger is, of course, simply finding another external form, a danger to which Beckett may have at least partly acceded in his more formalist drama and prose.

(Gontarski 1985: 5)

161

Michael Sherringham produced a monograph on the French version of *Molloy* **[66–8]** (*Beckett: Molloy*) in 1985: his short study set out to discuss Molloy as a novel, and not, as Sherringham put it, as 'a treatise, a symptom, a stage in the author's way' (Sherringham 1985: prefaratory note). In doing so, he examined the relation between Beckett's novel and those novels more usually described as post-modern. If a post-modern text was intertextual (that is, it contained a network of references and allusions to other texts), then Beckett's work could not be thought of as specifically post-modern. Beckett's work made use of references, but not in a particularly post-modern way

> In Beckett's fiction what is stressed is the arbitrariness; here intertextuality is not allusive; it is centripetal rather than centrifugal. But if, in a new dispensation, sometimes called 'post-modernist', writers as diverse as the *noveaux romanciers* in France, American fabulators like Pynchon, Barth and Gass, outsiders like Borges and Gombrowicz, have created fictions which, in various ways revel in the endless arbitrary profusion of representation, Beckett's name should not be to hastily allied with theirs. In his texts there is really no euphoric relinquishing of the bonds between the textual and the existential ...: nor, in the end, is there any attempt to instil new forms of consciousness, appropriate to a lucidly ludic vision. And there is none of that sense of conversion from one set of values (those of realism surrendering to the cult of subjectivity) which marks in some ways those works that we associate with modernism or post-modernism. By keeping resonant some of the voices of Western culture it helps to maintain, as powerful options, the claims of the individual subject to external mirrorings of itself, to a selfhood ontologically grounded. But at the same time it helps to undermine those claims, in their legitimacy and their efficacy, by manifesting itself, through the texts fictional structures, as a process rooted in the workings of reflexive consciousness itself. Beckett's fictions are haunted by a sense that the mind's quintessential mode is citation: in quest of the source of its own narration, it can only cite alien authorities. When it wishes to play the author, it can only quote.
>
> (Sherringham 1985: 82)

Peter Gidal's *Understanding Beckett* (1986) was a determinedly post-structuralist view of the author; it also attempted a political reading of Beckett's work, along the theoretical lines laid out in current post-structuralist and feminist criticism. For Gidal, Beckett's political importance lay not so much in the substance of his work as in its form; he argued that Beckett's writing, in destabilising the narrative, also destabilised the power structures whose interests were served by the idea of narrative (for Gidal, as for Kristeva or Cixous (see below), these power structures were capitalist and male). In a complex, closely written study, Gidal drew parallels between Beckett's work and Brecht's (both were interested in calling the nature of the theatrical event into question) and with the German comedian Karl Valentin (who had been an important early influence on the young Brecht).

Susan Brienza's *Samuel Beckett's New Worlds: Style in Metafiction* (1987) treated the later fiction **[39, 85–8]** as a complex interaction between the style of particular works and the process of writing itself. Beckett's late prose works (metafictions, because they dealt with the processes of creating fictions) did not, however, settle on a single style; rather, each one presented its own version of the interaction between style and writing

Samuel Beckett's fiction after *The Unnamable* can continue by photographing itself: style comments on writing in these new worlds. In *Texts for Nothing* Beckett 'goes on' artistically through linguistic sleights of hand with verbs and pronouns. *From an Abandoned Work* is the monologue of a disjointed narrator who speaks in distorted and inverted syntax. In *Enough* the narrator's self-delusion expresses itself in wistful and contradictory language. The self-destructive short novel *How It Is* spews out bits and scraps of a life in fragmented phrases of 'midget grammar' and thereby records the torture of composing. In *Imagination Dead Imagine* paradoxical language mirrors the impossible feat... of creating something out of nothing. The myth-like story of *The Lost Ones* tauntingly leads the reader on a search for meaning mirroring the climbers' attempts at escape) in language that mocks man's need for order and structure. The style of *Ping* embodies the suffering of the artist (represented as an imprisoned creature) as figure so constrained as the few recycled phrases of the text. By the time we get to *Lessness* the artist has regressed to a foetus, unable to stand, described with incomplete, 'issueless' phrases, as Beckett achieves the 'syntax of weakness' he set as his goal around 1960. In *Fizzles* the narrative voice is fizzling out, and bodies are either 'Still' or going in zig-zag paths as their sentences collapse and meander in parallel ways. Language itself is the narrator's only companion in *Company*, and both imagination and expression are doubted in the highly self-conscious prose of *Ill Seen Ill Said*. Finally, regressing from *The Unnamable*'s vow, 'I'll go on', the most recent piece promises only to move *Worstward Ho*, and manages to do so through the creation of 'worse' words and 'un-' words.

(Brienza 1987: 8)

Jane Alison Hale's *The Broken Window: Beckett's Dramatic Perspective* (1987) argued that Beckett's theatre disrupted the habitual structures of perception that had been common to all Western societies since the Renaissance: in his work, neither the characters nor the audience could rely on a stable perceptual system, in which every element was unambiguously fixed in space and time. Rather, Beckett's characters existed in a profoundly disorienting world that they tried and failed to order according to a stable perceptual system. Hale argued that this disorientation is most apparent in the disrupted vision manifested by many of Beckett's characters; unsurprisingly, Hale regarded *Endgame* **[36, 38, 76–8]** as a prime example of Beckett's disorienting theatrical world

Hamm has retreated to an enclosed shelter, perhaps in an effort to define a space for himself that would permit vision by affording a definable and stable point of view upon the world around him: he insists upon Clov's wheeling him around the limits of his room, then back to its exact centre, so that he can perceive and comprehend the space in which he exists. Yet the effort is futile, for the walls are boundaries between Hamm's universe and the nothingness that lies beyond ... His desire to be replaced in the exact centre of the room is just as vain, since a centre can be defined only in relation to precise boundaries, and boundaries can exist only if they delimit one space from another. So Hamm's attempt to separate his own space from the one he wishes to observe is a failure, since the only space available for observation is that in which he exists. In spite of his glasses, the windows of his room, and all his efforts to perceive the ends of the time and space of his life, he can put nothing in perspective, since he can attain no stable, exterior, definable point of observation ...

(Hale 1987: 60)

James Acheson and Kateryna Arthur's *Beckett's Later Fiction and Drama: Texts for Company* (1987) concerned itself with the post-trilogy prose and the post-*Endgame* drama: it contained essays by Brater on *Worstward Ho*; by Colin Duckworth, on Beckett's changes to the text of *Godot* for the San Quentin Drama workshop production in 1984); and Nicholas Zurbrigg, whose essay on *Ill Seen Ill Said* **[47, 95–6]** placed Beckett's work in an ambiguous relationship to both modernism and post-modernism

> Sometimes, Beckett's archetyphally post-modern evocations of perceptual confusion and delusion merely baffle us, and appear nothing more than 'Confusion amounting to nothing'. But on other occasions, they leave 'something there', and appear not so much the negation of the great modernist writers explorations of habitual perception, as an extraordinary extension and elaboration of Proust's and Eluard's meditations upon the mysteries of love ...
>
> (Acheson and Archer 1987: 152)

Steven Connor's *Samuel Beckett: Repetition, Theory and Text* (1988) took as its central premise the idea that repetition played a crucial part in the formation of the self

> It will be the argument of this book that repetition is a central and necessary concept within all attempts to understand individual and social being and representation. While to a large extent repetition determines and fixes our sense of our experience and representations of that experience, it is also the place where certain radical instabilities in these operations can reveal themselves. It is therefore no accident that Samuel Beckett, the writer who this century has most single-mindedly dedicated himself to the exploration of what is meant by such things as being, identity and representation, should have at the centre of his work so strong and continuous a preoccupation with repetition ...
>
> (Connor 1988: 1)

In classically deconstructive fashion, repetition both confirmed and undermined the original text. It confirmed the original, because without an original no copy can be made: but it also undermined the original, because it was indistinguishable from the original. The presence of repetition in a text, therefore, fatally destabilised that text's claims to represent an unambiguous truth about the world. For a writer as radically mistrustful of language as Beckett, the idea of repetition could not help but exercise a powerful influence

> Repetition in Beckett's work does not just involve the mirroring or duplication of situation, incident and character. From the beginning, repetition has been the dominating principle of his language: repetition of words, of sounds, of phrases, of syntactical

and grammatical forms. And as the consciousness of language as a
distorting or constricting force tightens its hold on Beckett ... so
repetition seems to become more and more necessary in his work
... [Where] repetition begins as a supplementary feature of language,
secondary to and derived from the uniqueness of particular utteran-
ces, it comes to occupy the centre of his work. Repetition comes
to be all there is, the only novelty being the variations in the forms
of sameness.

(Connor 1988: 15)

For Connor, this meant that Beckett's work undermined any notion
of the authentic and the unitary: repetition in Beckett was never stale,
because it drew attention to the process of writing and the process of
reading; and because the repetitions were never exact (and, arguably,
in the later work there was no 'original' for them to repeat) the works
themselves could never be completed.

Yet another theoretical approach to Beckett's work was taken by
Sylvie Debevec Henning, in *Beckett's Critical Complicity: Carnival,
Contestation, and Tradition* (1988). Henning's approach was heavily
influenced by the work of the Russian theorist Mikhail Bakhtin: in
particular, she utilised two terms associated with Bakhtin ('dialogue'
and 'carnival') in a reading of Beckett's work that did not treat the texts
as uninflectedly pessimistic statements about the Western condition.
For Henning, Beckett's work existed in a dialogue with the traditions
of Western thought; he both confirmed and overturned the assumptions
of the Western rational tradition, subjecting them to the kind of satirical
inversions that Bakhtin discerned in the practices of the medieval
carnival

Historically, the carnivalesque has always co-existed alongside our
sober rationalistic tradition. It has, however, been increasingly
confined and reduced. According to Bakhtin and others, an effort
to control and ultimately to eliminate all that does not conform
to the totalising (and not infrequently totalitarian) presumptions
of our cultural heritage has been operative on a fundamental level
within the historically predominant hermeneutic perspectives
whether, philosophical, religious, moral, scientific or literary.

For Beckett the task of creative thinking has always been to
conduct the search for ' a form that will accommodate the mess'
instead of repressing it through an excess of rationalist order. The
carnivalised satire comes to the fore in this context as a means of
playing out 'messy' relations such that the anxiety they engender

may be engaged in a more positive manner. An affirmation of their vital importance within the relative structures of temporal existence is in fact basic to this phenomenon, in as much as carnivalisation normally involves an open confrontation between contending forces, above all between those that strive for a full, harmonious unification and those that contest this desire.

(Henning 1988: 88)

Brian T. Fitch's *Beckett and Babel: an Investigation into the Status of the Bilingual Work* (1988) took as its starting point an interesting feature of Beckett's writing that had not been dealt with in any great depth by previous commentators (with some exceptions; see Cockerham, in Worth (1975)); Beckett's decision to write in both English and French **[33]**. He began by noting that the transition from English to French was not quite as extreme as it might have seemed to Beckett's early critics, as Beckett never really abandoned English (except for a relatively short period in the late Forties and early Fifties) as a literary language. The fact that he chose to translate his own work itself raised an interesting (and largely unconsidered) question about the status of the translation. Most translated texts exist in a hierarchical relation to the original: they are metatexts (texts formed from, and commenting on, other texts), but metatexts whose status is lower than the original, untranslated text. The fact that Beckett himself was the translator of his own work problematised this relation

... The situation [*Fitch has been discussing the reader's relation to the translated text*] changes radically once the reader knows that it is the author of the original who is responsible for the second version. The creativity he revealed in producing the original text continues quite naturally to be attributed to him, even if to a lesser degree, in his second incarnation as the author of the text in the second language ... In the first case it will be the second version's status as a metatext that will be lost sight of, and in the second, that of the 'normal' translation, it will be the workings of the writing process that will be concealed.

(Fitch 1988: 18–19)

To try to resolve these paradoxes, Fitch compared the versions of Beckett's work in either language with their respective translations. In doing so, he argued that Beckett's translations were, in effect, rewritings based on the original text and on the manuscript versions that Beckett himself had worked through while creating the original. Therefore, the translations had as much right to be thought of as originals as did the texts that Beckett had first created

> ... [One] thing from the preceding chapters has emerged beyond dispute, and its importance can hardly be over-emphasised. That is the need for both versions, both texts, of his work to be studied for their own sake. To take only one version of the work is to make a wholly arbitrary decision, for on what possible grounds would one take one rather than the other? To take the first is to fail to recognise that it is followed by another version; and to take the second is to fail to recognise that another version preceded it. *In other words, both versions are, in themselves, incomplete.*

> ... In other words, there is no shadow of a doubt that with Beckett the literary work has become something different. Just as his second versions are not translations like other translations and even his first versions are not texts like any other texts, sufficient to themselves, so too the literary work has become a translation unlike any other, arising, as it does, from the contiguity, if not the material coming together, of two distinct unilingual texts and the interaction of two separate linguistic systems.
>
> (Fitch 1988: 227, 228)

Lance St. John Butler and Robin Davis published a collection of essays from a 1986 conference at Stirling University, held to celebrate Beckett's 80th birthday. *Rethinking Beckett: a Collection of Critical Essays* (1988) dealt with the protean nature of the critical response to the author, and introduced a number of essays on Beckett's work from a variety of critical perspectives, from a post-structuralist analysis of Beckett's theatre as a theatre of self-erasure from Steven Connor, to Gottfried Buttner's mystic re-interpretation of *Watt*, to Michael Mooney's recasting of the same novel as a demonstration of sceptic philosophy (after the pre-Socratic philosopher Democritus). In the introduction, Butler sought to locate the sheer variety of critical approaches to Beckett in the author's implicit post-structuralism

> What is different about Beckett is not that he provokes a critical response ... but the protean, open-ended, 'undecidable' and inexhaustible quality of the challenge he offers. In this, it seems to us, he is the poet of the post-structuralist age. Not that he was *not* the poet of other ages too for he was – Beckett as the quintessential *nouveau romanice*r, Beckett the Cartesian, Beckett the Existentialist,

these have rubbed shoulders with Beckett the nihilist, Beckett the mystic and Beckett the explorer of the limitations of language. But, recuperating all of these and moving without apparent strain into new realms, deconstructionist avant la lettre, there is a new Beckett, thinkable only in the most recent terms, rethinkable now as, doubtless, also in the future.

(Butler and Davis 1988: ix)

Thomas Trezise's *Into the Breach: Samuel Beckett and the Ends of Literature* (1990) offered a by now standard post-modern reading, in which Beckett's writing was opposed to the Western metaphysical tradition; Carla Locatelli's *Unwording the Word: Samuel Beckett's Prose works After the Nobel Prize* (1990) focused mainly on the late Trilogy – *Company, Ill Seen Ill Said,* and *Worstward Ho.* Locatelli's study, although itself determinedly post-structuralist, took aim at a common post-structuralist assumption, that conventional literary forms took as their goal the precise imitation of the real world. She argued that Beckett's work was undoubtedly post-structuralist (because he could not accept that a sign unambiguously referred to an object) but that, at the same time, he was driven to try to reconstruct the idea that language could refer to an external reality, even though this attempt might not succeed.

Leslie Hill's *Beckett's Fiction: In Different Words* (1990) began from a position of some dissatisfaction with the current state of Beckett criticism. For Hill, Beckett's critics did not deal adequately enough with the radical nature of the texts; and, particularly, with the constantly uncertain, paradoxical and shifting nature of Beckett's language. The prose works gained their particular character from the tension between the thing described and the words that Beckett was forced to choose to describe it. Hill found a theoretical model for this constant uncertainty in Derrida: both subscribed to a theory of language in crisis

... it is a theory committed to defending the autonomy of literary texts and it defines fiction as an activity of language in which, paradoxically, the foundations of meaning are attacked by the uncontrollable, self-inverting character of meaning itself.

(Hill 1990: 6)

Jean Yamasaki Toyama's *Beckett's Game: Self and Language in the Trilogy* (1991) took as its starting point the often-employed 'Three Dialogues with Georges Duithuit' (in which Beckett discussed the idea of an art created from nothing but the obligation to express). Toyama took this as a signal that Beckett's work as a whole was an exercise in deconstruction: and, much like Brienza in 1987, came to the conclusion that Beckett's writing escaped all attempts to define it, leaving the reader to re-examine his or her own status as a reader. The Trilogy, for example, confused the reader's expectations of narrative linearity by consisting of a series of variations on a circle; the narratives were circular, the characters did not exist in a linear progression (that is, Molloy was not followed by Moran, who was not followed by Malone, and so on). Toyama argued (as Connor had done three years previously) that Beckett's work was based on an implicitly post-modern awareness of the importance of decentring and repetition.

In 1992, Steven Connor edited a collection of criticism on both *Waiting for Godot* and *Endgame* that demonstrated the impact that the theoretical debates of the 1980s had had on Beckett studies. It included work by Mary Bryden, Connor himself, Andrew Kennedy, Jane Alison Hale and Sylvie Henning. Anna McMullan's *Theatre on Trial: Samuel Beckett's Later Drama* (1993) argued that Beckett's theatre from *Play* onwards was subject to the same process of decentring and repetition that Connor had described in the prose works **[41–7, 88–93]**. McMullan's discussion of the later drama focused on the strategies that Beckett employed to undercut the idea of performance itself, and more particularly on the idea that a theatrical text could unambiguously represent the world. Representation in Beckett's theatrical universe was never a straightforward matter

> Representation is doubly framed in Beckett's late plays, as the text constitutes the characters' attempts to represent themselves, to bear witness to their existence through their narratives. The fictional world of the plays therefore revolves around the production and performance of narratives. In many of the plays, the performances occur on a stage which is primarily a scene of judgement, but in others, the performances constitute rites of passage or metamorphosis which resist the structures of identity and representation authorised by the dominant laws. The plays also draw attention to their own status as performances. In each case, the impulse or imperative to create order and coherence, on the part of the audience and characters, is set against the failure of both the characters and the visual/verbal text to achieve the fixity and mastery with which the traditional structures of narrative and visual representation are associated.
>
> (McMullan 1993: 4–5)

Beckett's later drama, therefore, put not only the idea of theatre itself, but also the idea that the self and the real world could be 'performed' (that is, that any representation could claim to describe and define that world), on trial

> Beckett's theatre can therefore be seen as the site of a confrontation between the attempt to assume a position of control and judgement in relation to the visual and verbal representations of self and the laws of representations of self and the laws of representation in general, and the opening up of spaces which challenge and disrupt the construction of the roles posited by representation, including those of the self and other, spectacle and spectator. Beckett's drama frames the operations of authority, but also stages the drama of a subjectivity which resists or exceeds the dominant codes of representation, questioning in the process the languages and limits of theatre itself.
>
> (McMullan 1993: 9)

Here, McMullan's study and Mary Bryden's (see below) began to reveal a common theoretical foundation; McMullan saw Beckett's work, as did Bryden, as an attack on the symbolic order, and a privileging of the semiotic (as described by Kristeva and Cixous).

---

## ii: Feminist criticism

---

The idea that the text itself now no longer had any authority proved influential in the development of a specific type of feminist criticism. In the work of theorists such as Julia Kristeva and Helene Cixous, the idea that a text produced a definite meaning was itself part of the subtle network of social constraints that ensured male dominance in society; they posited models of communication that sought to establish that communication itself was a form of social conditioning. Kristeva argued that, to learn a language, the individual had to pass from one linguistic state to another; the initial state, which Kristeva called the *semiotic*, produced linguistic constructions that, although they did not make formal sense, nevertheless conveyed meaning and significance (the most obvious examples would be a baby's cries, or a young child's idiosyncratic use of language); the second state was termed by Kristeva the *symbolic*, and was used to describe the use of language as social communication and conditioning (because, for Kristeva, to learn how to communicate in a particular society, one had also to learn the rules and agreed roles assigned to the individual in that society). The semiotic and symbolic layers of language existed in a hierarchical relationship, with the symbolic layer clearly dominant; however, the semiotic layer of discourse could be used to question and subvert the symbolic order, by calling into question its claim to be the only acceptable channel of communication. Kristeva, associated the symbolic order with those social positions that are usually characterised as typically male (and, because of this, she discusses the symbolic order as being fundamentally patriarchal; that is, concerned with establishing and defending male power). The semiotic layer as usually associated with typically female social positions; although, for Kristeva this did not have to be so – any text that subverted the normal, socially-acceptable channels of communication could be thought of as utilising the semiotic. Helene Cixous took this analysis a stage further; for her, there were clear, marked differences in the ways in which men and women used language. Men always sought to engage in conversations that defined their social status; male language sought to establish a position that could be defended, and did so by attempting to close communication down (having the last word, for example, could be thought of as a fundamentally male trait). Female conversation, on the other hand, sought to communicate without closure; female conversations overlapped, each other, and did not seek to establish a hierarchy of social status amongst the speakers. This trait also manifested itself in writing; for Cixous, male writing attempted to establish a position as clearly and conventionally as the current grammatical conventions would allow; female writing (the term is usually left untranslated, and appears in most critical works as *l'ecriture feminine*) is more fluid, less concerned with conventional analysis expressed in a conventional linguistic style, and more concerned with capturing the experience of expression.

In 1990, Linda Ben-Zvi edited a collection entitled *Women in Beckett: Performance and Critical Perspectives*. In her introduction, Ben-Zvi noted

> The metaphysical human condition Beckett describes is not gender-specific. All characters exist in a grey umbra, where 'perhaps' is the most surety they can muster; and all struggle with the vagaries of memory, time, and the perception of the self...
>
> Yet as much as they exist in a world of shared metaphysical uncertainty, they also exist in an everyday world – this world – shaped to a large degree by the societal constructs of gender that so often mark male and female behaviour and shape personality. Characters may go on, but the world is not some vague directional pointer through a theoretical terrain. In Beckett it is an imperative, prodding the traveller along an all too familiar way, demarcated by

alarm-clocks, benches, bicycles, bed-pans, tape recorders and mirrors. In such a world, to live is to get up, brush one's teeth and comb one's hair (or hairs); to survive is to 'play' the roles assigned or – if in doubt or in rebellion – to improvise, but always to be aware of the script already written, in which gender too often shapes the part.

Beckett's writings reflect this world, a fact critics tend to overlook in their rush to take the higher ground. For example, 'Astride of a grave' describes a metaphysical situation, but by choosing to omit the female from the description of birth, Beckett – or his character in *Godot* – makes a gendered comment ... Even the phrase 'this bitch of an earth', describing the scene of procreation and temporal decay, does not sidestep gender, since it indicates the coalescence of nature and the female, both denigrated by the phrase, spoken in a play in which no woman appears.

(Ben-Zvi 1990: 1x–x)

The collection was split into two sections: the first consisted of a series of interviews with a number of women who had acted in Beckett texts (Billie Whitelaw, Peggy Ashcroft, Madeleine Renaud, Nancy Illig, and others); and the second collected together a number of essays on women and the idea of gender in Beckett's work. These included Susan Brienza's re-examination of the female characters in Beckett's early fiction

In general, Beckett's characterisation of women alternates between stereotypes of femininity and bizarre reversals of the stereotypes. Whether paradigm or parody, the woman here is limited to the body and to the emotions. She is either too sensuous and too concerned with matters of appearance or totally unattractive – indeed, a grotesque victim of severe physical deformities ...

(Ben-Zvi 1990: 91)

Mary Bryden's *Women in Samuel Beckett's Prose and Drama* (1994) read Beckett's work through the filter of contemporary French theory (with particular reference to the work of the French feminists Julia Kristeva and Helene Cixous). In Bryden's view, the development of Beckett's work was marked by an interesting shift in the status and treatment of female characters

[The] evolution of Beckett's artistic practice is, I suggest, from an essentialist and often deeply mysoginistic construction of Woman

173

towards more erratic, often contingent or indeterminate gender configurations. In this, it may be set in parallel with a Western intellectual tradition which first of all Man-handles Woman into a sequestered space of dangerous alterity and then produces the tools necessary to dismantle – or at least disclose – that same accretive machinery ...

(Bryden 1994: 7)

In describing this movement, Bryden borrowed a term from the work of two French theorists, Gilles Deleuze and Felix Guattari; Beckett's writing, she argued, moved towards a state that Deleuze and Guattari had described as 'deterritorialisation', that is, a style of writing that existed outside familiar boundaries of gender and social organisation. The women in Beckett's later work seemed unconstrained by the usual dichotomies that structured their experience in the earlier work

Thus, as an illustration of the marked contrast between the women of Beckett's early fiction and those of Beckett's later writing (from his turn towards drama and thereafter), one many observe that the poles stasis/ movement, sterility/ fertility, absence/ presence do not operate in like fashion throughout the work. Further pairs could be added, but these alone make the point that, while both male and female are insistently and indiscriminately associated with the values of stasis, sterility and absence in the later work, it is their opposites – movement, fertility, presence – which contribute towards the differentiation of women as alien species in the earlier fiction ...

(Bryden 1994: 89)

In other words, men and women came to share characteristics in the later work that were, in the earlier work, almost exclusively male. This meant that, for Bryden, Beckett did not create women as female essences, incarnations of a peculiarly female life-force

On the whole, though, women are not spirit-guides, or even body-guides. They have their own spirits and bodies to energise as best they can. The route is full of setbacks for all, and they struggle alongside males in a hostile lifescape in which comradeship is sometimes a boon, sometimes a curse.

(Bryden 1994: 109)

## iii: Psychoanalytic/mythic criticism

Beckett, as a young man in London, had encountered the new science of psychology for himself, and that encounter had an undoubted influence over his development as an artist. In this, he was not alone; the impact of psychology on the cultural and artistic life of the twentieth century has been profound and far-reaching, stretching as far as the study of literature. The work of three psychoanalysts in particular have proved a fertile source of ideas for literary theorists. Sigmund Freud, the father of modern psychoanalysis, identified the human mind as driven as much by unconscious drives and desires as by rational decisions; for Freud, the work of art was a reflection of the psyche of the artist, and, by extension, an indication of the psychic life of the society in which that artist lived and worked. The value of art to a society was as a psychic safety valve, in which the reader or viewer experienced, from a position of relative safety, the unstated but powerful urges and drives that governed their own lives.

Carl Jung, on the other hand, saw the unconscious as universal; for Jung, an individual's behaviour was influenced by a variety of archetypal patterns and models that were common to all human societies, even though the precise constitution of those archetypes might vary from society to society. This construction, termed by Jung the 'collective unconscious', formed the backdrop to all branches of human behaviour; a work of art could not help but engage with it. In other words, for Jung the development of human consciousness obeyed certain patterns found in religious and spiritual myths; these myths were not simply inventive fictions, designed to explain the workings of a particular religion or a particular social structure, but themselves revealed and described fundamental patterns of human thought and behaviour.

Finally, the French psychoanalyst, Jacques Lacan, developed the idea of the unconscious mind (inherited from Freudian theory) along lines laid out by Saussure in the study of language. For Lacan, the unconscious developed as a language; the infant, learning how to speak, came to see itself as a linguistic sign, and came to deal with itself as a social construction independent of its original self. The learning of language was a crucial stage in a developmental process that began with the child's ability to recognise him or herself in a mirror; this crucial stage in infant development, called by Lacan the 'mirror stage' represented the first time that the growing child recognised itself as a separate being (in Lacanian terms, recognised itself as 'other'; as an object separate and distinct from other objects in the world, and from itself as a subject). An artwork replicated this fundamental split in the human mind, between the self as subject and the self as object; it can also provide a model for the social role that language plays in fixing the individual in a pre-existing social structure. Lacan's thought, as might be expected from the above description, proved very influential for feminist theorists. Lacan's work established language as primarily a socialising system, fixing the individual in a society already arranged in a hierarchy, in which authority was ultimately held by father-figures, and in which the idea of the feminine was a subordinate one.

Helene Baldwin's *Samuel Beckett's Real Silence* (1981) argued that Beckett's work was a version of the quest narrative, an underlying pattern of loss, searching and return that could be found throughout Western literature. However, Baldwin's analysis took this idea a stage further: for her, Beckett was engaged in a mystical search for the essential self. In contrast to the Jungian turn that such analyses would take later in the decade, she argued that the search was conducted within a fundamentally Christian worldview. Beckett's writing, for Baldwin, pursued a *via negativa*, a progress that allied it with mystical Christianity: it sought to discover *'Unconditioned Being'* (p. 16) by abandoning or negating the external world.

*Myth and Ritual in the Plays of Samuel Beckett* (1987), edited by Katherine Burkman, targued that Beckett's drama was a reworking of the mythic patterns that underlay Western culture. As Burkman put it in her introduction

> In the barren landscapes of Samuel Beckett's plays, dominated as they are by an ever more encroaching void, one may look in vain for rituals that bring renewal and myths that bespeak a meaningful redemption from that void. Yet Beckett's dramatic world is filled with ritual behaviour and is suffused with fragments of old myths ... Tempted as one might be to dismiss the kind of obsessive behaviours of Beckett's characters, from the vaudeville routines of *Waiting for Godot* or *Endgame* to the repetitive knocking of Listener in *Ohio Impromptu*, as habit, which is as Vladimir says 'a great deadener', one may not do so. For the dynamic of Beckett's plays continually reveals ways in which habit, as it fails to deaden, takes on a ritual aspect: and ritual in these plays moves always toward the meanings that linger in the mythical fragments that abound – and even toward the creation of new myths.
>
> (Burkman 1987: 13)

The collection included an essay by Stephen Watt, linking Beckett's work in the theatre to the work of the post-modern theorist Jean

Baudrillard ('Beckett by way of Baudrillard: Toward a Political Reading of Beckett's Drama'). Watt argued that the rituals in Beckett's plays were in themselves failures; if it was the goal of a religious ritual to achieve transcendence, then the rituals in Beckett denied transcendence, and simply made apparent, to the characters and to the audience, that the characters lived in the same material relation to the world as the audience did. Watt's essay, therefore, took a rather more political view of Beckett's work than most critics had: the character's relation to their possessions, for example, displayed the same acquisitive pride that could be found in the relation between man and his possessions in advanced capitalism.

A different approach to deconstruction was taken by Mary Doll, whose *Beckett and Myth: An Archetypal Approach* (1988) attempted to read Beckett's work as a characteristically post-modern reflection on the Jungian idea of the mythic archetype

> My critical approach to Beckett's work borrows from the implica-
> tions of post-modern thinking, of which deconstruction theory is
> a part. Like the postmodernists, I see Beckett debunking the systems
> of Western culture that perpetuate a closed system. Like the decon-
> structionists, I see Beckett presenting contextual encounters in
> every text, communicating from within the shattered pieces. Con-
> sistent with this post-modern, deconstructive approach, I break
> with traditional Jungian criticism as it has so often been applied
> to literary texts, reifying characters into stereotypes of archetypes.
> Jung's depth psychology became, in the hands of modernist critics,
> just another system, like that of Kantian idealism, that owed little
> to the phenomena of images, patterns or sounds. My claim, on
> the contrary, is that Beckett's work lends itself wonderfully to a
> mythopoetic method precisely because it breaks form. It not only
> eschews the established systems of Western philosophy, it also
> rejects other systems as Jungian criticism that impose themselves
> in gridlike certainty ... rather, Beckett's poetics of myth allows us
> to see patterns, and to hear patterns, and to read patterns afresh.
> (Doll 1988: 4–5)

So, therefore, Doll's Beckett walked the *via negativa* as surely as did Helene Baldwin's or Lance St John Butler's (1988: 7), but in a more decidedly post-modern way: his rejection of the modernist tools of structure and rationality, and his deconstruction of the characteristic literary and philosophical forms that were shaped by those tools, led him back to that which could be expressed, but could only be experienced

> ... Beckett's proposal is radical, in the same way that an archetypal approach is radical, for it is an urging to let go the literal way and to return instead to what one can neither hear nor see clearly: a return to the archetypes. But rather than reifying archetypes into such Jungian terms as anima, animus and trickster, Beckett's archetypal return takes away labels (which are, after all, only literature). His texts subvert, destroy, deviate: readers are torn from their safe resting places into the black pause. An archetypal approach to Beckett's texts is not interested in identifying archetypes but rather in allowing the coarse and violent images to come forth of themselves. For there, in the black pause, strange textual figures and images force us to acknowledge their otherness, and in otherness lives the soul. Beckett's regressive quest into empty space thus truly accomplishes a miracle ... We may not in Beckett's texts find our souls; but we may, at the very least, begin a journey that moves us from the rocky shore of egoism into the waters of all time.
>
> (Doll 1988: 7)

It can be seen that Steven Connor (see above) and Doll utilised the idea of the post-modern in radically different ways; in Connor's case, it was to destabilise all meanings and meaning systems: in Doll, it was to return to the underlying, pre-rational flood of images and figures that, for the Jungian, are part of the psychological inheritance of each human being.

David Watson's study of the prose, *Paradox and Desire in Samuel Beckett's Fiction* (1991) began by noting two main strands in Beckett criticism up to this point; one (the modernist approach) saw Beckett's work as engaged in a search for the essential self; and the second, described as existentialist by Watson, thought of it as an attempt to abolish the communicative power of language. For Watson, the second approach was by far the most useful, and during the course of his study he developed the idea in a distinctly post-modern direction. Using Lacan, Watson described the Beckett narrator as a shifting signifier; that is, as a character that had no essential, authentic self. The Beckett character, therefore, was a liar whose lies persisted; he or she recreated a life from moment to moment – and none of these moments had any more intrinsic claim to truth than any other. The character's speech created the character's life; but because he or she wanted to reach the end of speech, the subject in Beckett was trapped in a psychological paradox

The paradox of the Beckettian self is the paradox of desire: the desire for a silence which is beyond language is precisely the desire which maintains the subject in language, which obliges it to express ...

(Watson 1991: 44)

This had profound implications, not only on the characteristic concerns of the Beckett subject, but also on the structure of the novels themselves. Watson saw Beckett's writing as a denial of the symbolic order of language; the characters might wish to narrate, might feel themselves driven to tell and retell their experiences, but this did not mean that they would through telling their tales, achieve coherence. In fact, according to Watson, the texts were more likely to digress than to progress

[The] whole text is in a state of constant digression, indiscriminately setting off in all directions without any overall controlling influence on the presentation of information. Whereas the realist narrative text always strives to recuperate difference in sameness, Beckett's novels seem to take the opposite course, one of perpetual dispersal, of an anarchy of information that no narrative can ever bind ...

(Watson 1991: 76)

Eyal Amiran discerned a series of metaphysical oppositions (between the journey and the home; between the self and the other) that provided a structure for Beckett's work (*Wandering and Home: Beckett's Metaphysical Narrative* (1993)). Paul Davies' *The Ideal Real: Beckett's Fiction and Imagination* (1994) argued that Beckett's work bore striking similarities to gnosis (that is, with the revelation of spiritual mysteries). Beckett's writing, which rejected the physical body and dealt scathingly with rationality was, for Davies, an exploration of the deepest workings of the human imagination. As Davies acknowledged, this view of Beckett had an affinity with Mary Doll's work on Beckett and Jungian psychoanalysis (see above); however, this was because Beckett and Jung followed parallel paths

... I ... suggest that Beckett's interest and Jung's coincide on the issue of locating the self, whether it should be identified with the acculturated 'personality' or with something deeper which neither parents nor education nor milieu can do anything to define or modify other than to expedite or frustrate its development. These two possible 'selves' have rarely been more explicitly contrasted than in Beckett's short pieces ' Afar a Bird' and 'I Gave Up Before Birth [two of the *Fizzles*]. Here one self (the higher self) expresses a resentment nothing short of stinging toward the other 'social', 'cultured' self, which was stilted early on into almost total suspension. The question, as Beckett saw, is not the province of the psychologist alone. Perhaps Jung also appealed to Beckett precisely because he refused to exclude the arts, music, religion, alchemy, cosmology, and myth from his investigations of human identity, and indeed increasingly saw that the greatest need of our time was to give those things a central place in psychological work ...

(Davies 1994: 20)

---

## iv: Humanist/introductory/miscellaneous criticism

---

The theoretical debates outlined above did not entirely overwhelm the humanist approach to Beckett's work; indeed at the beginning of the 1980s Beckett criticism showed few signs of their influence. The decade began with the publication of Ruby Cohn's third book on the author, this time focusing exclusively on the theatre (*Just Play: Beckett's Theatre* (1980)). Cohn described the development of Beckett's theatre as a progression toward 'theaterreality'; in other words, Beckett's plays reduced theatre to its absolute essentials, and, in so doing, revealed the fundamental tensions within the theatrical event

> Beckett's plays are nourished on fundamental tensions – words wrung from silence, words belied by gesture, gestures wrestled from inertia, darkness invaded by light, hope betrayed by habit, passion eroded by compassion, mind divorced from feeling, mismatched couples straining to part. My words might read abstractly, but the tensions in the plays are excruciatingly concrete, and they are unique to each play ...
>
> (Cohn 1980: 12)

Interestingly, this commitment to the concrete experience enshrined in each play led Cohn to reject the idea that Beckett's work was at root existential, concerned with the description of human life as unfixed, engaged in the search for an essential, defining self that could not, in fact, be reached. For Cohn, the plays themselves had increasingly become dramatisations of essential existence

> Although Beckett has been confused with the philosophically existential, he has moved ever closer to the essential: events recede

180

into tones, characters precipitate into a single inward-looking mind, imagery approaches nudity, questions remain unanswered, sentences shrink to elliptical phrases, and yet Beckett continues to compose new configurations with a few tenacious words ...

(Cohn 1980: 13)

Cohn divided her study into a series of through views, on Beckett's use of stage space, stage time, soliloquy, dialogue, and language; in each, she discerned a gradual reduction to theatrical essentials. In addition, she analysed the fragment *Human Wishes*, the then-unpublished *Eleutheria*, and the substantially rewritten *Endgame*; and her final section dealt with the work in performance, including (for the first time in a work of Beckett criticism) analyses of Beckett's own directorial practice, and of the work of those with whom the author habitually worked (Blin, Magee, MacGowran, Schnieder, and Whitelaw) **[37–8, 44–5]**. She also included a chapter on cross-genre performances (which contains a full description of the American avant-garde Theatre Company, Mabou Mines', staging of *The Lost Ones*, one of the most renowned transpositions of Beckett's work). John Pierro's study *Structures in Beckett's Watt* and Eugene Kaelin's *The Unhappy Consciousness: The Poetic Plight of Samuel Beckett* (both 1980) both took a conventionally humanistic approach to Beckett's work. James Knowlson edited a volume on *Krapp's Last Tape* (1981) which blended discussion of the genesis of the play with descriptions of the text in performance; the book also included a selection of critical interpretations.

*Samuel Beckett: Humanistic Perspectives* (1983), edited by Morris Beja, S.E. Gontarski, and Pierre Astier, collected together papers delivered at a symposium on Beckett held at Ohio State University. The collection was, by and large, a restatement and expansion of the traditional approach to Beckett's work; the contributors included Ruby Cohn, James Knowlson, Richard Coe, Rubin Rabinowitz, H. Porter Abbot, Gontarski himself, Hersh Ziefman, Enoch Brater, and Nicholas Zurbrigg (all established, or soon to be established, Beckett scholars). All in all, the gathering was one of the most impressive in the history of Beckett scholarship up to this time (Beckett himself even contributed to it: the play *Ohio Impromptu* was written for, and first performed as part of, the symposium). James Knowlson's essay, 'Beckett's 'Bits of Pipe'', referred to a dismissive comment that Beckett had made to Knowlson about the status of quotations in his work: Beckett likened them to bits of pipe that he carried around with him, which were almost mechanically inserted into the text with no particular attention paid to their precise meaning. Knowlson developed this point, arguing that, in *Happy Days* **[40, 83–4]** for example

> Winnie's 'classics' differ hardly at all... from the remainder of the text. It may be said, of course, that part of their function is to add further levels of meaning. But the variation in voice, level, tone and register that they introduce tend to predominate over the actual 'references' themselves. The 'bits of pipe' of which Beckett speaks do not 'refer', as he suggests, therefore, in this sense. To extend the plumber analogy a little further, however, they are of exactly the right shape, length, thickness, bore, even ring, for the job in hand. And as much as they do point outside the play, it is as part of a dramatic technique that aims, above all, to involve the active imagination of the spectator, liberating it rather than imprisoning it with the shackles of reference.
>
> (Beja, Gontarski and Astier 1983: 23–4)

An interesting perspective on Beckett's drama was offered by Yasunari Takahashi, who compared the world of Beckett's drama to the world of the Japanese Noh play, a world as highly formalised and codified as any of Beckett's dramatic texts. The volume also included two interesting essays on Beckett's work in relation to the process of writing ('The Harpooned Notebook: *Malone Dies* and the Conventions of Intercalated Narrative', by H. Porter Abbot, and Frederick Smith's 'Fiction as Composing Process: *How It Is*').

Charles Lyons published a study of Beckett's drama in the Macmillan Modern Dramatists series (*Samuel Beckett* (1983)): Kirstin Morrison compared the narrative strategies employed by Beckett and Pinter (*Canters and Chronicles: the Use of Narrative in the Plays of Samuel Beckett and Harold Pinter* (1983)). Morrison argued that, for both Beckett and Pinter, narrative did not achieve its conventional dramatic aim of explaining and furthering the action: rather, narrative was a way of evading the world

> ... When characters in Beckett's and Pinter's plays shift into narrative, it is often because they have gotten too close to painful emotional issues, which the conventions of narrative allow them to disguise. They substitute narrative for the present moment; events become confronted (or affirmed) as story while they are evaded (or negated) as life. And since issues connected with death and sex are amongst the most painful and threatening for many people, the evasions and revelations of Beckett's and Pinter's storytellers,

usually centring on these issues, seem to an audience all the more plausible ...

(Morrison 1983: 8)

One finds in Morrison's study a recurrence of the liberal humanist reading of Beckett so prominent in the 1960s: Beckett's characters mirror the world of the reader precisely because they do not seek refuge in the traditional strategies of fiction or theatre. The figure of Beckett the existentialist *manque* returned in 1984, with the publication of Lance St John Butler's *Samuel Beckett and the Meaning of Being: A Study in Ontological Parable*. For Butler, Beckett occupied the same territory as Heidegger and Sartre; like them, he expressed dissatisfaction with rationalism, and was concerned with deeper questions, primarily about the formation of the self. However, such profound questions could not be answered (because, to do so, Beckett would have to concern himself once more with the rationalism that he had decisively rejected): rather, his work took the form of a series of parables – demonstrative stories that provided the reader with an experience of the irrational core of the self

If it is true that the meaning of being can only be experienced and not explained it is perhaps the case that literature can come closer to it than philosophy. Samuel Beckett may in fact offer us a purer insight into ultimate reality even than those philosophers most neatly attuned to it.

(Butler 1984: 205)

For Butler, as for Helene Baldwin (see above), Beckett's writing expressed the inaccessible mystery of being; it described a *via negativa*, a rejection of the world in favour of the spiritual truth contained, inexpressibly, in Being. In the same year, Sidney Homan followed Ruby Cohn's 1980 study, in treating Beckett's theatre works as evocations of the theatrical event itself (*Beckett's Theaters: Interpretations for Performance*). Rubin Rabinowitz published a study of the fiction up to *Watt* (*The Development of Samuel Beckett's Fiction* (1984)): the book contained a chapter on the as yet unpublished short story, 'Echoes Bones'. Matti Megged published a comparative study of Beckett and his friend, the artist Giacometti (*Dialogue in the Void: Beckett and Giacometti* (1984)): Harold Bloom edited a volume in the Modern Critical Views series: and James Knowlson edited the production notebooks that Beckett had used for the 1981 production of *Happy Days* **[40, 83–4]** Knowlson's study contained facsimile reproductions of Beckett's own directorial notebooks; in a short introductory essay, he discussed the realisation of Beckett's reinterpretation in performance

> In Beckett's Royal Court production, the contrast between aspiration upwards and movement downwards operated at a literal and metaphorical level, informing both Winnie's busy chatter and the most ordinary of her gestures. Often this would-be cheerfulness of her first act 'usual voice'... was pierced by darker tones, as sorrow repeatedly 'kept breaking in'. As is shown by the section of the notebook ... entitled +... – (that is, positive/negative oppositions) sadness intruded even into words and phrases not overtly scored in this way ... [The] frequent contrasts in the text between images of expansion and contraction were echoed in Winnie's own movements. So her gesture as she went to pray was halted and her swooping movements into the bag were arrested, as she confronted the danger or running out of things to say ...
>
> (Knowlson 1984: 16–17)

The study of Beckett's production notebooks was continued by Gontarski (*The Theatrical Notebooks of Samuel Beckett: Vol 2, Endgame* (1992) and *Vol 4: The Shorter Plays* (1994)) and by Knowlson himself (*The Theatrical Notebooks of Samuel Beckett, Vol 3: Krapp's Last Tape* (1992)).

Linda Ben-Zvi's *Samuel Beckett*, published in 1986, was an introductory study of the author; John Calder's festschrift, *As No Other Dare Fail: For Samuel Beckett on His 80th Birthday* (1986), included an essay by James Knowlson on the Beckett archive at Reading. Patrick McCarthy edited a volume of criticism (*Critical Essays on Samuel Beckett*): Eoin O'Brien's *The Beckett Country: Samuel Beckett's Ireland* (1986), a lavishly illustrated volume, demonstrated the importance of the Irish landscape (and especially the landscape around Dublin) in Beckett's work. Enoch Brater's *Beckett at 80/ Beckett in Context* (1986) was a collection of essays brought together (as the title suggests) to commemorate the author's 80th birthday: as well as a number of retrospective re-evaluations of his most famous text, *Waiting for Godot*, the book contained essays by some of the most prominent Beckett scholars of the previous two decades (James Knowlson, Charles Lyons, Martin Esslin). Kier Elam, better known as a performance theorist, produced an essay on the rhetorical structure of *Not I*, **[43–4, 90]** arguing that the play functioned because the spectator performed his or her traditional role of deciphering the performance: the difference between Beckett's play and conventional drama being that the spectator created the rhetorical structure of the play in the absence of a clearly defined, physically wholly present onstage character

> ... The great achievement of *Not I* is to free the spectator's *imaginaire* ... so as to operate the same kind of 'blurring of the oral, anal and genital' aspects of the body in the body's very absence. This has nothing to do with metaphor or allegory, but is the effect of an extraordinarily uncompromising and seductive engagement with the what-not, with that negative *rhetorica* out of which Beckett has made great *ars* ...
>
> (Brater 1986: 147)

By the mid 1980s, Beckett's work (and especially the plays of the 1950s) had become staples of the English literature syllabus, both in school and at university: S.E. Gontarski edited a collection of critical essays (*On Beckett: Essays and Criticism*) in 1986; and the canonical status of his work was marked in 1987 by the publication of no less than three volumes aimed at students (Harold Bloom's edited *Samuel Beckett's Waiting for Godot*, a collection of critical essays in the Modern Critical interpretations series: Ruby Cohn's *Samuel Beckett, 'Waiting for Godot': A Casebook*, which collected together contemporary responses to the first productions with critical analyses of the play; and Jennifer Birkett's *Samuel Beckett's 'Waiting for Godot'*, in the Macmillan Master Guides series).

Enoch Brater's *Beyond Minimalism: Beckett's Late Style in the Theater* (1987) adopted a subdued humanist approach to the later dramas: Beckett's works were lyrical poems, but poems made concrete through the act of staging

> What is at stake here, dramatically, is not so much the voice of the character, but rather the voice of the playwright. The role of the actor changes. Sometimes telling a story, sometimes reciting what sound like lines of verse, the actor here is always a vehicle for Beckett. The strongest actor in this drama is the playwright himself. Language becomes the centre of the action in these plays because, in an attempt to relyricize the genre, this is the only way the voice of the would-be poet can break open the constraints of a performing arts medium. This is not drama in the shape of poetry, but poetry in the shape of drama. The experience for the audience in the theatre is like the experience of reading a poem, except that in this instance the poem has been staged. Language art and theatre art draw together, progressively validating through stage time and our own

time the purity of the writer's voice as he builds a sustained dramatic metaphor. In his late plays Beckett will pursue the limits and
possibilities of such a unified dramatic form even further, challenging his audience to analyse and encounter with him the special
effects on a stage situation when one form breaks into another.

(Brater 1987: 17)

For Brater, the plays only revealed their essentially poetic character
in retrospect, when the audience could view the action as a whole

Unlike a lyric poem, however, the merged surface of sight and sound
in *Footfalls* cannot be fully perceived as an integrated image until
the time of the play is over. Time encapsulates the cycle: the title
of the play contains the whole idea. While Mouth complains of a
'dull roar like falls' and Winnie mentions 'little ... sunderings, little
falls apart', what is a footfall but the sound of a foot falling through
space in time?

(Brater 1987: 63)

*Beckett Translating/ Translating Beckett* (edited by Alan Friedman,
Charles Rossman, and Dina Sherzer (1987)) drew together an eclectic
collection of essays around the loose idea of translation; the essays
covered not only the bilingual status of Beckett's work, but also the
other 'translations' that his work had encountered. The collection
included a section on Beckett's work in translation (which included
Brian Fitch's detailed essay on the English and French versions of
*Company*, which argued that the text had been revisioned in French,
and could therefore not really be called a translation of the original
English work); a section on the philosophical and cultural references
in Beckett's work; a section on Beckett's use of generic conventions
(which included an essay by Angela Moorjani on his use of the 'Magna
Mater' myth in *Molloy* and *Ill Seen Ill Said*); and sections on Beckett's
work in other media, and on the relation between his work and fine
art. The collection concluded with Ruby Cohn's tribute to Alan
Schneider, to whom the book as a whole was dedicated.

Rosemary Pountney's *Theatre of Shadows: Samuel Beckett's Drama
1956–1976* (1988) had been written, in fact, at the end of the 1970s; it
took the same approach to the drama as Gontarski had taken to the
prose in 1985, following the genesis of Beckett's drama from *All That
Fall* to *Footfalls* from the original manuscripts to the printed and performed text. Pountney noted, as Gontarski did, that Beckett 'vaguened'
his texts in the process of revision. Valerie Topsfield's *The Humour of*

*Samuel Beckett* (1988) seemed to look further back, to Hugh Kenner and to Cohn's first study: Beckett's work was a grimly comic existential quest for non-existent meaning, heavily influenced by Joyce, Descartes, Geulincx and the pre-Socratics: his laughter moved toward the laugh identified in *Watt* as the 'risus purus'; the laugh that laughed, desperately and yet heroically, at that which was unhappy. Nicholas Zurbrigg in *Beckett and Proust* (1988) found that Beckett's early monograph on the French author was an interesting misreading of Proust's work; Zurbrigg argued (as had Steven Rosen in the 1970s) that Beckett's study was heavily influenced by his concurrent reading of Schopenhauer, which led him to overestimate the tragic import of Proust's work.

Jonathan Kalb's *Beckett in Performance* (1989) began from a slightly different viewpoint than most works on Beckett's stage plays: whereas the common tendency was to analyse the content of the plays, Kalb set himself the task of describing the plays as theatrical constructs, texts that demanded a particular style and strategy in performance if they were going to succeed. This could only be found, Kalb argued, if the director and the actor approached Beckett's work with few of the preconceptions implicit in either traditional approaches to the dramatic text (Beckett did not supply the director and the actor with the conventional props of psychological realism) or the theatrical avant-garde (Beckett was not interested either in disrupting the theatrical event, or in the expressive freedom of the director and the performer)

> Part of Beckett's importance as a cultural figure is that he blurs ordinary distinctions between mainstream and avant-garde. Because he was embraced so readily as a classic he was able, in effect, to smuggle certain progressive ideas across the border of mainstream culture, and that achievement is, rightfully, his most celebrated: he has actually changed many people's expectations about what can happen, what is supposed to happen, when they enter the theatre. Not surprisingly, then, many avant-gardists, true to the bohemian habit of mind that considers any work compromised as soon as it attracts a wide audience, perceive this achievement as already ancient history and assume that their own work represents a radical departure from Beckett's. Actually, though, his work, particularly the media and late plays, remains in certain ways just as radical, as unassimmilable into traditional structures of theatrical production, as theirs.
>
> (Kalb 1989: 157–8)

Beckett's theatre, for Kalb, did not coincide with any of the major models of twentieth century drama: those involved in it found themselves face to face with the basic nature of the form itself. So, therefore, the actor discovered that he or she is put onstage to act; the awareness that nothing more was required of him could in itself be a profoundly disorienting realisation

> Unlike in classic roles ... actors in Beckett are barely even given opaque surfaces to hide behind if necessary; for the author's habit is to make the actor's denuding a part of his subject matter. Performers in the early works have found that they can progress only so far by imagining and imitating specific personalities; even after developing strong characterisations, they find themselves facing an emptiness onstage that is unbearable for them as actors. That emptiness is the essence of what Robbe-Grillet called their 'irredeemable presence', also a primary experience for spectators, a condition of acting ... that makes it impossible for audiences to believe completely in either the action's lifelikeness or its illusionism ... The general dilemma of the Beckett actor is subsumed in this problem of suspension; he need not convince anyone of particular truths (that his character or situation is real, for instance, or that we should accept this or that ideology), he need only keep on going, keep on acting, but with conviction and clown-like charisma if he is not to lose his audience and with it his *raison d'etre*.
>
> (Kalb 1989: 146)

1989 also saw two full-length studies: Andrew Kennedy's *Samuel Beckett* (a lucid untheoretical introduction to Beckett's work), and Paul Foster's *Beckett and Zen: A Study of Dilemma in the Novels of Samuel Beckett*. Finally in this year, Laurence Graver published an introductory study of *Godot* (*Samuel Beckett: Waiting for Godot*).

Thomas Coisineau's *Waiting for Godot: Form in Movement* (1990) was a guide, aimed at students, to Beckett's most famous play; its slant was rather more obviously theoretical than previous volumes (perhaps inevitably, given the drift in Beckett studies toward literary theory in the 1980s). Katherine Worth's *'Waiting for Godot' and 'Happy Days': Text into Performance* (1990), part of Macmillan's Text and Performance series, provided the student not only with a discussion of both texts, but with descriptions and analyses of productions (including two directed by Beckett: *Godot* at the Schiller Theatre in Germany in 1975, and *Happy Days* at the Royal Court in London in 1979); Cochran provided a discussion of the full range of Beckett's shorter prose. P.J.

Murphy (in *Reconstructing Beckett: Language for Being in Samuel Beckett's Fiction* (1990)) uncovered a fundamentally realistic strand in Beckett's writing; this realism came from Beckett's continuing engagement with ideas of representation, and with the idea of a life lived in time. He argued that Beckett's writing had, as its goal, an attempt to reintegrate life and art; and that the drift of Beckett's fiction was towards a guardedly positive relation between the writer and the written world. The study contained detailed analyses of *From an Abandoned Work* and *All Strange Away* – two of the shorter prose texts that had been rather ignored by Beckett scholars.

Shimon Levy's *Samuel Beckett: The Three I's* (1990) took a rather different theoretical perspective; Levy's study of the drama was heavily influenced by hermeneutics, a philosophical school particularly concerned with the problem of interpretation. In line with this Levy examined the interpretive strategies in Beckett's theatre; he argued that, in order to be understood, a drama requires the interaction of author, actor and audience (the three I's of Levy's title)

> Beckett as author is never totally eliminated from his works. Indeed, in the plays where the playwright rather than the implied author is the central subject behind the characters, Beckett draws particular attention to himself. The playwright is the maker of all the semantic content, to which the plays are respectively linked. In fact, only the literary work can be objectively self-referential. The essence of theatre involves a tripartite relationship between playwright, actor and audience. The notion of audience, from Beckett's point of view, is an implied figure: it is to be detected and discovered. In the same way, the playwright can be discovered by examining the text from the audience's point of view. Beckett actors are not only intermediaries of texts, but through their own self-referentiality they are intermediaries of self-consciousness: from that of the playwright to that of the audience. The playwright can be detected in his plays by examining the I of the role, which in Beckett's plays ... is a triple I. It is the 'I' of Beckett, the 'I' of the actor (as both person and role) and, finally and hopefully, the 'I' of the audience.
> (Levy 1990: 98–9)

In 1991, Enoch Brater and June Schlueter edited a useful volume on the use of Beckett's most famous text in the classroom (*Approaches to Teaching Beckett's* Waiting for Godot). In the same year, Beckett's Irish heritage was marked; he was included in the third volume of an anthology of Irish Writing, edited by Seamus Deane under the aegis of the theatre company Field Day; and John Harrington published a study of Beckett from the perspective of Irish literature and culture (*The Irish Beckett*). The year also saw a study of the earlier Beckett (Anthony Farrow's *Early Beckett: Art and Allusion in* More Pricks Than Kicks *and* Murphy).

Rubin Rabinowitz had been publishing articles on Beckett's work throughout the 1980s; these were reworked and collected together in *Innovation in Samuel Beckett's Fiction* (1992). The study made use of a relatively recent innovation in literary studies; the computer assisted concordance, which allowed Rabinowitz to describe the recurrence of terms and phrases in Beckett's work. The technique was most closely applied to the Trilogy; Rabinowitz was able to discover a network of repetitions that underlay each of the three novels, providing them with, if not a conventional structure, then at least with a common language and phraseology. John Pilling and Mary Bryden produced an edited study of the Beckett archives held at Reading University ('*The Ideal Core of the Onion': Reading Beckett Archives* (1992)) which contained one of the first readings of Beckett's final prose work *Stirrings Still* by Paul Davies. Sidney Homan and Kees Hessing produced work on the as yet underwritten area of Beckett's media plays; Homan assessed the texts from a director's standpoint (*Filming Beckett's Television Plays: A Director's Experience* (1992) and Hessing provided a useful listing of all Beckett's work to have appeared in the media (*Beckett on Tape: Productions of Samuel Beckett's work on Film, Video and Audio* (1992)). Steve Wilmer edited a collection of essays on Beckett's relation to his home city (*Beckett in Dublin* (1992)).

Lawrence Miller's *Samuel Beckett: The Expressive Dilemma* (1992) focussed mainly on the trilogy **[30–4, 66–72]** in discussing the novels, he discerned the presence of an unresolvable dilemma

> The novels carry out increasingly deep excavations of expressive dilemmas – the dilemmas that strand the author of a narrative, the writer of a text, and the speaker of a word between the terms that their expressions sought to connect ...
>
> (Miller 1992: xi)

The argument, then, recast Beckett's often quoted statements on the necessity and impossibility of expression; however, this did not mean that Beckett's work could be neatly slotted into the by-now conventional argument, posed by deconstructionists, that the text was merely indeterminate. Beckett's work posed incisive questions about the nature and meaning of art; in other words, there was more to Beckett than a writer's struggle with his writing

> At the end of the trilogy we seem to be offered only two options: more or less elaborate re-enactments of the recognition of dilemmas, or simple silence, a deliberate refusal to allow our reading to become writing, and art to become criticism. In the current critical climate, this is a choice between a professionally respectable exercise of deconstructive irony and an unprofessional display of amateurish embarrassment. But the force of Beckett's critique would be misspent if it were merely to urge such a choice. The difficulty of going on as writers and as readers indicates the need to entertain alternative ways of talking about art, and to redirect philosophical and cultural criticism towards the demands that we make of artistic production and reception ... The difficulty of determining a place of Samuel Beckett in literary history, then, is finally the difficulty of rethinking literary history, and discovering an organisation of our literary experience that does not repeat inexorably the conditions of literary production.
>
> (Miller 1992: xi)

In 1993, Lance St John Butler edited another collection of Beckett criticism, this time for the Critical Thought series published by Scolar Press (*Critical Essays on Samuel Beckett*); and Marius Buning and Lois Oppenheim co-edited *Beckett in the 1990s: Selected Papers from the Second International Beckett Symposium*. S.E. Gontarski assembled a *Beckett Studies Reader*; and Charles Krance edited a bilingual edition of two of Beckett's shorter works (*Samuel Beckett's* Company/Compagnie *and* A Piece of Monologue/Solo: *A Bilingual Variorum Edition*).

Christopher Ricks' *Beckett's Dying Words* (1993) was written from a traditional standpoint (during the course of the study, Ricks was rather scathing about the work of critics who were, for him, too committed to theory). The study, originally delivered as the Clarendon lecture series in 1990, began by declaring that Beckett's work manifested an apparently contradictory but nevertheless real human desire, the wish to die

> Most people most of the time want to live for ever. This truth is acknowledged in literature, including Beckett's. But like many a truth, it is a half-truth, not half true but half of the truth, as is the truth of a proverb. For, after all, most people some of the time, and some people most of the time, do not want to live for ever.

This counter-truth – that, on occasion and more than moodily, we want oblivion, extinction, irreversible loss of consciousness – is insufficiently, or is mostly prophylactically, rendered by literature. Authorities, sacred and secular, do not care for the thought; they do not want you to be dead. Except, perhaps, as a martyr, and even this they have their doubts about.

(Ricks 1993: 1)

From this starting point, Ricks went on to discuss the various ways in which Beckett's fiction rehearsed and enacted the desire to die. This desire manifested itself mainly on the level of language; for Ricks, Beckett's work abounded in linguistic redundancies, in phrases that missed their mark or that failed to express, in words that seemed to lose their meaning as soon as they were uttered.

*The Cambridge Companion to Beckett*, edited by John Pilling, collected together a series of accessible essays by, amongst others, Paul Davies on thN *nouvelles* and the *Trilogy*; Anna McMullan on Beckett the director; Kier Elam on the later plays, and P.J. Murphy, on Beckett's relation to philosophy. Lois Oppenheim edited *Directing Beckett* (1994) a collection of essays and interviews that dealt, in various ways, with the vexed question of the individual director's freedom to re-interpret Beckett's work. In her introduction, Oppenheim discussed the impact that the rise of the director as *auteur* (that is, as the author of the theatrical event) had had on the production of Beckett's plays

The matter of directorial freedom is highly complex, and any temptation to view it merely as generational, reflecting a movement from a pre-auteur aesthetic of directorial anonymity to the individualism of auteur direction ... is misleading. It is true that Roger Blin and Alan Schnieder, Beckett's foremost first-generation directors, though strikingly different in their artistry (the one resolutely anti-realist, the other pure Stanislavski) did not see themselves as invisible orchestrators: Schnieder viewed his role of director to be that of 'playwright's surrogate', and Blin thought his directorial contribution should go virtually unnoticed ... But their work could hardly be thought to represent some mainstream of Beckett directing against which a younger generation would be collectively reacting. The diversity of viewpoints represented in this volume clearly attests to the fact that the increased number of directors taking liberties with Beckett's plays in recent years is attributable only to the larger number and divergence of directors now working with them.

(Oppenheim 1994: 3–4)

Alongside interviews with contemporary directors of Beckett's work, the collection also included a number of essays, most of which argued that Beckett's work should be staged as written. For example, Robert Scanlon's 'Performing Voices: Notes from Stagings of Beckett's Work', noted that in Beckett's work the voice and the actor were always placed in a very precise relation on stage

> Beckett himself has said to me (and to others) that certain texts come from 'things heard' and others from 'things seen'. Some texts are generated by a visible figure, and others are heard only by an invisible auditor. These distinctions, in fact, define the difference between the dramatic and the non-dramatic texts ... If a voice cannot be located, then its text cannot be 'staged' by a live actor without disrupting the action (and thereby the intrinsic nature) of the piece. Since all the Beckett works are fundamentally structured around the voice, any handling of the text that fails to locate the voice accurately will disrupt the formal coherence of the work.
>
> (Oppenheim 1994: 3–4)

Enoch Brater's *The Drama in the Text* (1994) covered precisely the territory outlined in Scanlon's essay; Brater was concerned with the persistent presence of the voice in Beckett's later fiction, but was convinced that this did not mean that the prose works were themselves simply theatre works waiting for reinterpretation

> No wonder so many theater practitioners have been tempted to adapt Beckett's late prose works for the stage. There is indeed a drama to these little texts, one that looks, at first *aperçu*, very much like the Beckett we recognise in the theater. Fiction and drama, theatricality and textuality, seem to come together here ... and yet the drama is written into prose, based so securely on the sound of the human voice, and is not necessarily performable in the technical stage sense. For as it materialises in sound, Beckett's voice is a mise en abime without the accompanying mise en scene. Such prose is, in fact, a discourse in sound: no theater image takes centre stage – 'A voice comes to one in the dark', and though that is where theater takes place, in the dark – as the director Frederick Neumann reminded Beckett when he set about adapting *Company* for his company, Mabou Mines – the darkness is in this case more strictly imagined. Sound makes all the sense there is ...
>
> (Brater 1994: 12)

But, for Brater, the drama in the text is not simply in the unexpected presence of a voice in these texts; it is in the words themselves, and in the way Beckett creates patterns of sound an sense from their combination; as, for example, in the late prose work *Still*

> Set not in stone, but as prose on a page, *Still* makes us hear words interact: the process is a verbal kineticism whose protagonists are verbs, adverbs, adjectives and nouns. The drama is the spectacle and speculum of Beckett's language; the only hero in the play is the uncertain word. A *nature morte* [dead nature] 'impossible to follow let alone describe', *Still*, ironically, is not still at all. 'Trembling all over', the words of this piece quiver onto actuality. The word *still* itself, like the hours of a day, is sounded twenty-four times, a verbal journey in disorienting repetition that highlights inversion, opposition, and indeterminacy rather than stasis or immobility ...
>
> (Brater 1994: 70)

The year also saw the publication of a *Critique of Beckett Criticism: A Guide to Research in English, French and German*, a monumental undertaking co-written by P.J. Murphy, Werner Huber, Rolf Bruer and Konrad Schell.

---

## (d) RECENT CRITICISM: 1995–

---

In the past few years something of the heat of the theoretical debates of the mid and late 1980s has drained away from Beckett studies. Partly, this reflects the fact that deconstruction, post-structuralism, psychoanalytic criticism and feminist theory have themselves made their way into the critical mainstream, and are no longer regarded (for the most part) as outlandish and controversial; partly, Beckett studies has been altered by the publication of biographical studies that have provided a more rounded portrait of Beckett's life and work. In the late 1990s, debates over Beckett's place in theory have given way to studies that re-examine Beckett's work in the light of the new information contained in Lois Gordon's, Anthony Cronin's, and especially James Knowlson's biographies.

This is not to say that the theoretical debates have subsided altogether. H. Porter Abbott's *Beckett Writing Beckett: The Author in the Autograph* (1996) took issue with those critics who argued that Beckett's work was an intrinsically post-modern response to the problem of writing. Beckett did not produce work that treated language as a game, and that tried to subvert it

> ... [A] view of Beckett which features primarily the Beckett of linguistic and tropological subversion may fail to account for the intense earnestness that distinguishes him from so many of his post-modern contemporaries ...
>
> (Abbot 1996: 50)

Beckett was in earnest because his work was neither fiction nor autobiography; it was *autography*, or an attempt to create the self in the moment of writing

> In summary, what I am proposing is a fundamental categorical shift in our reading of Beckett, one that moves him out of fiction altogether and relocates him in that rarely occupied subset of autography ... These texts are as distant from fiction as they are from conventional autobiography ... Beckett's subset is writing governed not by narrative form nor any species of tropological wholeness but by that unformed intensity of being in the present which at every point in the text seems to approach itself ...
>
> (Abbot 1996: 17–18)

– an approach that developed the idea of 'imitative form' in Abbott's previous (1973) study.

Richard Begam's *Samuel Beckett and the Ends of Modernity* (1996) set the theoretical argument over Beckett's status in modernity and post-modernity in a historical context. He examined the sequence of novels from *Murphy* to *The Unnamable* as 'the most influential expression we have of the "end of modernity" '; in opposition to the texts of the nineteenth century (and the work of Joyce and Proust), Beckett's work stressed diversity over unity, and the unfinished over the finished text

> ... For Proust and Joyce, the truth of art ultimately consists in an act of finding ... But for Beckett art is generative rather than recuperative. The *Unnamable* delivers us, in a way no previous novel ever has, into a new literary domain where we explore a world not of transcendence but of contingency, a world not of truth but of fiction, a world not of finding but of making.
>
> (Begam 1996: 183)

Lois Oppenheim and Marius Bruning's co-edited collection *Beckett On and On* .... (1996) consisted of two sections; the first, on gender and genre, included essays from Johanneke Van Slooten ('Beckett's Irish Rhythms Embedded in His Polyphony'), and from Angela Moorjani ('Mourning, Schopenhauer, and Beckett's Art of Shadows'); the second on textuality and theatricality, contained essays by Gerry McCarthy ('Rehearsals for the End of Time; Indeterminacy and Performance in Beckett') and Krill O. Thompson ('Beckett's Dramatic Vision and Classical Taoism'). Gonul Pultar argued that the Trilogy was firmly placed in a Continental tradion of philosophical literature (*Technique and Tradition in Beckett's Trilogy of Novels* (1996)); and Hwa Soon Kim, in a study influenced by Derrida, Lacan and Bakhtin, argued that Beckett's work in the theatre enacted a dialogue between the characters' sense of hope, their compulsive need to act, and their strongly expressed wish for extinction (*The Counterpoint of Hope, Obsession and Desire for Death in Five Plays by Samuel Beckett* (1996)).

1997 brought two studies of Beckett's relation to psychoanalysis; but, as with Begum's study in the previous year, both contextualised their approach to Beckett's work in a historically grounded concept of psychoanalytic criticism. Phil Baker's *Beckett and the Mythology of Psychoanalysis* argued that Beckett was influenced not so much by the specific theories of one particular psychologist, but by the idea of psychoanalysis as a myth; that is, as a set of commonly held social assumptions about the structure of the mind

> ... [The] mythic aspect of psychoanalysis has become something of a commonplace. The reified concepts within psychoanalysis – the ego, the id, the instincts and so on-can be said to constitute a mythology ... But there is a larger, more pervasively ambient, sense in which the discourses of psychoanalysis have become mythological, which has to do not with its conclusions but with its legacy, and it is with this that the present study is concerned.
>
> There is a whole retrospective landscape of loss in mid-twentieth century culture constituted by notions such as the paradise of the womb, pre-Oedipal plenitude, parental prohibition, oceanic regression, narcissism, and the narratives of mourning and melancholia. Taken together, these constitute a distinctive terrain, and I shall argue that much of Beckett's major work has deep investments in this landscape ...
>
> (Baker 1997: xv)

J. D. O'Hara's *Samuel Beckett's Hidden Drives: Structural Uses of Depth Psychology* argued that Beckett's knowledge and use of psychoanalytic themes and motifs was in some ways purer than the commonly accepted view of Freudian thought, even though it was influenced by his reading of Schopenhauer

> Beckett's multitudinous uses of Freud sketch his sense of Freud. This Freud is a remarkably central version, free from the distortions of his early discoverers and from the overthrowings and alterations of recent times. The skeletal structure of Beckett's Freud is provided by the basic tenets of depth psychology: much of our psychic identity is *unbewussie*, beyond knowing and beyond control. Especially beyond control are those libidinal impulses basic to our existence. Beckett's reading of Schopenhauer undoubtedly made easy his acceptance of those elements; Schopenhauer's description of an amoral and almost omnipotent will and subservient intellect had prepared him, as they had prepared Freud himself.
>
> (O'Hara 1997: 281)

James Acheson's *Samuel Beckett's Artistic Theory and Practice* (1997) took an overview of Beckett's work from the earliest criticism to the end of the author's life; Acheson argued that Beckett's work was fundamentally concerned with the relationship between art and the limits of human knowledge.

Knowlson's biography (O'Hara 1997: 281) had reminded Beckett scholars of the author's debt to other artforms, particularly to painting and music. Two recent essay collections have analysed the influence of these artforms on his writing. Mary Bryden's *Samuel Beckett and Music* (1998) dealt with not only the use of music in Beckett's work, but also with the inherent musicality of his writing

> ... Beckett's sensitivity to a broad range of music was part of a much wider attainment to the aural medium, to ambient sounds, and to silence. The implications of this are multiple. Perhaps the musicality of Beckett's writing finds its clearest manifestation within the dynamics of theatre or live reading ...
>
> Nevertheless, all of Beckett's texts, whether they be prose, poetry, or drama, are the product of one who, by his own account, heard them in advance of writing them ...
>
> (Bryden 1998: 1)

Lois Oppenheim's collection *Samuel Beckett and the Arts: Music, Visual Arts and Non-Print Media* (1999) cast its net wider, taking in the influence of music, painting, and film on the development of Beckett's texts; it contained an interesting section on the television plays. In her introduction, Oppenheim noted a paradox in the Beckett text; it was intensely visual and musical, but these elements already existed in the text, and did not have to be teased out in performance

> ... Beckett was the consummate artist: extraordinary is the fact that his visionary use of such diverse modes of creative expression as stage, radio, television, and film emanated from within the confines of the printed page. The written word was his medium. Actors did not initially appear before him like dancers or other performance artists, the very sight of whom might help to shape ... the choreographic effect. Voices and sounds made music in his head; images from life and art he treasured remained inspirational throughout his career.
>
> (Oppenheim 1998: xx)

John Pilling's *Beckett Before Godot: The Formative Years (1929–1946)* (1998) provided a useful and interesting analysis of the formation of Beckett's writing before the intense burst of creativity following his return to Paris in 1946. Pilling argued that Beckett's early writing life could be divided into three sections; 1929 to 1932, when the young Beckett produced work in a volatile, if unfocussed manner; 1932–1936, the years in which Beckett wrote *Murphy,* and was forced to earn money by reviewing; and 1937–1946, the years in which Beckett came to accept failure, and began his struggle to find a voice based on that acceptance. Mary Bryden's *Samuel Beckett and the Idea of God* (1998) dealt with the persistent echoes of religion in Beckett's work. Jennifer Jeffers' edited collection *Samuel Beckett: A Casebook* (1998) brought together essays on Beckett's drama; the collection contained two notable contributions from Anna McMullan ('Performing Vision(s); Perspectives and Spectatorship in Beckett's Theatre') and from Christine Jones ('Bodily Functions: A reading of Gender and Performance in Samuel Beckett's *Rockaby*').

## (e) BIOGRAPHICAL STUDIES

Beckett's life – at least in outline – had been known to scholars from the 1950s to the 1970s; some studies (in particular Laurence Harvey's

*Samuel Beckett: Poet and Critic*) had contained quite detailed accounts of parts of it. Deidre Bair's biography (*Samuel Beckett*, first published in 1978) was the first full length study of Beckett's life to be published in any language. The work grew from Bair's doctoral thesis. Dissatisfied with existing studies of Beckett (that seemed to her to get lost in theoretical abstraction, as the authors used Beckett's work as a springboard from which to dive into the wilder seas of philosophical speculation), she approached Beckett, who told her that he would *'neither help nor hinder her'* (Bair 1978: 9). His diffidence concerning the project can be gauged from Bair's own comments

> Samuel Beckett was kind enough to see me whenever I went to Paris, even though I soon realised how much pain and embarrassment some of my questions caused him. Nevertheless, he answered them patiently and honestly. He introduced me to his family and wrote letters on my behalf and, all the while, I am sure he did not want this book to be written and would have been grateful if I had abandoned it.
>
> (Bair 1978: 10)

The Bair biography has become rather notorious amongst Beckett scholars: its numerous factual inaccuracies were discussed in articles by Martin Esslin (amongst others) and, at great length, in the newsletter *The Beckett Circle*. This first biography was undoubtedly flawed (P.J. Murphy called it 'thoroughly botched'(Murphy, Huber, Bruer and Schell 1994: 11)); and the portrait it paints of Beckett is, in some respects, rather lurid and overdramatic. Something of its flavour can be gleaned from the following description of Beckett during the few months he spent in Ireland at the end of the war

> The fragmentation of his life contributed to the 'sense of pain and urgency' [John Fletcher, *Samuel Beckett's Art*, p. 82] that drove him to recklessness and excess. He careened about the countryside with his cousin, William Heron, usually ending up in a pub called the Brazen Head, where drinks were served after closing time as long as there was someone to buy them. Often automobiles were wrecked, clothing lost or destroyed, and sometimes jewellery was removed from the body of a senseless drunk. Casual sexual encounters occurred in a haze of whiskey and were unremembered when the participants were sober ...
>
> (Bair 1978: 297)

It is not that Beckett was completely incapable of riotous behaviour (none of his biographers could claim this) or that he did not pass through periods of severe mental strain. The problem is that, for Bair, there sometimes seems to be little else in Beckett's life. The image of Beckett that emerges from the pages of Bair's biography is of a self-obsessed neurasthenic constantly haunted by the thought of death; even his writing is a source of danger (a breakdown accompanies the composition of *Watt*, and *Malone Dies* nearly finishes Beckett off). However, the biography did contain much that was interesting (particularly in relation to Beckett's wartime activities); and, even if Bair's work was fundamentally a missed opportunity, it was at least the first attempt to put the details in Beckett's life in some kind of accessible order.

Between the Bair biography and the biographies published after Beckett's death, an interim study appeared: Enoch Brater's *Why Beckett* was a relatively slim amalgamation of already available biographical information and quick literary analysis; its main interest lay in the copious illustrations that provided the reader with a visual record of Beckett's life and work.

Lois Gordon's study *The World of Samuel Beckett* set out to be a corrective to Bair's view of Beckett the inward-looking neurotic

> The present book, collating details from a wide assemblage of Beckett scholarship and focusing on the historical events through which he lived, creates an entirely different profile. My basic assumption is that despite Beckett's artistic images of debilitation and impotence – too often taken as projections of Beckett's own mental state – the public record describes a man of courage and resilience. This volume proposes that Beckett was a gentle but heroic man with a reservoir of toughness and strength that enabled him to pursue both an altruistic bent and the need for personal and artistic fulfilment. I would venture to say that Beckett's life – even in brief summary – was inspiring.
>
> (Gordon 1996: 3)

Gordon's was not a biographical study *per se*; rather, she placed Beckett firmly in the particular historical context of European political, social and cultural life, from Beckett's birth in 1906 to the period immediately preceding 'the siege in the room'. The study, although it did not contain any new biographical detail (and occasionally seemed to leave Beckett behind altogether) provided ample evidence of the traumatic historical periods through which Beckett had lived, from the Easter uprising in Ireland in 1916 to the end of the Second World War.

1996 was the year of the Beckett biography: in addition to Gordon's work, two more conventional biographical studies appeared, each one marking an advance on Bair's book. Anthony Cronin's *Samuel Beckett: The Last Modernist* benefited from the author's knowledge of the Irish milieu that had formed the backdrop to Beckett's early life; Cronin, a poet and novelist, shared some acquaintances with Beckett (Thomas McGreevy, Con Leventhal, John Calder and Barney Rosset, amongst others). The study contains much in the way of interesting detail about Beckett's life and times over the same period covered by Gordon; the latter part of his life is not dealt with in the same depth, and the chronology (particularly the order of publication and first performance of Beckett's various works) is sometimes rather confused.

James Knowlson's *Damned to Fame: The Life of Samuel Beckett* is as close as we are likely to come to an authorised biography: Knowlson began work on it in the year of Beckett's death, and told Beckett that he would only write a biography with his subject's express approval. Beckett sent back a message, that said '*To biography of me by you it's yes*' (Knowlson 1996: xix). Knowlson benefited from greater access to primary sources, and to Beckett's own diaries, than had his other biographers. The portrait of Beckett is in consequence that much more detailed (even if it is coloured by Knowlson's obvious affection for his subject). The Beckett of Knowlson's biography is much calmer and tougher (particularly in the second part of his life) than the Beckett described by Bair; he is also more engaged in the world. In one of Knowlson's biographical *coups*, Beckett's trip to Germany in 1937 is described with the aid of Beckett's own diaries, which reveal a far more alert and antagonistic reaction to Nazism than had previously been thought (thus making Beckett's activities in the resistance during the war more comprehensible). Knowlson also revealed Beckett's low-key support of Amnesty International, the anti-apartheid movement, and of movements protesting the French involvement in Algeria. The years of Beckett's fame are given as much weight as those of his obscurity; and the nature of his relationships with his family and with his wife are delineated carefully and (as far as it is possible to judge) fully. The Knowlson biography is liable to remain the standard biographical work on Beckett for quite some time.

In 1998, the first collection of Beckett's letters was published; *No Writer Better Served* (edited by Maurice Harmon) collected together Beckett's correspondence with Alan Schneider from the first American production of *Godot* to Schneider's death in 1984. The collection tended to favour Schneider, whose letters were longer and more garrulous (especially towards the correspondence's end, when Beckett's replies became increasingly telegrammatic); but it contained much that was interesting, especially on the first American production of *Godot* and on the production of *Film*.

## Further Reading

As Beckett's work has figured in some of the more abstruse theoretical debates of the past two decades, the following works might be useful in explaining the key terms of those debates in more depth. Peter Barry's *Beginning Theory* (Manchester University Press, Manchester, 1995) and Jonathan Culler's *Literary Theory: A Very Short Introduction* (Oxford University Press, Oxford, 1997) are useful introductions and guides to the field in general. Terence Hawkes *Stucturalism and Semiotics* (Methuen, London, 1977) remains a useful introduction to semiotic analysis; Christopher Norris' *Deconstruction: Theory and Practice* (Routledge, London, 1991) is a readable guide to Derrida and to the development of post-structuralism. Anthony Eliot's *Psychoanalytic Theory: An Introduction* (Blackwell, Oxford, 1994), Michael Jacobs' *Sigmund Freud* (Sage, London, 1992) and Madan Samp's *Lacan* (Harvester Wheatsheaf, London, 1992) will provide helpful information on the development of psychoanalytic theory; Susan Rowland's *C.G. Jung and Literary Theory: The Challenge from Fiction* (Macmillan, Basingstoke, 1999) is an interesting recent contribution to Jungian textual analysis. Finally, feminist theory is a large and complex field; Mary Eagleton's *Feminist Literary Theory: A Reader* (Blackwell, Oxford, 1996) and Ed David Lodge's *Modern Criticism and Theory: A Reader* (Longman, 1988) are both a good introduction and a useful guide to further reading.

# CHRONOLOGY

| | |
|---|---|
| 1906 | Samuel Beckett (SB) born (13 April) in Foxrock, Co. Dublin, youngest son of May and Bill Beckett (one older brother, Frank). |
| 1920 | SB attends Portora Royal School, Enniskillen, Co. Fermanagh. |
| 1923 | SB attends Trinity College Dublin, reading French and Italian. |
| 1928 | SB moves to Paris for the first time, to take up lectureship at the Ecole Normale Superieure. In Paris, he meets Thomas MacGreevy, who introduces him to James Joyce. |
| 1929 | 'Dante...Bruno.Vico..Joyce' (essay) and 'Assumption' (short story) published. |
| 1930 | 'Whoroscope' published. SB returns to Dublin to take up post at TCD. |
| 1931 | *Proust* published. |
| 1932 | SB resigns post at Trinity College Dublin and moves to Paris. *Dream of Fair to Middling Women* composed (unpublished in his lifetime). Returns to Dublin. |
| 1933 | Deaths of SB's father and of Peggy Sinclair (cousin). *More Pricks than Kicks* (short stories) accepted for publication. SB leaves for London at the end of the year, to undergo psychoanalysis (treatment lasts until 1935). |
| 1934 | *More Pricks than Kicks* published. |
| 1935 | SB attends Tavistock lecture given by C.G. Jung, and composes *Murphy*. *Echoes Bones and Other Precipitates* (poems) published. At the end of the year, SB returns to Dublin. |
| 1936 | SB visits Germany. |
| 1937 | SB returns to Dublin and, in October, moves to Paris. *Murphy* accepted for publication. |
| 1938 | SB stabbed while walking in Paris at night; during recovery, he forms a relationship with Suzanne Descheveaux-Dumesnil, which lasts until her death. *Murphy* published. |
| 1940 | Hitler invades France. SB flees Paris, and meets Joyce for the last time; subsequently, he returns to the capital, and joins the Resistance. |
| 1942 | Resistance cell betrayed; SB and Suzanne flee to Roussillon, a village in the Vaucluse. |
| 1942–5 | In Roussillon: SB writes *Watt*. |
| 1945–6 | At the end of the war, SB visits family in Ireland; while there, he gains a fundamental insight into the nature of his writing. |

He works for Irish Red Cross, building a hospital in Saint-Lo.

1946–53 'The Siege in the Room'. Period of intense creative activity. SB writes the *Nouvelles* ('First Love', 'The Expelled', 'The Calmative', 'The End'); *Mercier et Camier*; The Trilogy (*Molloy*, published 1951; *Malone Dies*, published 1951; *The Unnamable*, published 1953); *Texts for Nothing*; and two plays *Eleutheria* and *Waiting for Godot*.

1950 Death of SB's mother.

1953 *Godot* produced in Paris.

1954 Death of Frank, SB's older brother.

1955 First production of *Godot* in London. SB begins *Endgame*.

1956 SB writes *All That Fall*.

1957 *Endgame* staged (in French) in London.

1958 *Endgame* in English produced in London, on a double bill with *Krapp's Last Tape*.

1959 SB writes *Embers*, and begins writing *How It Is* (*Comment C'est*).

1960 SB begins *Happy Days*.

1961 *How It Is* published. SB writes *Words and Music* and *Cascando*. Marriage to Suzanne.

1962 SB writes *Play*. *Happy Days* produced in London.

1964 Shooting of *Film* (directed by Alan Schnieder). *Play* produced in London.

1965 SB writes *Eh Joe* and *Come and Go*. *Imagination Dead Imagine* published.

1966-7 Short fiction collected in *Tetes-Mortes* (in French) and (*No's Knife*) in English.

1969 SB wins Nobel Prize for Literature. Short dramatic sketch *Breath* produced in London as part of revue (*Oh! Calcutta*)

1970 *Le Depeupleur* (*The Lost Ones*), *Mercier et Camier* and 'Premier Amour' ('First Love') published.

1972 *Not I* written and produced.

1974 SB writes *That Time*.

1975 SB writes *Footfalls*.

1976 *For to End Yet Again and Other Fizzles* and *All Strange Away* published. *That Time* and *Footfalls* produced in London, on triple bill with Not I. SB writes *Ghost Trio*.

1977 SB Writes *...but the clouds...*; produced by BBC alongside *Ghost Trio* and *Not I* under the collective title *Shades*. Begins *Company*.

1979 *A Piece of Monologue* staged. *Company* published.

1980 SB writes *Rockaby* and *Ohio Impromptu*.

1981 *Mal Vu Mal Dit* (*Ill Seen Ill Said*) published. *Quad* filmed for German Television. SB begins *Worstward Ho*.

1982    SB writes *Catastrophe*. *Nacht und Traume* produced for German Television.
1983    *Worstward Ho* published. SB writes *What Where*.
1986    SB begins *Stirrings Still*.
1988    Diagnosed as suffering from Parkinson's Disease. *Stirrings Still* published. SB writes 'What is the Word'.
1989    Death of Suzanne Beckett (17 July); SB dies (22 December).

# BIBLIOGRAPHY

Abbott, H. Porter *The Fiction of Samuel Beckett: Form and Effect*. Berkley, Los Angeles, and London: University of California Press (1973)
—— *Beckett Writing Beckett: The Author in the Autograph*. Ithaca: Cornell University Press (1996)
Abel, Lionel *Metatheater: A New View of Dramatic Form*. New York: Hill and Wang (1963)
Acheson, James *Samuel Beckett's Artistic Theory and Practice: Criticism, Drama and Early Fiction*. New York: St Martin's Press (1997)
Acheson, James, Arthur, Kateryna (eds) *Beckett's Later Fiction and Drama: Texts for Company*. London: Macmillan (1987)
Alvarez, Al *Samuel Beckett*. New York: Viking (1973)
*AMULA*. No. 55: Samuel Beckett Special Issue (1981)
Amiran, Eyal *Wandering and Home: Beckett's Metaphysical Narrative*. University Park: Pennsylvania State University Press (1993)
Andonian, Cathleen Culotta *Samuel Beckett: A Reference Guide*. Boston: Hall (1989)
*Art Press*. No. 55: Samuel Beckett Special Issue (1981)
Astro, Alan *Understanding Samuel Beckett*. Colombia, SC: University of South Carolina Press (1990)
Bair, Deidre *Samuel Beckett: A Biography*. New York: Harcourt Brace Jovanovich (1978)
Baker, Phil *Samuel Beckett and the Mythology of Psychoanalysis*. London: Macmillan (1997)
Baldwin, Helene L. *Samuel Beckett's Real Silence*. University Park: Pennsylvania State University Press (1981)
Barale, Michele A. and Rabinwoitz, Rubin *A KWIC Concordance to Samuel Beckett's Trilogy: 'Molloy', 'Malone Dies', 'The Unnamable'*. 2 vols. New York: Garland (1988)
Barge, Laura *God, The Quest, The Hero: Thematic structures in Beckett's Fiction*. Chapel Hill: University of North Carolina Press (1988).
Barnard, G.C. *Samuel Beckett: A New Approach*. New York: Dodd (1970)
*Beckett Circle, The*. No 1 (1978)
Begam, Richard *Samuel Beckett and the End of Modernity*. Stanford: Stanford University Press (1996)
Beja, Morris, Gontarski, S.E., Astier, Pierre *Samuel Beckett: Humanistic Perspectives*. Colombus: Ohio State University Press (1983)
Ben-Zvi, Linda *Sameul Beckett*. Boston: Hall (1986)
—— (ed.) *Women in Beckett: Performance and Critical Perspectives*. Urbana and Chicago: University of Illinois Press (1990)
Birkett, Jennifer *'Waiting for Godot' by Samuel Beckett*. Macmillan Master Guides. London: Macmillan (1987)

Bloom, Harold (ed.) *Samuel Becket. Modern Critical Views.* New York: Chelsea House (1985)
—— (ed.) *Samuel Beckett's 'Waiting for Godot'.* Modern Critical Interpretations. New York: Chelsea House (1987)
—— (ed.) *Samuel Beckett's 'Endgame'.* Modern Critical Interpretations. New York: Chelsea House (1988)
Brater, Enoch *Beckett at 80/Beckett in Context.* Oxford: Oxford University Press (1986)
—— *Beyond Minialism: Beckett's Late Style in the Theatre.* Oxford: Oxford University Press (1987)
—— *Why Beckett.* London: Thames and Hudson (1989)
—— *The Drama in the Text: Beckett's Late Fiction.* Oxford: Oxford Univerity Press (1994)
Brienza, Susan *Samuel Beckett's New Worlds: Style in Metafiction.* Norman: University of Oklahoma Press (1987)
Bruning, Marius and Oppenheim, Lois (eds) *Beckett in the 1990s: Selected Papers from the Second International Beckett Symposium, held in the Hague, 8–12 April, 1992.* Amsterdam and Atlanta: Rodopi (1993)
Bryden, Mary *Women in Samuel Beckett's Prose and Drama: Her Own Other.* London: Macmillan (1993)
—— *Samuel Beckett and the Idea of God.* Basingstoke: Macillan (1998)
—— (ed.) *Samuel Beckett and Music.* Oxford: Oxford University Press (1998)
Burkman, Katherine H. *The Arrival of Godot: Ritual Patterns in Beckett's Drama.* London and Toronto: Associated University Press (1986)
—— (ed.) *Myth and Ritual in the Plays of Samuel Beckett.* London and Toronto: Associated University Press (1987)
Busi, Frederick *The Transformations of Godot.* Lexington: University Press of Kentucky (1980)
Butler, Lance St. John *Samuel Beckett and the Meaning of Being: A Study in Ontological Parable.* London: Macmillan (1984)
—— *Critical Essays on Samuel Beckett.* Critical Thought Series, 4. Aldershot: Scolar Press (1993)
—— and Davis, Robin J.(eds) *Rethinking Beckett: A Collection of Critical Essays.* London: Macmillan (1988)
Calder, John *Beckett at Sixty: A Festschrift.* London: Calder and Boyars (1967)
—— *As No Other Dare Fail: For Samuel Beckett on his 80th Birthday.* London: Calder (1986)
*Centerpoint,* Vol 4, No2: Samuel Beckett Part Issue (1981)
Chevingy, Belle Gale *Twentieth Century Interpretations of Endgame.* Eaglewod Cliffs, NJ: Prentice-Hall (1969)
Cochoran, Robert *Samuel Beckett: A Study of the Short Fiction.* New York: Twayne (1990)
Coe, Richard N. *Samuel Beckett.* New York: Grove Press (1964).
Cohn, Ruby *Samuel Beckett: The Comic Gamut.* New Brunswick, NJ: Rutgers University Press (1962)
—— (ed.) *A Casebook on 'Waiting for Godot'.* New York: Grove Press (1967)

—— *Back to Beckett*. Princeton: Princeton University Press (1973)

—— (ed.) *Samuel Beckett: A Collection of Criticism*. New York: McGraw-Hill (1975)

——*Just Play: Beckett's Theater*. Princeton: Princeton University Press (1980)

—— (ed.) *Samuel Beckett, 'Waiting for Godot': A Casebook*. London: Macmillan (1987)

Coisineau, Thomas *'Waiting for Godot': Form in Movement*. Boston: Twayne (1990)

*College Literature*, Vol 8, No 3: Samuel Beckett Special Issue (1981)

Connor, Steven *Samuel Beckett: Repetition, Theory and Text*. Oxford: Blackwell (1988)

—— (ed.) *'Waiting for Godot' and 'Endgame'*. New Casebooks. New York: St Martin's Press (1992)

Cooke, Virginia (ed.) *Beckett on File*. London: Methuen (1985)

Copeland, Hannah-Case *Art and the Artist in the Works of Samuel Beckett*. Paris: Mouton (1975)

Cronin, Anthony *Samuel Beckett: The Last Modernist*. London: Harper Collins (1996)

Davies, Paul *The Ideal Real: Beckett's Fiction and Imagination*. London and Toronto: Associated University Press (1994)

Davis, Robin J. *Samuel Beckett: Checklist and Index of His Published Works, 1967–1976*. Stirling: The Library, University of Stirling (1979)

——, Butler, Lance St. John (eds), *'Make Sense Who May: Essays on Samuel Beckett's Later Works*. Gerrards Cross: Colin Smythe (1988)

Dearlove, J.E. *Accomodating the Chaos: Samuel Beckett's Nonrelational Art*. Durham: Duke University Press (1982)

DiPierro, John C. *Structures in Beckett's 'Watt'*. York, SC: French Literature Publications (1981)

Doherty, Francis *Samuel Beckett*. London: Hutchinson (1971)

Doll, Mary A. *Beckett and Myth: An Archetyphal Approach*. Syracuse: Syracuse University Press (1988)

Duckworth, Colin *Angels of Darkness: Dramatic Effect in Beckett with Special Reference to Ionesco*. New York: Barnes and Noble (1972)

Eliopulos, James *Samuel Beckett's Dramatic Language*. The Hague: Mouton (1975)

Esslin, Martin *The Theatre of the Absurd*. New York, Doubleday (1961)

—— (ed.) *Samuel Beckett: A Collection of Critical Essays*. Eaglewood Cliffs, NJ: Prentice-Hall (1965)

*Europe*, No 71 Samuel Beckett Special Number (June–July 1993)

Farrow, Anthony *Early Beckett: Art and Allusion in 'More Pricks then Kicks' and 'Murphy'*. Troy, NY: Whitson (1991)

Federman, Raymond *Journey to Chaos: Samuel Beckett's Early Fiction*. Berkley and Los Angeles: University of California Press (1965)

Federman, Raymond and Fletcher, John *Samuel Beckett: His Works and His Critics*. Berkley, Los Angeles and London: University of California Press (1970).

Finney, Brian *Since 'How It Is'; A Study of Samuel Beckett's Later Fiction*. London: Convent Garden Press (1972)

Fitch, Brian *Beckett and Babel: An Investigation into the Status of the Bilingual Work*. Toronto: University of Toronto Press (1988)

Fletcher, Beryl, *et al. A Student's Guide to the Plays of Samuel Beckett*. London: Faber and Faber (1978)

Fletcher, John *The Novels of Samuel Beckett*. London: Chatto and Windus (1964)

—— *Samuel Beckett's Art*. London: Chatto and Windus (1967)

Fletcher, John *Beckett: A Study of His Plays*. New York: Hill and Wang (1972)

Friedman, Alan Warren, Rossman, Charles, Sherzer, Dina and Spurling, John *Beckett Translating/Translating Beckett*. University Park: Pennsylvania State University Press (1987)

Friedman, Melvin J. (ed.) *Samuel Beckett Now: Critical Approaches to His Novels, Poetry, and Plays*. Chicago and London: University of Chicago Press (1970)

*Gambit International Theatre Review*. Vol 7, No 28: Samuel Beckett Part Issue (1976)

Gidal, Peter *Understanding Beckett: A Study of Monologue and Gesture in the Work of Samuel Beckett*. London: Macmillan (1986)

Gontarski, S.E. *Beckett's 'Happy Days': A Manuscript Study*. Colombus: Ohio State University Press (1977)

—— *The Intent of 'Undoing' in Samuel Beckett's Dramatic Texts*. Bloomington: Indiana University Press (1985)

—— (ed.) *On Beckett: Essays and Criticism*. New York: Grove Press (1986)

—— (ed.) *The Theatrical Notebooks of Samuel Beckett, Vol 2: 'Endgame'*. London: Faber and Faber (1992)

—— (ed.) *The Beckett Studies Reader*. Gainesville: University Press of Florida (1993)

—— (ed.) *The Theatrical Notebooks of Samuel Beckett, Vol 4: The Shorter Plays*. London: Faber and Faber (1993)

Gordon, Lois *The World of Samuel Beckett*. New Haven: Yale University Press (1996)

Graver, Lawrence *Samuel Beckett: 'Waiting for Godot'*. London: Thames and Hudson (1989)

—— and Federman, Raymond *Samuel Beckett: The Critical Heritage*. London, Henley and Boston: Routledge and Kegan Paul (1979)

Gluck, Barbara R. *Beckett and Joyce: Frendship and Fiction*. Lewisburg, PA: Bucknell University Press (1979)

Hale, Jane Alison *The Broken Window: Beckett's Dramatic Perspective*. West Lafayette, IN: Purdue University Press (1987)

Hamilton, Alice and Hamilton, Kenneth *Condemned to Life: The World of Samuel Beckett*. Grand Rapids, MI: Eerdmans (1976)

Harmon, Maurice (ed.) *No Author Better Served: The Correspondence of Samuel Beckett and Alan Schneider*. Cambridge, MA: Harvard University Press (1998)

Harrington, John P. *The Irish Beckett*. Syracuse: Syracuse University Press (1991)

Harrison, Robert *Samuel Beckett's 'Murphy': A Critical Excursion*. Athens: University of Georgia Monographs (1968)

Harvey, Lawrence E. *Samuel Beckett: Poet and Critic*. Princeton: Princeton University Press (1970)

Hassan, Ihab *The Literature of Silence: Henry Miller and Samuel Beckett*. New York: Knopf (1967)

Hayman, Ronald *Samuel Beckett*. London: Heinemann (1968)

Henning, Sylvie Debecque *Beckett's Critical Complicity: Carnival, Contestation, and Tradition*. Lexington: University Press of Kentucky (1988)

Hesla, David *The Shape of Chaos: An Interpretation of the Art of Samuel Beckett*. Minneapolis: University of Minnesota Press (1971)

Hessing, Kees *Beckett on Tape: Productions of Samuel Beckett's Work on Film, Video and Audio*. Leiden: Academic Press (1992)

Hill, Leslie *Beckett's Fiction: In Different Words*. Cambridge: Cambridge University Press (1990)

Hoffmann, Frederick J *Samuel Beckett: The Language of Self*. Carbondale: Southern Illinois University Press (1962)

Homan, Sidney *Beckett's Theaters: Interpretations for Performance*. Lewisburg, PA: Bucknell University Press. (1984)

—— *Filming Beckett's Television Plays: A Directior's Experience*. Lewisburg, PA: Bucknell University Press (1992)

Jacobsen, Josephine and Mueller, William R. *The Testament of Samuel Beckett*: New York: Hill and Wang (1964)

Jeffers, Jennifer M. (ed.) *Samuel Beckett: A Casebook*. Levittown, PA: Garland (1998)

*Journal of Beckett Studies*, Vol 1- (1976)

Kaelin, Eugene F. *The Unhappy Consciousness: The Poetic Plight of Samuel Beckett*. Dordrecht and Boston: Reidel (1981)

Kalb, Jonathan *Beckett in Performance*. Cambridge: Cambridge University Press (1989)

Kennedy, Andrew *Samuel Beckett*. Cambridge: Cambridge University Press (1989)

Kennedy, Sighle *Murphy's Bed: A Study of Real Sources and Sur-Real Associations in Samuel Beckett's First Novel*. Lewisburg, PA: Bucknell University Press (1971)

Kenner, Hugh *Samuel Beckett* New York: Grove Press (1961)

—— *A Reader's Guide to Samuel Beckett*. New York: Farrar (1973)

Knowlson, James *Light and Darkness in the Plays of Samuel Beckett*. London: Turret Books (1972)

—— *Happy Days/Oh Les Beaux Jours*. London: Faber and Faber (1978)

—— *Krapp's Last Tape: A Theatre Workbook*. London: Brutus Books (1980)

—— *'Happy Days': the Production Notebook of Samuel Beckett*. London: Faber and Faber (1985)

—— (ed.) *The Theatrical Notebooks of Samuel Beckett, Vol 3: 'Krapp's Last Tape'*. London: Faber and Faber (1992)

—— and Pilling, John *Frescoes of the Skull: The Later Prose and Drama of Samuel Beckett*. London: John Calder (1979)

Krance, Charles (ed.) *Samuel Beckett's 'Company'/'Compagnie' and 'A Piece of Monologue'/'Solo': A Bilingual Variorum Edition*. New York and London: Garland (1993)

Levy, Eric P. *Beckett and the Voice of Species:A Study of the Prose Fiction*. New York: Barnes and Noble (1980)

Levy, Shimon *Samuel Beckett's Self-Referential Drama: The Three I's*. New York: St Martin's Press (1990)

Locatelli, Carla *Unwording the World: Samuel Beckett's Prose Works After the Nobel Prize*. Philadelphia: Philadelphia University Press (1990)

Lyons, Charles *Samuel Beckett*. London: Macmillan (1982)

McCarthy, Patrick (ed.) *Critical Essays on Samuel Beckett*. Boston: Hall (1986)

McMillan, Dougald and Fesenfeld, Martha *Beckett in the Theatre: The Author as Practical Playwright and Director: Volume 1: From 'Waiting for Godot' to 'Krapp's last Tape'*. London: Calder (1988)

McMullan, Anna *Theatre on Trial: Samuel Beckett's Later Drama*. London: Routledge (1993)

Megged, Matti *Dialogue in the Void: Beckett and Giacometti*. New York: Lumen Press (1985)

Mercier, Vivian *Beckett/Beckett*. Oxford: Oxford University Press (1977)

Miller, Lawrence *Samuel Beckett: The Expressive Dilemma*. New York: St Martin's Press (1992)

*Modern Drama* Vol 9, No 3: Samuel Beckett special issue (1966)

—— Vol 19, No 3: Samuel Beckett part issue (1976)

—— Vol 25, No 3: Samuel Beckett part issue (1982)

—— Vol 28, No 2: Samuel Beckett part issue (1985)

*Modern Fiction Studies* Vol 29 Part 1: Samuel Beckett special issue (1983)

Moorjani, Angela *Abysmal Games in the Novels of Samuel Beckett*. Chapel Hill: University of North Carolina Press (1982)

Morrison, Kirstin *Canters and Chronicles: The Use of Narrative in the Plays of Samuel Beckett and Harold Pinter*. Chicago: University of Chicago Press (1983)

Morot-Sir, Edouard, Harper, Howard and McMillan, Dougald *Samuel Beckett: The Art of Rhetoric*. Chapel Hill: Department of Romance Languages, University of North Carolina (1976).

Murphy, P.J. *Reconstructing Beckett: Language for Being in Samuel Beckett's Fiction*. Toronto: University of Toronto Press (1990)

——, Huber, Werner, Breuer, Rolf and Schoell, Konrad (eds) *Critique of Beckett Criticism: A Guide to Research in English, French and German*. Colombia, SC: Camden House (1994)

Murray, Patrick *The Tragic Comedian: A Study of Samuel Beckett*. Cork: Mercier Press (1970)

*New Theatre Magazine* Vol 2 No 3: Samuel Beckett Special Issue (1972)

O'Brien, Eoin *The Beckett Country: Samuel Beckett's Ireland*. Dublin: Black Cat Press; London: Faber and Faber (1986)

O'Hara, J.D. (ed.) *Twentieth Century Interpretations of 'Molloy', 'Malone Dies' and 'The Unnamable'*. Englewood Cliffs, NJ: Prentice-Hall (1970)

—— *Samuel Beckett's Hidden Drives: Structural Uses of Depth Psychology*. Gainesville: University of Florida Press (1997)

Oppenheim, Lois (ed.) *Directing Beckett*. Ann Arbor: University of Michigan Press (1994)

—— (ed.) *Samuel Beckett and the Arts: Music, Visual Arts and Non-Print Media*. New York: Garland (1998)

*Perspective* Vol 11 No 3: Special issue on Beckett (ed. Ruby Cohn) (1959)

Pilling, John *Samuel Beckett*. London: Routledge (1976)

—— (ed.) *The Cambridge Companion to Beckett*. Cambridge: Cambridge University Press (1994)

—— *Beckett Before Godot: The Formative Years (1929–1946)*. Cambridge: Cambridge University Press (1998)

—— and Bryden, Mary (eds) *'The Ideal Core of the Onion': Reading Beckett Archives*. Reading: International Foundation (1992)

Pultar, Gonul *Technique and Tradition in Beckett's Trilogy of Novels*. Lanham, MD: University Press of America (1996)

Pountney, Rosemary *Theatre of Shadows: Samuel Beckett's Drama 1956–1976: from 'All That Fall' to 'Footfalls' with Commentaries on the Latest Plays*. Gerrards Cross: Colin Smythe (1988)

Rabinowitz, Rubin *The Development of Samuel Beckett's Fiction*. Urbana: University of Illinois Press (1984)

—— *Innovation in Samuel Beckett's Fiction*. Urbana: University of Illinois Press (1992)

Reid, Alec *All I Can Manage, More Than I Could: An Approach to the Plays of Samuel Beckett*. Dublin: Dolmen Press (1968)

Ricks, Christopher *Beckett's Dying Words*. Oxford: Oxford University Press (1993)

Robinson, Michael *The Long Sonata of the Dead: A Study of Samuel Beckett*. London: Rupert Hart-Davis (1970)

Rosen, Steven J. *Samuel Beckett and the Pessimistic Tradition*. New Brunswick, NJ: Rutgers University Press. (1976)

*Samuel Beckett Today/Aujourd'hui* Vol 1 (1992)

Schlueter, June and Brater, Enoch (eds) *Approaches to Teaching Beckett's 'Waiting for Godot'*. New York: MLA (1991)

Scott, Nathan A *Samuel Beckett*. London: Bowes and Bowes (1965)

Sherringham, Michael *Beckett: 'Molloy'*. London: Grant and Cutler (1985)

Smith, Joseph H. *The World of Samuel Beckett*. Psychiatry and the Humanities, 12. Baltimore and London: Johns Hopkins University Press (1991)

Solomon, Philip H. *The Life After Birth: Imagery In Samuel Beckett's Trilogy*. University, MS: Romance Monographs (1975)

Spurling, John and Foster, Paul *Beckett and Zen: A study of Dilemma in the Novels of Samuel Beckett.* Boston: Wisdom Publications (1989)

States, Bert O. *The Shape of Paradox: An Essay on 'Waiting for Godot'.* Berkeley: University of California Press (1978)

Tindall, William York *Samuel Beckett.* New York: Columbia University Press (1964)

Topsfield, Valerie *The Humour of Samuel Beckett.* London: Macmillan (1988)

Toyama, Jean Yamasaki *Beckett's Game: Language and Self-Referentiality in the Trilogy.* New York: Lang (1991)

Trezise, Thomas *Into the Breach: Samuel Beckett and the Ends of Literature.* Princeton: Princeton University Press (1990)

Via, Dan O. *Samuel Beckett's 'Waiting for Godot'.* New York: Seabury Press (1968)

Watson, David *Paradox and Desire in Samuel Beckett's Fiction.* London: Macmillan (1991)

Webb, Eugene *Samuel Beckett: A Study of His Novels.* Seattle and London: University of Washington Press (1970)

—— *The Plays of Samuel Beckett.* Seattle: University of Washington Press (1972)

Wilmer, Steve (ed.) *Beckett in Dublin.* Dublin: Lilliput Press (1992)

Worth, Katherine (ed.) *Beckett the Shape Changer.* London: Routledge and Kegan Paul, (1975)

—— *'Waiting for Godot' and 'Happy Days'. Text and Performance.* Basingstoke: Macmillan (1990)

Zilliacus, Clas *Beckett and Broadcasting: a Study of the Works of Samuel Beckett for and in Radio and Television.* Abo: Abo Akademi (1976)

Zurbrigg, Nicholas *Beckett and Proust.* Gerrards Cross: Colin Smythe (1988)

# INDEX